# Living in London

## A Practical Guide

Ninth Edition

Written and Publishe

THE JUNIOR LEAGUE OF

D1112940

Registered Charity No. 288427

About the Junior League of London:

The Junior League of London is an international organisation of women committed to promoting voluntary service and to making a difference in the community through effective action and leadership of trained volunteers. Its purpose is exclusively educational and charitable. The organisation has been operating in London since 1979.

First Edition, 1981
Second Edition, 1984
Third Edition, 1988
Fourth Edition, 1990
Fifth Edition, 1993
Sixth Edition, 1995
Seventh Edition, 1997
Eighth Edition, 1999
Ninth Edition, 2002

The contents of this book are believed to be correct at time of printing. However, The Junior League of London can accept no responsibility for errors, omissions, or changes in the information contained herein.

Cover design by Alison Tilley Design; (07900) 216 610; info@alisontilleydesign.co.uk

ISBN 0-9525195-3-4

In keeping with our belief that "when in Rome...", we have used English spelling and terminology throughout the book. As it is frequently used in the United Kingdom and Europe, we have also given all times in 24-hour time; thus, 2:00 a.m. is written 02.00 and 2:00 p.m. as 14.00.

Regional dialing codes for all telephone numbers outside the 020 Central and Greater London districts have been listed parenthetically before the telephone numbers. Street addresses followed directly by a postal code with no city mentioned imply that it is a London address.

Living in London would like to thank Merrill Corporation, Park Communications and London Central Portfolio for all of their help and guidance with this new edition.

Living in London would like to offer a special thank you to Pamela Plant who has been an enormous supporter of the Junior League of London and Living in London for the past twenty years. Her continuous contributions have made a difference in our lives and those we help in and around London.

The Junior League of London thanks the following sponsors for their generous contributions towards the 9th edition of *Living in London*

**THE INTERNATIONAL HERALD TRIBUNE**

...investing in London

Specialists in property search, refurbishment, letting and management

**LONDON CENTRAL PORTFOLIO LTD**

# MERRILL CORPORATION

**MERRILL LTD**

**PARK COMMUNICATIONS**

**Corporate Benefactor**

**THE AMERICAN SCHOOL OF LONDON**

# Corporate Sponsors

## Corporate Sponsor

Cleary Gottlieb & Hamilton

Citigroup

## Corporate Donor

American Psychotherapy Associates Ltd

Fried, Frank, Harris, Shriver & Jacobson

## Corporate Friend

The History of Art Studies

Focus Information Services

Kuhnke Communications

Tesco Stores Ltd

# Individual Sponsors

## Gold Patron
Candy Beeny
Jerry & Sandra del Missier
Lisa Kleinknecht

## Benefactor
Robert & Brittan Chepak
Catherine FitzMaurice
Mr & Mrs Karp
Dorothy H Leonard
Mr & Mrs James J Morreale
Dona Phelan
Ingrid Jacobson Pinter

## Patron
Lisa Allen
Cathleen Avila
Mr & Mrs Charles S Bowen
Kevin & Sheree Bryant
Ersel Buckley-Sharp
Mrs Barry Bruckmann
Lisa P Carlson
Jennifer & Martin Fisher
Alexandra Hallen
Binney & Jeff Huffman
The Korde Family
Dan & Huntley Kubitza
Dermot and Paula McNulty
Patricia F Mendelsohn
Mrs Robert C Olney
Noelle Pierce
Brooke A Russell
Rosemary Sandars
Cheryl L Stevens
Kerey Toms
Kelly & Rick Welch
Carlyn Barr Zehner

## Friend
Monique Bahadur
Carolyn Temple Cohen
Beth Forfang
Miss Lynne Frawley
Eileen Glynn
Catherine W Hays
Barbara Ilias
Dina Keller
Ashley Klaasmeyer
Heather Russel Koenig
Vernon & Joli Mauldin
Betsy Olson
Carolynn C Reynolds
Colleen Shaw
Jessica Stewart
Rebecca P Thomas
Patricia A Wallace
Katherine Wood

# Contents

*Embassy of the United States of America*

My wife, Sarah, and I were delighted and honoured when President Bush asked me to serve as U.S. Ambassador to the Court of St. James's.

We have known and loved the United Kingdom for many years, and we already had many happy memories of time spent on these shores.

Of course, as all seasoned expats know, living here, as opposed to just visiting, turns out to be – while still wonderful – a whole different ball game. I mean that in part literally: It took some time before we remembered when to say "football," or got even a rudimentary understanding of "wickets." It took time, too, to get used to light switches that flipped down to turn on, and having the hot-water faucet on the other side.

Such things may sound trivial to people who plant new roots in countries where the culture and language are dramatically different from our own. But getting accustomed to little everyday differences is also part of how expats finally begin to feel at home abroad. And a guide such as this is invaluable in dealing with hurdles both little and big, like finding child-care and schooling, or getting a car on the road, whatever side.

Sarah and I extend our sincere congratulations to the Junior League as it celebrates 25 years of voluntary service in London. Their contributions to community life here in our host country are a credit to all Americans lucky enough to be living here.

William S. Farish
U.S. Ambassador to the Court of St. James's

Welcome to London - one of the greatest cities in the world! And welcome to *Living in London* - a wonderful, resourceful and personal guide to help you settle in quickly and provide you with relevant information. Whether you are new to London or someone who has lived here for years, you may wonder…

What events take place throughout the year & how to get tickets?
What schools to consider and how to begin the process?
What caterer to use?
What to do about your taxes now that you're living and earning in London?
How would you like a personal referral?

You've got it as well as much, much more! All of the contents of *Living in London* are based on personal recommendations and advice from The Junior League of London volunteers - individuals, numbering in the hundreds, whose experiences will make discovering London exciting and far easier. Imagine… since 1981, when the first *Living in London* edition was published, our volunteers have been compiling their recommendations regarding life in London. You are in good hands.

Having both lived in London for five years plus, we recognise that London is a large, complex and sometimes, bewildering city… and we know how that feels! It takes time to understand its complexities, to identify its charms and to discover its hidden secrets. *Living in London* is designed to help you make the most of your time in this captivating city from the moment you find out your moving until it is time for you to move on. It is pragmatic, inspiring and a great resource to read cover-to-cover or to dip in and out of from time to time.

You may be interested to know, the Junior League of London is self-funded and self-governed by our volunteers. Profits from our leading fundraisers, *Living in London* and Boutique de Noel, a fabulous holiday shopping fair, help us to make a substantial impact in our community. Through the purchase of this book, you are assisting us to make an impact on our community focus area - helping families in need.

We support programmes and collaborative efforts with local agencies, schools and refuges to benefit the community and the families within it. Activities include lunch-time and after-school learning programmes, a befriending scheme for the elderly, an awareness raising initiative to break the cycle of domestic violence and programmes that help families/women to make the transition to economic self-sufficiency.

We are proud to introduce the ninth edition of Living in London. Thank you to all of the dedicated volunteers, past and present, whose energies, resourcefulness and dedication to voluntary service have not only helped to create this guide, but also have made an impact on the community within which we all live.

And, mostly, we thank you for your support and wish you well as you explore the following pages and enjoy *Living in London* in all its senses!

Barbra Lewis-Green
President 2001-2002
Junior League of London

Lisa Irwin
President 2002-2003
Junior League of London

# Chapter One: Moving

## Immigration

Before moving to the United Kingdom, you must ensure that you have permission from the British government to do so. Immigration into the UK is the remit of the Home Office's Immigration and Nationality Directorate. Details, application forms, and instructions for applying to live and/or work in the UK can be found at: http://www.ind.homeoffice.gov.uk. Please note that if you do not arrive in the UK under the correct category, you will most likely not be allowed to enter or will be deported. It is imperative to organise the process correctly before moving.

Information about immigration is often the subject of rumour and it is wise to ensure that the advice you are getting is from a reliable source. If you are moving in connection with a job, the Human Resources department often organises the process for you. If you need independent advice, be wary. If your advisor is not a lawyer, solicitor, barrister or legal executive you should ask if they are "OISC authorised." A list of OISC authorised advisers is on The Office of the Immigration Services Commissioner's website at www.oisc.gov.uk. In addition, you may wish to contact the British Consulate or Diplomatic Post closest to where you live for advice. See the Foreign and Commonwealth Office's website for a list of all diplomatic missions. http://www.fcogov.uk. Also, Embassies often have lists of attorneys practising in London who can assist with immigration matters.

### Work Permit Holders and Their Families

Most people moving to the UK come under the work permit scheme. The employing company must apply for the work permit through the Work Permits (UK), a division of the Home Office, prior to your arrival. The permit applies specifically both to the job and to the individual. Once the application has been approved, a work permit is issued and sent to you. It must then be presented to the immigration authorities upon entry into the UK and your passport will be stamped accordingly.

Spouses, dependants and children of overseas nationals who hold a work permit can apply for leave to enter at a British Consulate or Diplomatic Post *before* moving to the UK. See the Home Office's visa website for more information http://www.ukvisas.gov.uk. A same-sex partner who can demonstrate that he or she has been in a relationship akin to marriage for at least two years, can also obtain entry clearance. For specific advice about immigration to the UK as a same-sex partner please see http://www.stonewall-immigration.org.uk. Allow at least one week to apply for leave to remain. The application should be done after the spouse or partner's work permit is approved.

Spouses, dependants and same-sex partners of work permit holders with a correct entry clearance can work in the UK without being issued a work permit.

## Overseas Visitors Registration and Police Registration

A limited number of non-EEA nationals are required to register with the police. If you are a national of a country required to register, you and members of your family residing with you in the UK must register with the Overseas Visitors Records Office (OVRO) within seven days of your arrival in the country. Children under the age of 16 do not need to register. You should contact your local police station for information about where you need to register.

You will be given a green booklet (certificate) that you must produce within 24 hours, if asked to do so by the police or immigration officers. It is best to carry this certificate with you always while in Great Britain. Also, the certificate will make re-entry into the UK easier when you travel abroad on trips lasting less than two months. The certificate should be submitted to the Immigration Office on departure if travelling abroad for more than two months.

Any change of address or name change must be given to the OVRO within seven days. Only if a stamp requiring registration is endorsed in their passport must children register with the OVRO when they turn 16.

## Extensions of Stay; Change of Employment

The endorsement, stamp or certificate in your passport indicates how long you may remain in the United Kingdom. In order to stay longer, your employer must apply to Work Permits (UK) for an extension (within two months of the expiration of your stay).

A work permit is issued for a particular position. If your employment ends, your work permit is no longer valid and you should make arrangements to leave the UK within a reasonable amount of time. If you switch employers, your new employer must apply for a work permit before you begin working. A work permit cannot be 'rolled-over' into another job. Please note it is simpler to get a work permit for an employee if he or she had one before.

After four years of residence in the UK, a work permit holder and his or her dependants may apply for Indefinite Leave to Remain (ILR), permanent residence status, which will lift the need for a work permit and entitle the holder to certain public benefits. However, be aware that lengthy delays are probable, and it is not at all unusual to wait longer than 6 months for the Home Office decision. It may be possible to expedite the process by applying in person at the Home Office, Immigration and Nationality Department, Lunar House, 40 Wellesley Road, Croydon, Surrey CR9 2BY, (0870) 606 7766 or through hiring the services of a solicitor or lawyer. Before going to the Home Office in person ensure that you have all the correct information with you and be prepared to spend the entire day there.

## EEA Nationals and Their Families

A national of a member state of the European Economic Area (EEA) is free to enter the UK work and live. No prior permission is required and no work permit is needed for employment.

EEA nationals exercising their rights of free movement are entitled to bring with them to the UK their dependants, even where they are non-EEA nationals. Non-EEA family members require entry clearance in the form of a family permit. The non-EEA dependants of an EEA national may stay in the UK so long as the EEA national spouse is exercising his or her treaty rights by working in the UK. After living in the UK for four years, the non-EEA national is entitled to apply for Indefinite Leave to Remain, permanent residence status (see 'Extensions of Stay' above).

If you are a citizen of the EEA, you can apply for a resident's permit when you arrive in the UK. The application is made to the Home Office (see above) on form ECC1. You will need to submit your and your family members' passports or national identity documents and two passport size photographs of yourself and any of your dependants over the age of 16. The Home Office may take 6 to 12 months to process your application. Therefore, if you are a frequent traveller, be sure to make the application using your national identity card or a notarised photocopy of your passport.

## Other Immigration Categories

There are many other categories under which people can live in the UK including: British ancestry, working-holiday makers, students, retired persons of independent means, innovators, highly skilled migrant workers (HSMP), investors, and sole representatives of an overseas firm. For details about any of these schemes, please see the Home Office website address listed above. Please note that most of these categories are paper intensive and require you to apply at a British Consulate or Diplomatic post before arriving in the UK. Be sure to reserve plenty of time to gather all supporting evidence and documents and have your application reviewed. Again, your local British Consulate or Diplomatic Post will be able to advise you on these schemes.

## Climate and Weather

Weather in London is unpredictable; however, there are no extreme conditions. The average temperature varies from a low of 0C (32F) to a high of 24C (about 75F). July is the warmest month and January is the coldest and rainiest month. One common climate condition is the very soft drizzle. An umbrella is a must. Purchase one that is convenient to carry.

Temperatures are usually reported in Celsius. An approximate conversion from Celsius to Fahrenheit is to double the Celsius and add 30.

*Fahrenheit to Celsius (Centigrade)*

| | | |
|---|---|---|
| 20F | = | -6.67C |
| 30 | = | -1.11 |
| 32 | = | 0.00 (Freezing Point) |
| 40 | = | 4.44 |
| 41 | = | 5.00 |
| 50 | = | 10.00 |
| 59 | = | 15.04 |
| 60 | = | 15.56 |
| 68 | = | 20.00 |
| 70 | = | 21.11 |
| 77 | = | 25.00 |
| 80 | = | 26.67 |
| 90 | = | 32.22 |
| 98.6 | = | 37.00 (ave. human body temperature) |
| 212 | = | 100.00 (Boiling Point) |

*Celsius (Centigrade) to Fahrenheit*

| | | |
|---|---|---|
| -3C | = | 26.66F |
| -1 | = | 30.2 |
| 0 | = | 32.0 (Freezing Point) |
| 1 | = | 33.8 |
| 5 | = | 41.0 |
| 10 | = | 50.0 |
| 15 | = | 59.0 |
| 20 | = | 68.0 |
| 25 | = | 77.0 |
| 30 | = | 86.0 |
| 37 | = | 98.6 (ave. human body temperature) |
| 100 | = | 212 (Boiling Point) |

**MOVING**

## What to Bring and What Not to Bring

What to bring when you move to London is an individual decision. Obviously, your decisions will be based on the anticipated length of time you will reside in the UK. It will also depend upon your housing, whether furnished or unfurnished, house or flat.

## What to Bring

The following items may not be readily available or easily replaced in the UK. If they are available, they may be considerably more expensive than they are abroad.

## Personal Items

✓ Eye glasses, contact lenses, and related products

✓ Special cosmetics and beauty products, particularly dermatologist-recommended ones

✓ Medical prescriptions – wise to bring with you on the aeroplane

✓ Children's/adult over-the-counter medicine that you particularly like (See Chapter 8: Children for list of medicines not available in the UK).

## For the Home

European and English beds and bedding vary greatly in size from those sold elsewhere, particularly the United States, and are relatively expensive. If you bring your beds, bring the appropriate bedding.

If you are moving from the US, you also may wish to bring a set of measuring cups and spoons along with your favourite cookbooks. British recipes use imperial and metric measurements, and some UK measuring utensils differ in size from those sold in the US. (See Chapter 10: Cooking, Food and Drink for cooking tips).

## Miscellaneous

Children's games, sports equipment (baseballs, softballs, bats, footballs and basketballs, and bicycles). Special decorations for holidays including Halloween, Easter egg kits, and a Christmas tree stand and decorations.

## What Not to Bring

Cordless telephones
Light bulbs (except appliance bulbs – see following section for explanation of electrical differences)
Christmas tree lights
Electric clocks (will not work even with a transformer)
Liquor/Spirits (excluding wine), except duty free allowance
Cigarettes, except duty free allowance

Perfumes, except duty free allowance
Paints, cleaning agents or other combustible or flammable items
Plants and bulbs
Meat, fruits and vegetables
Certain fish and eggs
Most animals and all birds
Items made from protected species including reptile leather, ivory and fur skins

> **Did you know...** The law regarding firearms being brought into Great Britain for sports purposes and/or decorative sports equipment are extremely restrictive. You are advised to check the current law when you move.

## Electrical Differences

Deciding which electrical appliances and equipment to bring to England or leave home can be confusing, especially if you are relocating from the United States. US current is 110 volts and 60 Hz (frequency or cycles per second) while English current (and most of Europe) is 220/240 volts and 50 Hz (frequency or cycles per second). Understanding what voltage and frequency is compatible with your electrical devices will facilitate your decision making. Some devices, if made for several voltages, can be used directly in the UK. Some can be used with a voltage transformer, and some cannot be used at all.

## Adaptors

Most UK plugs have three square prongs. Electrical devices that do not need voltage transformers may require a plug adaptor. Or, you can simply replace all of the non-UK plugs on voltage compatible appliances with UK plugs. The latter option is the cheapest.

## Transformers

In general, most non-European electrical goods are incompatible with UK electrical supply because of the voltage difference (220/240V for UK vs 110V for US, for example). This means that if you try to use them in the UK they will burn out. You can get them to work if you use a transformer. A transformer is a plug in device that will convert 220/240V to 110V. Transformers are available in London and the surrounding area. Transformers are sized from 30 watts to 1,500 watts and are priced from £15 to £75, depending on the size. A hair dryer or electric curler will require up to a 250 watt transformer. A blender or food processor will require up to a 500 watt transformer, while a refrigerator will require up to a 1,500 watt transformer.

Transformers, depending on the size, can be used to power several appliances so you don't necessarily need one transformer for each device. However, they are bulky and heavy and not very portable.

## Dual Voltage Appliances

Some appliances, such as VCRs, TVs, stereos, can function on 120 or 240V merely by adjusting a switch on the appliance. Check your appliances for this feature because it will allow you to use it in the UK without a transformer.

## Appliances incompatible with the Frequency

All US appliances are 60 Hz while the electrical supply in the UK is 50 Hz. This frequency difference comes into play in appliances with a motor where speed of the motor is important. There is no simple device that will convert 50 to 60 Hz, so any device with a motor will run at a bit more than 80% of its normal speed, even if it is run on a transformer. For hair dryers, fans, washers, blenders, refrigerators, and dryers that might not be a problem. For analogue clocks, it is a problem.

In using certain devices with motors, like VCRs, personal computers, tape decks and CDs, the frequency difference is not an issue because the electrical current is converted to Direct Current in the machine so the device will run at the right speed, independent of frequency. So if they are 110-120V machines, they can be run on a transformer. If they are 120 or 240V machines, with a switch, they can be run directly in the UK. Also be aware that some devices, like battery chargers or power packs for camcorders will run on any voltage up to 240V, so can be run directly in the UK.

## Specific Appliances

### Refrigerator

To convert to English voltage, a refrigerator can be run on an appropriate size transformer. You may purchase a new refrigerator for UK 220/240 volts, 50 cycle current before moving. American refrigerators may be purchased in the UK, but they are very expensive. If you are renting, make sure there is space in the kitchen for a large refrigerator; English refrigerators often are small.

### Washing Machine and Electric Dryer

To use in the UK the washer can be run on a transformer. The dryer will probably be 240V so may be able to be used without a transformer, but the dryer should only be installed by a qualified electrician. Again, American washers and dryers are larger than UK appliances and may not fit in your particular house or flat. Gas dryers can be used in the UK, if your flat or house is serviced with gas, but will need a transformer for the motor and may need a different pressure regulator for the gas.

> *Did you know...*If you are interested in buying American appliances during your stay in the UK, try www.americanappliances.com.

## TVs, VCRs and DVDs

It may be wise to sell these appliances before moving and buy new or used ones when you arrive. While TVs, VCRs and DVDs purchased abroad can be run in the UK with a transformer, they have limited use because of the differences in broadcasting standards. The TV will not pick up British stations, by antenna or cable, unless it is a "multi system" TV, equipped with a switch for PAL system, which is the UK standard. Similarly, American VCRs will not play British videos unless it is a "multi system" VCR equipped with a switch for PAL system.

*Did you know...*DVDs are coded differently for different regions of the world. North America is coded as zone 1 while Europe is coded as zone 2. If you are bringing your US DVDs over, make sure the DVD player you purchase can play zone 1 disks. Likewise, don't buy disks in the UK and expect to be able to play them back in the States.

## Telephones

Do not bring cordless telephones.

US telephones may be used in the UK after purchasing an adaptor – although the price of an adaptor may be more expensive that the price of a new phone. Otherwise US telephones are not compatible with the UK system.

## Computers

Your computer, monitor and printer will run on a transformer in the UK. Bring your surge protector.

## Lamps

All lamps can be used in the UK, provided they are used with an adapter or are fitted with UK plugs. US light bulbs will explode if used in the UK, because of the voltage difference, so leave your light bulbs at home.

## Miscellaneous Electrical Information

Some electrical appliances purchased in the UK do not come with socket outlet plugs. Attaching a plug is an easy procedure but keep a store of plugs with both 3 amp and 13 amp fuses. Different appliances require different size fuses. Be sure to have the correct fuse for each appliance. If your appliance fails to work, check the fuse and plug before calling the electrician. Obviously, all electrical appliances are potential fire hazards and should be used with caution. Always consult an electrician if you are not absolutely certain how an appliance should be correctly operated.

If you have American electrical appliances that require appliance bulbs, bring the bulbs with you, such as bulbs for sewing machines, refrigerators and freezers.

Wall outlets in a flat or house may not be of a uniform size. For this reason, when you shop for plug adaptors, appliances or electrical needs, check the outlets in the room where the appliance/adaptor will be used. While the 13 amp square, 3 prong (pin) plugs are becoming standard, you may also find 2 amp, 5 amp and 15 amp round pin plugs.

American appliances are available in the UK in some of the larger department stores (although very expensive) and some used appliances may be purchased through various American organisations, including The American School in London newsletter, the Kensington and Chelsea Women's Club newsletter, The American Women of Surrey newsletter.

For your electrical questions and needs, Ryness Electrical Supplies has branches throughout London.

*Did you know...*If you plan to rent accommodation, keep in mind that most flats and houses come furnished with basic appliances.

### Shipping Household Effects

Shipping of household effects depends on the anticipated length of your stay and the type of house to be maintained. If it is a total move, start making arrangements and organising the move at once. If it is only temporary or short term, remember to include some favourite personal possessions, so your home away from home has your personality.

Start your plans by making lists:
What is going with you on the aeroplane?
What is needed soon after you arrive (if you are going into temporary housing, it may be necessary to bring these items with you via excess baggage or air shipment)?
What is being shipped in a container via sea/air?
What is going into storage?
Things to give away?
Things to sell?
Things to discard?

*Did you know...*It is important to remember when choosing items to bring that many flats are converted 19th century houses. They are very beautiful, however the hallways and doors can be very narrow and it may be difficult to get large pieces of furniture in.

Once you have finally made all of these decisions it is a good idea to have the lists duplicated. There is nothing more frustrating than misplacing your only copy of one of these important lists.

## Selecting a Moving Company

When selecting a moving company, choose a reputable one. Investigate the company's performance record; check references. Go over all items in detail with the moving company's representative and have everything in writing. Get more than one estimate. Do not choose a firm simply because it is the cheapest; it may turn out to be a 'penny wise, pound foolish' decision.

Decide when items for storage are to be packed and placed in storage. Decide when the shipment is to be packed and when the container is to be loaded at your home. Know which ship is going to carry your container and when it is scheduled to depart and to arrive in England. Plan the unloading in England so the moving company can make arrangements with British Customs and the British removal company. After your goods have arrived in Great Britain, it can take several weeks before you receive them.

Be knowledgeable about the company's loss and damage protection – read all the small print on any contract. Be sure to know the scope and coverage of the insurance for the shipment. It is essential to have insurance. It might be wise to check with one or more private insurance companies, rather than relying on the moving company's insurance programme.

For insurance purposes it is necessary to have an itemised inventory. This might be done by categories, such as furniture, silver, paintings, and accessories, or room by room. Pick the system that best suits your needs and have everything appraised. Remember to value all items at replacement value. One good idea is to record everything with photographs. Make several copies of the inventory. One copy has to go to the insuring company, whether it be the moving company or an insurance agent. Take more than one copy with you for use when the shipment arrives in England. This inventory makes it easy to record any possible damages which might require repairs and an insurance claim.

## Packing Your Household

Make sure your specifications and instructions are being carried out to your satisfaction. Make sure each box is labelled with contents and destination (even the room).

If you are doing any of the packing or unpacking, check for insurance coverage. Usually breakables are covered only when packed and unpacked by the moving company. The shipping charges normally include all packing and unpacking.

## Packing Your Luggage for the Plane

Some items that might go into your luggage are a sewing kit and a small first aid kit, umbrella, address book, extra pair of glasses, extra prescriptions, small tool kit, carrying bag for groceries or laundry, the baby's stroller, books you have wanted to read, plus some old clothes for cleaning or painting and comfortable shoes. Do not ship jewellery – carry it with you.

Take copies of any important legal documents with you. Foremost, make a full copy of your passport and any visa or work permit information. Additionally, you should have copies of any wills, insurance policies, rental contracts on properties, investments, and a list of current charge accounts with their account numbers. Make sure a trusted friend or attorney knows the whereabouts of the originals. You may also want to carry copies of family medical records with you.

## Customs and VAT

The British Government allows importing of all household or personal effects duty free – providing they have been owned six months prior to the date of entry into the UK. Proof of purchase must be available on items less than six months old. Certain other household items may be dutiable. There are also special regulations regarding the importing of inherited goods and antiques into Great Britain. There are restrictions on liquor and cigarettes. You are allowed the duty free amount of one quart of liquor and one carton of cigarettes per adult, which must accompany you on the airplane. Liquor and cigarettes which are shipped will be charged with the normal British duty, which is very costly. No living plants, meat, fruit and vegetables are allowed into the UK. Refer to the list of "What Not to Bring" on page 5.

If at all possible have a file with a copy of the bill of sale for every valuable item, such as cameras, watches, jewellery, silver, major appliances, etc. If you do not have these bills of sale, an alternative is a copy of an old insurance policy that itemises these articles. Carry these documents with you, do not ship them. If you will be travelling with jewellery or cameras, for example we suggest you carry that portion of the insurance policy or the bill of sale.

All items which are not at least six months old are subject to duty charges and VAT (Value Added Tax – currently 17.5%). Check with your moving company or the closest British Consulate, who will be able to advise you on which items may be subject to duty and excise tax plus VAT, as the customs and duty charges can vary from three to 24% depending on the item in question. Duty on tobacco products, however, is as high as 90%. For additional information contact *General Inquiries, H.M. Customs & Excise Department*, Dorset House, Stamford Street, London SE1; (020) 7928 3344 (Excise Advice Centre).

## Shipping Your Pet and Quarantine

Domestic pets entering Great Britain require a six-month quarantine. Presently there is discussion to reduce the length of or eliminate quarantine. Be sure to check prior to departure. Penalties for smuggling animals are severe. Such an offence will result in a heavy fine, a prison sentence for yourself, or the destruction of the animal. It is a legal requirement to obtain a British Import Licence for your pet prior to your animal's arrival.

Arrangements for boarding kennels must be made and confirmed by letter before you leave your home. Allow four to six weeks to complete all paperwork and keep in mind that the most accessible kennels may have waiting lists.

Whether you vaccinate your animal or not (as required by the airlines), vaccination must take place again upon arrival in Great Britain.

A list of boarding kennels can be obtained by calling or writing to *The Ministry of Agriculture, Fisheries and Food*, The Government Building, Hook Rise South, Tolworth, Surbiton, Surrey KT6; (020) 8330 4411 (Rabies Section). See Chapter 11: Services for several kennel suggestions.

Do consider the proximity of the kennel to your residence, as you may wish to visit your animal regularly. If your animal has favourite toys and/or a bed, you may wish to bring these items on the plane with you. Do not bring tinned or dried foods as they will require an export/import licence, as well as a veterinary certificate stating that the tinned food has been heat-treated in an hermetically sealed tin.

> *Did you know...* A six-month quarantine sometimes can be very hard on a pet, especially if they are older. If you have the opportunity beforehand, it is a good idea to visit the quarantine facilities before deciding to proceed.

Check with the airlines for the carrier dimension requirements for your animal. Such carriers can be purchased directly from the airlines after you have booked your flight. The carrier will travel air freight, as animals are not allowed in the cabin on flights into Great Britain. The carrier must be tagged with the kennel destination and the animal's import licence number. Your pet is met upon landing by a representative from the boarding kennel. You are not allowed to see your pet for one week, so you might consider sending your pet early to avoid the trauma of moving day. Check also with your vet as to the possibility of medication to prevent trauma/air sickness to your pet while in transit.

### Arrival at the Airport

The majority of people moving to London arrive by aeroplane. There are two main airports for London: Heathrow, which is 18 miles west of London, serves most major airlines; Gatwick, which serves many major airlines and charter flights, is located 30 miles south of London.

It is quite a long walk from the gates to the Immigration and Customs Control. If you have a large amount of hand luggage or a small child, it is a good idea to have luggage wheels and a baby's pushchair. Larger pushcarts/trolleys are available near the gates at Heathrow. Arrange in advance with the airline if you will need a wheelchair, are travelling with a new-born infant or have medical problems.

If you are a non-EU passport holder, at the Immigration Desk (Passport Control) you will submit the British Landing Card given to you on the flight. Your passport will be stamped by the Immigration Officer at this point. Remember that the Immigration Officer's stamp in your passport indicates how long you may stay in Great Britain. The officer will ask to see your travel documents or work permit so that he can stamp your passport accordingly. He may ask you a few questions regarding the reasons for your entrance into the country.

After you are through Passport Control, check the electronic board to find out the area for your flight's baggage claim. It is good to know that in the UK, and in many other European International Airports, pushcarts or "trollies" are free of charge. If your luggage or part of it does not arrive, contact a representative of your airline. Lost luggage can usually be traced within 24 hours.

## Customs

If you have nothing to declare and are arriving from a non-EU country, proceed through the area marked with the green sign. If you are arriving from another EU country, proceed through the area marked with the *blue* sign.

If you have items to declare, you must go to the area marked with the *red* sign. The customs inspector will probably ask you a few questions and may ask to see these items. You are required to pay any duty or tax at the time the belongings are brought into the country. Be sure to travel with English money. Foreign currency or travellers cheques can be cashed at the airport banks.

For further information on transportation to London see Chapter 6: Transportation.

## Important Personal Data

The following lists pertain to personal matters and information. We recommend that you complete the necessary information for each member of your household and then make one or more copies to keep in a safe place. In the case of an accident, a fire, theft, or an emergency, these lists will be helpful in filing claims. Certain information will have to be added when you arrive in London.

It may be useful and convenient to list the information directly onto these pages.

## General Information

Identity or Social Security Number:

Passport Number and Renewal Date:

Employee Identification Number:

Insurance Policies:

Health Insurance Number:

Major Medical Policy Number:

National Health Insurance Number:

## Financial Information

Current (Chequing) Account:

Savings Account:

Other Bank Accounts:

Certificate of Deposit:

Safe-Deposit Box:

Address of Bank:

Location of Key:

Brokerage Account:

Mutual Fund Account:

Securities (serial numbers):

## Automobile Information

Driving Licence:

Car Identification:

Car Registration:

Licence Plate Number:

Car Insurance and Renewal Date:

Car Tax Renewal Date:

AA/RAC Membership Number and Renewal Date:

MOT (Ministry of Transport) Test Certificate Renewal Date:

Area Parking Permit Renewal Date:

## House Information

Title (Land) Deed:

Mortgage:

Buildings Insurance:

Contents Insurance:

Landlord:

Serial Numbers of all major appliances, such as:

    VCR:

    DVD:

    Computer:

    Printer:

    Camera:

    Stereo:

Television Licence Renewal Date:

## Credit Cards

List name, account number, and address to report loss:

Bank Cards:

Travel and Entertainment Cards:

Store Charge Account Cards:

## MOVING WITHIN LONDON

Moving within London can sometimes be as big a production as moving to the United Kingdom. Some things to remember are:

- If you need to secure parking for unloading or loading a truck or van make sure to contact your Borough at least two weeks ahead of time. For free, or a small fee, your Borough will block parking spaces for you.

- Transfer your TV licensee to your new home. Cancel all direct debits for services to your former home.

- Try to set up utilities (i.e. cable and telephone) before you move into your new home.

- The Post Office offers a mail forwarding scheme that is extremely efficient and reliable. For a fee, they will forward all of your mail – including magazines and packages- to your new address. Any branch Post Office will have the requisite forms for you to fill out.

- When hiring a moving company, be sure to check references and inquire about insurance limits. Many moving companies will move boxes that you have packed yourself. This is often much less expensive than purchasing a full moving service. Also, prices are sometimes lower if you move during the week rather than on the weekends.

# Chapter Two: Housing

What makes London such a wonderfully liveable city is that it is made up of many small 'villages', each with its own particular charm. Deciding on the best location for you and your family is difficult only because the choices are so great. You must consider a number of factors: high cost of certain areas, proximity to work and schools (or easy transportation to them), convenience of shopping facilities, and atmosphere. If it is at all possible, any house-hunting trip should begin with a morning spent driving around the city, taking in the flavour and overall feel of each area. By the time your tour ends, your list of areas in which to search may be considerably shorter than it was earlier. Those few hours can save you days of wasted time and energy, not to mention frayed nerves.

The first decision to make is whether you want to live in Central London, in one of the smaller outer suburban communities of Greater London or in the country.

Another factor to consider is which London borough you live in. London is divided into 32 boroughs, which provide local public services such as street cleaning, social housing, libraries and parking. To pay for these services, each borough sets its own level of local "council tax", which can vary significantly even between neighbouring boroughs. It is worth bearing in mind that boroughs of City of Westminster and Wandsworth have very low council tax rates, while Islington, Southwark and Camden are high. There are also differences in the quality of services, particularly in the local schools, which are mostly run by the borough. State schools in the London Boroughs of Kingston, Richmond and Sutton rank among the best in the country.

Parking within certain London boroughs, notably the City of Westminster and the Royal Borough of Kensington and Chelsea, is allowed only at meters (always scarce) unless a car displays a valid resident's parking permit issued by the borough.

The following short descriptions of some of the London areas may be of assistance.

## LIVING IN LONDON

### Central London (SW and W postcodes)

The communities of Central London are expensive but convenient for shops, theatres, restaurants, clubs and often public transportation. These areas have a high proportion of international residents.

### *Belgravia (SW1)*

Near Buckingham Palace and Hyde Park, this area consists of magnificent Regency squares, late Georgian terraces and mews houses. Some of the larger houses are now used as embassies and consulates: others have been divided into flats. Belgravia is one of the more expensive and desirable areas of London, and similar to Mayfair, large grocery shopping is limited. This area is served by Victoria and Sloane Square tube stations.

### Chelsea (SW3 and SW10)

South of Knightsbridge and South Kensington and bordering the Thames, Chelsea features a range of mostly low rise period buildings, including Victorian cottages and mansion blocks. Sloane Square and King's Road are convenient for shopping, although the latter's reputation as one of London's trendiest areas is now more tradition than fact. Chelsea also boasts many cosy local pubs and restaurants, as well as excellent antique shops and markets. The area is not well served by public transport as there is no tube station.

### Kensington (W8)

South and west of Kensington Gardens, Kensington features tree-lined residential streets and squares: a mixture of Georgian and Victorian terraced houses, red-brick mansion blocks and elegant villas. Kensington High Street and Notting Hill Gate offer convenient shopping and access to public transport. There are also three cinemas and numerous restaurants and pubs in the area.

### Knightsbridge (SW1, SW3 and SW7)

Bordering Hyde Park to the south, this expensive area features Victorian terraces and squares, cobbled mews and red brick Victorian mansion blocks. Once part of a forest on the outskirts of London, today Knightsbridge is home to Harrods and other fine stores, making it one of the world's most famous shopping destinations. The tube station is on the Piccadilly line, serving the West End and Heathrow.

### Maida Vale (W9)

Maida Vale has a rich supply of flats of various sizes and types. The area's wide streets are lined with large terraced houses and red-brick mansion blocks, often with access to large private gardens, some with tennis courts. The area surrounding the Grand Union Canal, known as 'Little Venice', has many large stucco houses, some of which remain single family homes while others have been converted into flats.

### Marylebone (W1)

North of Oxford Street and south of Marylebone Road, this area has many 18th century streets and squares, mews houses and portered Edwardian mansion blocks. It is convenient for the West End shops, and has excellent public transport links to the City and to nearly all London's main line rail stations. Marylebone High Street has recently become a fashionable spot for shopping and dining. Regent's Park is also very convenient.

## Mayfair (W1)

Bordered by Hyde Park, Oxford Street, Regent Street and Piccadilly, Mayfair has been a fashionable central neighbourhood since the 1700s. Many of the large Georgian houses have been divided into flats, available for long or short lets, or have been converted into luxury hotels and offices. There is a good supply of flats in large, well-maintained mansion blocks. The area is limited for grocery shopping (the local custom of daily shopping still prevails); however it is well situated for many of the finest clubs, restaurants, antique shops and designer boutiques. The US Embassy is located here.

## Pimlico (SW1)

South of Victoria Station, bordering the Thames, this area has lovely white stucco squares and terraces. Its quietness owes much to the complicated one–way street system. Pimlico is a more affordable alternative to its neighbouring communities of Belgravia and Chelsea, and is popular with Members of Parliament and other government workers based in Westminster.

## South Kensington (SW3, SW5 and SW7)

South Kensington's streets feature large terraced houses, many converted into flats, often with access to private garden squares. One of the most central residential areas in London, South Kensington benefits from plentiful tube and bus services, providing easy access to the West End, the City and Heathrow airport. The area is also home to four of the capital's major museums, as well as the Lycée Français, which attracts many French families to the area.

## West London (W/SW postcodes)

In addition to the west/central neighbourhoods listed below, going westward from Knightsbridge are the residential areas of Brook Green, Chiswick, Hammersmith, West Kensington and Shepherds Bush. These contain tree-lined streets with large houses, many of which have been converted into flats. These neighbourhoods are well served by public transport with the Central, Piccadilly and District lines running through the vicinity. It is also on the right side of London for a quick journey on the M4 to Heathrow Airport. With riverside walks and pubs and excellent facilities for shopping, leisure and health this area is ideal for families planning to settle in London for a considerable amount of time.

## Bayswater and Paddington (W2)

West of Marble Arch and to the north of Hyde Park, this area has modern blocks of flats, as well as some squares mostly rebuilt after the war. It is convenient for Oxford Street shopping and Mayfair and is considerably cheaper than neighbouring Notting Hill. Paddington is nearby and is benefiting from widescale development and urban regeneration of the Paddington Basin, as well as the new Heathrow rail link. It also has some very pretty period cottages and magnificent stucco terraces.

### Fulham (SW6)

Just West of Chelsea, Fulham has a number of large parks. It is home to many young English professionals and their families, as well as increasing numbers of expatriates who are attracted by the larger private gardens and better value for money. The typical Fulham street is lined with two and three-storey Victorian terraced houses, many of which have been converted into flats. Several large mansion blocks are located near the river.

### Holland Park (W14)

Surrounding Holland Park, this area features leafy streets and some of the largest detached and semi-detached houses in London. The area also offers a good supply of flats in large mansion blocks and converted Victorian houses. It is also convenient to the shopping and entertainment facilities of Kensington High Street and Notting Hill Gate, and there is easy access to the West End and the City by public transport.

### Notting Hill (W11)

Just north of Kensington, Notting Hill has large houses, often with good size private or communal gardens, and easy access to the West End and the City by public transport. The area is close to both Holland Park and Kensington Gardens, and has a large variety of local restaurants, trendy shops, bars and antique shops. Notting Hill also hosts the largest annual street party and carnival in Europe, held normally over the last weekend in August.

## North London (N and NW postcodes)

### Hampstead (NW3)

North of Swiss Cottage, this suburban village has a quaint feel. The high street is dominated by exclusive boutiques, cafes and restaurants. Its winding and hilly streets feature brick townhouses and large detached houses, many of which have been converted into flats. It is adjacent to Hampstead Heath which has many walking paths, golf club, art shows and outdoor concerts in summer.

### Hampstead Garden Suburb (NW11)

North of Hampstead this area is definitely a suburban enclave. It features cottages and beautiful four, five and six bedroom homes, many stately Georgian and ambassadorial types, with well-manicured gardens. It has two small but varied shopping areas. Many homes back on to Hampstead Heath, however in some parts it is necessary to have a car.

### Highgate (N6)

Northeast of Hampstead Heath, Highgate Village is quietly residential with a definite country atmosphere. It has a golf club and many homes, both old and new, with large gardens. Parking and driving are quite easy.

### Islington (N1)

East of Regent's Park, Islington is a friendly, lively place with modern terraced houses, Victorian villas and smartly restored Georgian squares. It is close to Camden Passage, noted for its antique shops and market and enjoys easy access to the City and the West End. The restaurants and bars along Upper Street are the centre of the area's vibrant night life.

### Regent's Park (NW1)

The elegant residential area around Regent's Park is most famous for its Nash Terraces overlooking the park. Its impressive homes include Winfield House, the residence of the American Ambassador. Modern blocks of flats, the London Zoo and the Open Air Theatre all add to its diversity.

### St. John's Wood (NW8)

Northwest of Regent's Park and suburban in feeling, St. John's Wood has many large detached and semi-detached houses as well as large blocks of flats with good views over the park. The American School in London is located here.

### Swiss Cottage (NW3)

North of St. John's Wood, and less expensive, this area has large blocks of flats, low terraced houses and modern townhouses with a cosmopolitan flavour. The heart of Swiss Cottage is dominated by a large public leisure centre attached to the main library.

### East London

To the east of Tower Hill, is a newly developed area known as Wapping and the Docklands. Housing here is mainly either converted warehouses, which have been converted in the last ten years to a very high standard, or new developments – often with a river view. Some have off-street parking, 24 hour porters, indoor swimming pools and other fitness facilities. Transport is improving and the Docklands Light Railway runs a service between Tower Hill, Bank, Beckton, Stratford and Island Gardens. Canary Wharf, in the heart of the Docklands, is the new home to a number of banks and other financial institutions, which has made East London particularly appealing to professional young couples. In this up and coming area, new shops and restaurants are opening all the time.

### South London

### Battersea (SW8 and SW11)

On the south side of the Thames from Chelsea Harbour, Battersea is dominated by Battersea Park and the now derelict Battersea Power Station. Battersea is cheaper than living north of the river, with many brick Victorian mansion blocks and larger late Victorian properties. With excellent facilities for shopping, parking, education, health and sports, it is very popular with young Londoners due to its parks and bar and restaurant scene.

## Clapham (SW4 and SW9)

Always popular with families, this area surrounds Clapham Common, featuring large Victorian family properties, on tree lined streets with on-street parking. Clapham's three tube stations are served by the Northern line, making this a recommended location for young City professionals who are looking to buy rather than rent.

## Putney (SW15)

Bordering the south bank of the Thames, Putney has a chain of attractive open spaces with extensive sporting grounds, especially rowing clubs. It contains the first high-rise flats in London as well as many two-storey homes with gardens. There is a busy and convenient street for shopping as well as the Putney Exchange, an enclosed shopping mall. Putney has main line and bus links to Central London as well as a tube station, but this is not so close to the area's residential neighbourhoods.

## Shad Thames (SE1)

This riverside neighbourhood on the south bank of the Thames stretches east from Tower Bridge. The area boasts a high concentration of warehouse conversions and newly constructed apartment complexes. It is also home to the Design Museum, and there is a Friday antiques market nearby. There are four local Terence Conran restaurants, as well as speciality food shops, clothing stores and bookshops. There is easy access to the City and the Docklands.

## Greater London

More and more newcomers to London are moving to communities farther from the centre. These communities are often less expensive, have fewer foreigners and retain more of their historic character. They are generally regarded as good places to bring up families, as in general, houses have larger gardens, there is less crime and schools are better. Most have every type of housing, from rows of brick terrace houses to tall stately Georgian terraces to large detached houses.

Perhaps the only disadvantages are the longer commute to Central London and the City and the necessity for a car in most locations.

## Barnes (SW13)

Located west of Putney, on the Thames, this area features low terraced houses from the late Victorian and Edwardian eras. It has a wonderful 'wilderness' Common, sporting grounds and swan pond. Barnes offers bus and train transportation, but not a tube station.

## Richmond (TW10)

Southwest of Barnes, Richmond is a lovely suburban village with large houses and beautiful gardens. Its many parks add a delightful 'country' atmosphere. Richmond Park comprises 2,000 acres of parkland, and Richmond Green is often the setting for cricket matches.

**HOUSING**

## Wimbledon (SW19)

Wimbledon, famous for the tennis tournament held here every summer, is located eight miles southwest of Central London. Wimbledon has a suburban atmosphere, with Wimbledon Common comprising 1,200 acres of land for riders, walkers and picnickers. The Village has a wide range of shopping and the train and tube station offers convenient transportation to London. Centre Court is a new shopping complex next to the station.

Other equally charming areas worth considering are *Blackheath (SE3)*, *Dulwich (SE21)*, *Kew (TW9)*, *Greenwich (SE10)* and *Wandsworth (SW18)*.

## Living in the Country

Within commuting distance of London are some wonderful suburban communities with large houses and enormous gardens. There is no question that for what one has to pay for a house in London, one can find almost palatial splendour in the rural areas. But yet again, the commute into London must be considered.

Surrey, south of London, encompasses many charming villages - Cobham, Esher, Walton-on-Thames, Weybridge, West Byfleet and many others - all with good public transportation into London. The American Community Schools, the TASIS England American School, and Marymount International Schools are also located in Surrey.

Northwest of Central London are the communities of Wembley, Harrow, Pinner and Ruislip. These areas are popular for their suburban atmosphere and more garden-for-the-money value. They primarily contain semi-detached and small detached houses.

Further northwest are the communities of Northwood, Chorleywood, Moor Park and Watford with large houses and gardens. These areas are convenient to the London Orbital (M25) and the many suburban superstores.

---

*Did you know...* The term "High Street" refers to the main shopping street of an area, borough, or town. There are often many shops, restaurants and banks located on the High Street.

---

## INTRODUCTION TO RENTING AND BUYING PROPERTY

Once you have narrowed your list of areas, there are many crucial issues to consider. These will depend on whether you are going to rent or buy a home in London. Indeed, once you are established in London, you may see what a unique and exciting investment opportunity London can offer.

## RENTING/LETTING PROPERTY

If you are planning to rent rather than buy, you should be aware of the Housing Act 1988 which regulates your right to extend your tenancy and the landlord's right to re-possess the property or increase the rent. Your solicitor (lawyer) or relocation agent can explain this in detail. You should not sign a tenancy agreement or lease without first having it approved by a solicitor familiar with such documents. Your company may have an in-house lawyer who can do this for you, or you can contact the Law Society, 113 Chancery Lane, WC2A; (020) 7242 1222, for names of firms specialising in such work.

There are two important aspects of the housing market you may encounter:

A.  Many rentals are fully furnished (down to dishes, sheets, towels, etc.) which can make your move very uncomplicated. You only need to bring your clothes, the children's toys and other personal items. But sometimes the furnishings may not be of a very good quality. It may be possible to negotiate with the owner to remove the furnishings and move in your own, provided you are prepared to pay for the storage costs. If you find you need additional storage for furniture that will not fit into your house/flat, see Chapter Eleven: Services for self-storage locations.

B.  Some rentals are only available as a 'company let', which means that the lease is made out to your corporation and must be signed by the Managing Director or his/her appointee. The company therefore guarantees the tenancy.

### Defining your rental checklist

For happy renting, it is important to get the legal and practical aspects right. Negotiation is all about striking a balance between your needs and requirements and those of the landlord. Here are a few tips.

### *Read the Small Print*

There are three main types of tenancy agreements:

An Assured Shorthold Tenancy (AST) for rents up to £25,000; a Standard Tenancy Agreement for rents above; and a Company Tenancy Agreement where the company is the tenant and you are "the permitted occupier". Wording is very similar but watch out for the following:

• Do you have a break clause? Job mobility makes it sensible to be able to terminate early and this is usually granted subject to a minimum tenure of six months.

- Do you have an <u>option to renew</u>? You may want an option to extend for a second or third year.

- What is the level of annual rent increase? It is likely to be no less than the RPI (inflation) but a minimum of either 3% or 5%.

## Be Prepared

- Rent is expressed on a "per week" basis. As there are 52 weeks in a year, your monthly rent is equivalent to 4.3 weeks not 4 weeks.

- The deposit required against dilapidations is normally six weeks. If pets are allowed, this may go up to eight weeks. It may not be returned until you have proved you have settled your utility bills.

- If you are asked for a holding deposit to secure a tenancy, make sure it is refundable against the full deposit.

- Sort out your "wish-list" at negotiation stage e.g. linen, microwave. It is difficult to go back to the landlord later.

- There may be additional charges, for example drawing up tenancy agreements and check-ins.

## Best Practice

- Set up a standing order to pay the rent. You have an obligation to pay on time.

- You have no legal right to withhold rent, whatever your grievance, so discuss any problems with your agent.

- Ensure your check-in is conducted by an independent inventory clerk, as this will form the basis of the dilapidation charges.

- Take care with picture hooks or you may end up redecorating.

- Make sure the utilities (gas, water, electricity, telephone, and council tax) are transferred into your name at the onset and out of your name when you leave.

- Get to know your managing agents and be realistic about what they can achieve – that way you will get the best out of them.

- Protect your belongings with tenants contents insurance. If your London office cannot recommend an insurance broker, you might telephone the British Insurance Broker's Association, 14 Bevis Marks, EC3A; (020) 7623 9043, for a recommendation.

- Always get your property professionally cleaned when you leave. Domestic cleaning is no substitute.

## Know your Neighbourhood

- Proximity to schools/parks/playgrounds.

- Proximity to amenities – shops, restaurants and pubs.

- Is there a local supermarket?

- Proximity to the tube – is it an easy link to work?

- Availability of on street/off street parking.

- Level of crime in the area – check with local police if needed.

## Household Tips

Look out for:

- Storage space and bedroom wardrobe (closet) space.

- Points for appliances, PC, TV & video, stereo, etc.

- Burglar alarm and smoke alarms.

- Separate washing machine and dryer (often they are all in one).

- Refrigerator/freezer size (often they do not meet American specifications).

- Shower pressure (power showers).

- Access – are there too many stairs? Are the common areas of a good standard?

- Height and width of the corridors and stairwells (especially in conversions).

- Outside space – do you have access to the garden/will you have to share?

Much of the 'Renting Property' information has been provided by Naomi Heaton, London Central Portfolio Ltd.

## BUYING PROPERTY

For those not familiar with buying property in London, the experience can be daunting, distressing and expensive. It will pay dividends to acquaint yourself with basic procedures and terms and to obtain good professional advice.

### Acquisition Costs

| | |
|---|---|
| Finders Fee: | The fee paid to a property search or purchase management company for representing you, the buyer, and finding your property. You do not have to pay such a fee if you register with a normal estate agent and/or reply to an advertisement for a property. Remember that an estate agent represents the seller's interest – not yours. |
| Legal Fees: | The solicitor's fee for acting for you in the purchase. These can vary quite significantly so it is advisable to obtain a quotation before proceeding. |
| Lenders Arrangement Fee: | Lenders may charge you for organising your house loan. This may be a flat fee or a percentage of the total advance. They may also require legal representation using a solicitor from their designated panel. |
| Local Searches: | These are searches undertaken by your solicitor of the local Council to ensure there are no apparent reasons for not proceeding with the purchase. These take about two weeks and cost in the region of £180 to £200. |
| Stamp Duty: | A government tax levied on the purchase price. 1% for purchases between £60,001 - £250,000, 3% between £250,001 - £500,000 and 4% on the purchase price thereafter. |
| Survey Fees: | The cost of the survey conducted to determine that the property has no significant structural faults. |

## Conveyancing (Legal) Process

| | |
|---|---|
| Estate Agent: | The selling agents who receive a fee from the vendor to achieve a sale at the best possible price. |
| Formulating the Offer: | Your bid will be given to the Estate Agent who will forward it to the vendor for acceptance. There is very little price negotiation in the marketplace and if you like something, it is often best to offer the asking price. In return you should ask for a period of exclusivity when another contract cannot be issued. (This is not legally binding). |
| Gazumping: | Prior to exchange of contracts, the vendor may accept another offer, usually as a result of receiving a higher bid. |
| Legal Exchange of Contracts: | At this stage, which takes approximately one month, providing you have received your mortgage offer, you will enter into a legally binding contract with the seller who can no longer accept other offers. You will normally pay a 10% deposit although 5% is increasingly acceptable. |
| Legal Completion: | This usually occurs one month after exchange of contracts at which time you become the legal owner of the property and obtain possession. |
| Insurance: | If you are buying a house you are responsible for buildings insurance from exchange. With flats, you pay for this via the service charge. You will require contents insurance at completion to cover your belongings. |
| Mortgages: | The term for a housing loan, normally up to 70-80% of the purchase price and for a period up to 30 years. Lenders normally require 25 years on the lease at the end of the term. |
| Capital Repayment: | Instalment covers interest as well as repaying the capital borrowed. |
| Endowment: | This uses the maturity value of an endowment policy to pay off the borrowing at the end of the term. Be aware that at maturity, the assurance policy may not cover the full loan sum. |
| Interest Only: | Covers the interest only that is accumulating on the loan. In this case it is advisable to have collateral security to pay off the capital at the end of the term. |

## Surveys

| | |
|---|---|
| Mortgage Valuation: | A visual inspection carried out by the Bank to confirm the property valuation. |
| Homebuyer's Report And Valuation: | Normally used by the homebuyer to obtain basic structural information. |
| Full Structural Survey: | A more expensive but comprehensive report highlighting significant faults which may lead to further negotiation on the property purchase price. |

## Types of Property Charges

| | |
|---|---|
| Service Charges: | Annual contribution to the running costs of a building e.g., porter, lift, lighting, cleaning. |
| Sinking Fund: | Reserve fund collected annually to provision for major works e.g. external redecoration. |
| Ground Rent: | Sum paid to owner of the freehold for use of the land over which your property is built. |

## Types of Tenure

| | |
|---|---|
| Freehold: | Outright purchase of a building, normally a house, and land "in perpetuity." |
| Leasehold: | Purchase of a right to occupy a house or, more normally, a flat, for a specified number of years, up to 999. The land and main structure of the property is owned by the freeholder who charges ground rent. Leases confer obligations on the lessee and the landlords. Property values diminish as leases shorten but owner occupiers have a statutory right, subject to certain terms, to extend their lease for a further 90 years. |
| Share of Freehold: | In some cases, the building lessees combine together to buy the freehold. A Management Company is normally set up to purchase it and the lessees take a share. Amongst other benefits, it is then possible to extend the lease term without payment of a premium. |

\* Buying Property information provided by Naomi Heaton, London Central Portfolio Ltd.

## ENGLISH TERMINOLOGY

The following list of real estate "jargon" will hopefully eliminate any confusion in communication and help you "read" your property particulars.

### A home by any other name

There are a whole host of different descriptions for property, especially in London. Here are a few of the most common:

| | |
|---|---|
| Bungalow: | One level ground floor house, very rare in central London. |
| Conversion: | A flat in a house that was originally for single family occupation. |
| Cottage: | Small rustic-style house, generally old, often with garden. |
| Detached House: | A house that stands apart from any others; generally surrounded by its own garden. |
| Duplex: | Apartment on two floors. |
| Flat: | Apartment, usually on one floor. |
| Maisonette: | Apartment on two or more floors. |
| Mansion Block: | Period apartment building often Victorian, Edwardian or "Art Deco", built specifically to provide flats. |
| Mansion Flat: | Large, traditionally old-fashioned apartment, usually in a good area. Often possessing large rooms, good storage space and lacking modern conveniences, until refurbished. |
| Mews House: | Converted "carriage" house, small rooms and lots of "character", archetypal English, often with garage. |
| "New Build": | A property, either in a new development of flats or houses. |
| Purpose Built Block: | A modern block of flats built specifically for this purpose. |
| Semi-Detached House: | A house that is joined to another house on one side only, generally with its own garden. |
| Studio Flat: | A one roomed flat with a separate bathroom and kitchen or kitchenette. |
| Terraced House: | One of a row of similar houses joined together. |
| Town House: | Typical central London home, often located in a Georgian or Victorian terrace, usually 2-5 floors high. |

## The ABC of Property

Know your abbreviations. Below are some of the most commonly used.

| | |
|---|---|
| CH: | Central Heating. |
| CHW: | Constant hot water. |
| F/F: | Fully furnished: equipped with furniture, soft furnishings and accessories for immediate occupation. |
| GFCH or GCH: | Gas-fired central heating. |
| OSP: | Off-street parking, which is free and unrestricted. Mostly found in mews or private roads. |
| Respark: | Residents Parking: Council approved on-street parking. Usually unrestricted access in allocated areas for 2 vehicles per household for small annual fee. |
| U/F: | Unfurnished: no furniture but generally with carpets, light fixtures and appliances. |
| WC: | Literally "water closet" but really a room with toilet and wash basin. |

## English as a foreign language

Here is some property "lingo" you may be unfamiliar with:

| | |
|---|---|
| Airing Cupboard: | Cupboard housing the hot water tank, with extra space suitable for drying damp and pressed clothes. |
| Boiler: | Furnace usually combined with hot water heater. |
| Communal Gardens: | Landscaped area in most "squares" that provides outdoor space for residents of the square. Access is by key and an annual fee is charged for maintenance. All have rules regarding access for dogs and permitted children's activities. |
| Common Parts: | The common area of a block of flats looked after by the building owner/managing agents. |
| Communal Heating & Hot Water: | Provided by a central source and included in the "building maintenance charge", paid directly by the landlord and not the tenant. |
| Courtyard: | Central area surrounded by flats and houses for the use of residents. Often paved with ornamental gardens. |
| Fireplace: | The burning of wood is banned in London by the air pollution laws, but "smokeless fuel" may be purchased. The fireplace may be fitted with gas jets. The term may also refer to the ornate surround. |
| Fixtures and Fittings: | This term may include anything from major appliances to carpets, curtains, and lighting fixtures. These may be excluded in the sale price and your solicitor will receive a list for checking. As a tenant, they will be included on the inventory. |
| Reception Rooms: | General term for living room, drawing room, sitting room, dining room and study. |
| Self-Contained: | Has its own separate entrance. |

No list would be complete without mention of the diverse descriptions of the "little room"!

| | |
|---|---|
| Bathroom: | A room used for bathing: always contains a tub and wash basin, very often has a toilet, sometimes a bidet. Sometimes incorporates the shower. |
| Cloakroom: | Toilet and wash basin, often with space to store outerwear. |
| Loo/WC: | Toilet with wash basin. |
| Shower room: | Room with shower cubicle, generally with toilet and wash basin. |
| Shower: | Maybe self-contained cubicle or small hose with showerhead attached to tub taps, often affording minimal pressure. Increasingly American style "power showers" are being installed. |

* English Terminology provided by Naomi Heaton, London Central Portfolio Ltd.

## AGENTS LISTINGS

Hopefully, you have now a flavour of what living in London is all about – both in terms of the areas and the basic issues involved in buying and renting. Below is a brief list of agents that other readers have found helpful.

## RELOCATION FIRMS

Enquire whether your company recommends a relocation firm in London. If this service is available to you, by all means look into it. These firms can introduce you to the local real estate market, explain the UK educational system, make appointments at schools, acquaint you with driving test requirements and provide information on leisure and sports facilities. Such firms are particularly useful in the absence of a multiple listing system as they will contact all estate agents in an area.

*Anglo Relocations,* 34 Meadway, Esher, Surrey, KT10, (01372) 469 019.

*Cendant Relocations,* Framewood Road, Wexham, Slough, SL3, (01753) 834 000; (www.cendantrelocation.co.uk)

*Team Relocations Ltd.,* Unit 1, 91-97 Freston Road, W11, (020) 7221 4867; (Ers@execrelo.demon.co.uk)

*Karen Deane Relocations Ltd.,* Plaza, 535 King's Road, SW10, (020) 7352 4114; (www.karendeane.com)

*Karen Phillips & Co.*, 15 Park Drive, NW11, (020) 8731 7370; (karenphillipsuk@aol.com). Specialises in St. John's Wood, Hampstead and surrounding areas.

*Key Relocation Services*, (020) 8748 3232; contact Nanouk Busck-Neilsen.

*LSS Relocation*, Surrey House, 114 Tilit Road, Cobham, Surrey, KT11 3JH, (01932) 868 608; (Info@lssrelocation.co.uk)

*People and Property*, 18 Coulson Street, SW3, (020) 7225 1313; (www.peopleandproperty.net)

*Premier Relocation Management*, 111 Station Road, Hampton, Middlesex, TW12, (020) 8941 7195.

*The Relocation Company*, 2/10 Harbour Yard, Chelsea Harbour, London SW10 0XD, (020) 7761 9420.

*Relocation Resources International*, First Floor, 56 Buckingham Gate, SW1E, (020) 7802 2500; (www.rriworld.com)

*UK Relocation Services Ltd.*, 58 Grand Avenue, N10, (020) 8442 0044; (www.ukrelocation.com)

## TEMPORARY ACCOMMODATIONS AND SERVICED FLATS

Serviced flats are fully furnished apartments that can be rented by the week or by the month. This accommodation provides maid and porter service. If you have not been able to come to London on a house-hunting trip and arrive with the whole family, serviced flats can be much more pleasant than staying in a large commercial hotel. Many companies deal with these on a regular basis, so enquire at your London office.

*The Apartment Service*, 5-6 Francis Grove, SW19; (020) 8944 1444, (www.apartmentservice.com)

*Draycott House*, 10 Draycott Avenue, Chelsea, SW3, (Sloane Square tube), (020) 7584 4659.

*Go Native Limited*, 26 Westbourne Grove, W2, (020) 7221 2028; (www.gonative.co.uk)

## ESTATE AGENTS

Estate agents generally only have a listing of homes in their immediate area although many firms now have offices scattered throughout London. There is no established multiple listing system in London, although many agents have good working relationships with certain agents in other areas and can set up a network of agents for you. Most estate agents work Monday through Friday, but weekend hours are becoming more common.

The following is a list of some of the estate agencies we have found to be helpful. In case of agencies with several locations, we have listed the full address and telephone number of the main office, and their branch locations; ring the number shown for additional details. It should be noted that estate agents are not required to have a licence or undergo training.

Please note that as a buyer or renter you generally should not have to pay a fee to the estate agent for finding a property for you. The agent's fees are paid by the landlord or vendor.

## Central London

*Allsop & Co.*, 100 Knightsbridge, SW1 (Knightsbridge tube); (020) 7584 6106; (www.allsop.co.uk). Also in the West End and the City.

*AMA International Property Services*, 20 Seymour Street, W1 (Marble Arch tube), (020) 7724 4844; (www.ama-international.com). Specialises in luxury short-term accommodation.

*Aylesford & Co.*, 440 King's Road, SW10 (Sloane Square tube and No. 11 or 22 bus); (020) 7351 2383; (www.aylesford.com). Also in Kensington and Wimbledon.

*Chestertons Residential*, 2 Cale Street, SW3 (Sloane Square or South Kensington tube); (020) 7589 4585; (www.chesterton.co.uk). Also in Barnes, Battersea, Bayswater, Chiswick, Docklands, Fulham, Hampstead, Kensington, Little Venice, Mayfair, Pimlico, Putney, Tower Bridge and Wimbledon.

*Churchill House Lettings*, 6 Pownall Road, Hounslow, Middlesex, TW3; (020) 8570 3655; (www.tower-bridge.co.uk). Specialises in Tower Bridge/Shad Thames - London SE1 and Waterloo.

*Douglas & Gordon*, 21 Milner Street, SW3 (Sloane Square tube); (020) 7730 0666; (www.douglasandgordon.com). Also in Battersea, Clapham, Fulham, Putney and Wandsworth.

*Farrar & Co.*, 152 Fulham Road, SW10 (South Kensington tube); (020) 7373 8425; (www.farrarandco.co.uk). Covers SW3, SW7 and SW10 areas.

*FPD Savills*, 20 Grosvenor Hill, W1 (Bond Street or Green Park tube); (020) 7499 8644; (www.fpdsavills.co.uk). Also in City, Docklands, Fulham, Hampstead, Kensington and Sloane Street and throughout England.

*Friend & Falcke*, 293 Brompton Road, SW3 (South Kensington tube); (020) 7225 0814; (www.friendandfalcke.co.uk). Also in Barnes, Belgravia, Brook Green, Clapham, Fulham and Wandsworth.

*Gerald Kay*, 64 Bury Walk, SW3 (South Kensington tube); (020) 7823 3113.

*Hamptons International*, 168 Brompton Road, SW3 (Knightsbridge or South Kensington tube); (020) 7584 2014; (www.hamptons.co.uk) Also in Chelsea, Wimbledon, Hampstead and Kensington.

*John D. Wood & Co.*, Lincoln House, 296-302 High Holborn, WC1V (Chancery Lane tube); (020) 7430-2100; (www.johndwood.co.uk). Also in Battersea, Chelsea, Fulham, Kensington, St. John's Wood, Wandsworth and Wimbledon.

*Knight Frank*, Kings House, 36 King Street, EC2V (Oxford Circus tube); (020) 7606 0606; (www.knightfrank.com). Also in Chelsea, City, Docklands, Knightsbridge and Wapping.

*London Central Portfolio Ltd*, 39 Crawford Street, W1H (Marble Arch Tube); (020) 7723 1733; (www.londoncentralportfolio.com). Specialists in property search, refurbishing, furnishing and lettings in prime central London.

*Marsh & Parsons*, 9 Kensington Church Street, W8 (Kensington High Street tube); (020) 7368 4454; (www.marshandparsons.co.uk). Also in Bayswater, Chelsea, Holland Park, Notting Hill and Shepherd's Bush.

*McGlashans Property Services*, 43 Marylebone Lane, W1U (Bond Street tube); (020) 7486 6711. Primarily in West End, Hampstead, Swiss Cottage, Amersham, Ruislip, Finchley and Chalfont.

*Susan Rafi*, 12 Mercers Place, W6 (Hammersmith tube); (020) 7602 8579. Individual property consultant who specialises in finding, vetting and selecting high quality houses and apartments for rent mainly in Central London (fees payable).

*W. A. Ellis*, 174 Brompton Road, SW3 (South Kensington or Knightsbridge tube); (020) 7581 7654; (www.wa-ellis.co.uk). Handles properties primarily in Knightsbridge, Chelsea, Belgravia, Kensington and South Kensington.

*Winkworth & Co.*, 123A Gloucester Road, SW7 (Gloucester Road tube); (020) 7373 5052; (www.winkworth.co.uk). Branches across London.

## Greater London and the Home Counties

### Surrey

*Countrywide Residential Lettings*, 42 High Street, Esher, KT10; (01372) 466 110; (www.cwrl.co.uk).

*John D. Wood*, 53A High Street, Esher, KT10; (01372) 462 211; (www.johndwood.co.uk)

*Hamptons International*, 51 High Street, Esher, KT10; (01372) 468 411; www.hamptons.co.uk

*Your Move*, 69 High Street, Walton-on-Thames, KT12; (01932) 220 548; (www.your-move.co.uk)

### Buckinghamshire

*Bradford & Bingley/Rafferty Buckland*, 7 Burkes Parade, Beaconsfield, HP9; (01494) 675 432; (www.marketplace.co.uk)

*Hamptons International,* 10 Burkes Parade, Beaconsfield, HP9; (01494) 671 511; (www.hamptons.co.uk)

## Berkshire

*Barton & Wyatt,* 2 Station Approach, Virginia Water, GU25; (01344) 842 857, (www.bartonwyatt.co.uk)

*Chancellors Residential,* 31 High Street, Ascot, SL5; (01344) 872 909; (www.chancellors.co.uk)

*JSC Lettings,* 23 Station Approach, Virginia Water, GU25; (01344) 845 535; (www.jsclettings.co.uk)

Additional information on estate agents throughout the UK

*ARLA (Association of Residential Letting Agents),* Maple House, 53-55 Woodside Road, Amersham, Bucks HP6; (01494) 431 680; (www.arla.co.uk)

*NAEA (National Association of Estate Agents),* Arbon House, 21 Jury Street, Warwick CV34 4EH; (01926) 496 800; (www.naea.co.uk)

## PROPERTY INVESTMENT CONSULTANTS

Once you have settled in London, you may wish to consider the unique investment opportunity central London offers. There are specialist companies that can help you identify a suitable property and assist you in fitting it out for rental, letting and management. Whilst financially rewarding, it can be a difficult and daunting market to enter and requires local knowledge and expertise to maximise the opportunity.

*London Central Portfolio (LCP) Ltd,* 39 Crawford Street, W1H (Marble Arch Tube); (020) 7723 1733; (www.londoncentralportfolio.com). Consultants who specialise in property search, refurbishment, furnishing, letting and management of residential property for investors. A one-stop, in-house service which covers all of prime central London.

*\* Much of the information in this chapter has been contributed by Naomi Heaton, London Central Portfolio Ltd.*

# Chapter Three:
# Money, Banking and Taxation

## British Currency

British currency, normally referred to as sterling, comprises two monetary units: the penny (called the 'p') and the pound. Like the US dollar, the pound is spilt into 100 smaller units. The smallest unit is the penny, so one hundred pennies equal one pound, however, all other coins are referred to as pence. Coins include the penny, two pence, five pence, ten pence, twenty pence, fifty pence, the one pound coin, and the two (£2.00) pound coin. The notes (bills) are called pounds (£) and come in five pound, ten pound, twenty pound and fifty pound notes. You may hear a pound called a 'quid'.

> *Did you know...*The term 'quid' comes from the Latin expression 'quid pro quo' meaning one thing in return for another, no doubt dating back to the Roman occupation of Britain.

> *Did you know...*Many services, for example shops and taxis especially, don't like to or can't change large notes. Asking for smaller notes when banking will make life easier.

## The Euro

The Euro is a common currency adopted by several European countries that are member states of the European Union. As of January 1, 2002, the Euro notes and coins replaced the national currencies of: Austria, Belgium, Finland, France, Germany, Greece, Ireland, Italy, Luxembourg, The Netherlands, Portugal, and Spain.

The Euro is divided into 100 cent with coins and notes issued in a similar fashion to the British pound. In addition to the cent coins (issued in denominations of one, two, five, ten, twenty, fifty) there is a one Euro coin and a two Euro coin. Each coin carries a common European design on one side and designs created by each Member state on the other side. All coins are valid in all twelve countries regardless of the Member state specific design on one side of the coin. Bills are issued in denominations of five, ten, twenty, fifty, one hundred, two hundred, and five hundred.

The transition to a common currency is called The European Monetary Union (EMU) and is one of many objectives facing the European Union (EU). Another way to think about the EMU is as the Unification of several currencies. This is not to be confused with the European Union itself which, to save confusion, is described below. In January 2002, the Economic and Monetary Union entered the final phase when the Euro was introduced in physical form.

Three member states of the EU decided not to enter the EMU and thereby retain their national currencies. They are: Denmark, Sweden, and The United Kingdom.

There has been and continues to be fierce debate in the United Kingdom regarding participation in the Euro. Although most support strengthening ties between European states in a political sense, many question the merits of joining the monetary unit of the Euro. The main cause for concern is the relative strength of the British Pound today in comparison to the Euro. Abandoning the pound and joining the Euro is synonymous to many as propping up Europe's economy at the expense of the UK. However, it will likely become increasingly difficult for the UK to effectively participate in other issues facing the EU without adopting the unified currency.

---

### The European Union

The European Union is an institutional system with Member states aiming to represent the interests of the Union on issues of interest to all. France first suggested the creation of the union in 1950. Since the original six countries, the total number of Members is now 15. The Member States are: Austria, Belgium, Denmark, Finland, France, Germany, Greece, Ireland, Italy, Luxembourg, The Netherlands, Portugal, Spain, Sweden, and The United Kingdom. Current objectives of the EU include, establishing European citizenship, ensuring freedom, security and justice, promote economic and social progress, and asserting Europe's role in the world.

---

### Conversions

From the moment you arrive in the UK, one question you will be confronted with time and time again is 'How much does this cost in US dollars?' Since your frame of reference of what you consider to pay for an item is in dollars, you will most likely frequently convert prices from pounds to dollars. Given the exchange rate (at the time of printing) of 1.45 GBP to 1.00 USD, to convert from pounds to dollars, simply multiply the price in pounds by 1.45. However, the quicker you get a feel for what is cheap, expensive, or appropriate in terms of pounds, the more comfortable you will feel. Given that the USD is a weaker currency than the GBP, most items will seem expensive when you covert the GBP price into USD. Therefore, the sooner you get accustomed to prices in GBP and stop converting, the better.

As a point of reference, one Euro is the equivalent of about 0.90 USD at the time of printing.

## Banks in London

Much of your banking needs will likely be determined by your main source of income. If you are moving to the UK as an expatriate, your company may choose to continue to pay your salary in USD to a US bank account providing an adjustment for the difference in cost of living. If this is the case, note that although many of the major US banks have branches in London, many of them do not offer 'retail' or personal banking services. Contact your London Branch to see if they will provide chequing and savings account services and importantly 'plastic' compatible with the UK network of ATM's and accepted in most shops.

It is generally a good idea to open a local currency account with a UK bank. Some of the largest UK banks are:
* Barclays Bank (www.barclays.com, www.internationalbanking.barclays.com)
* Lloyds TSB Bank (www.lloydstsb.com)
* National Westminster Bank (www.natwest.co.uk)
* HSBC (www.hsbc.co.uk). They have numerous branches throughout London and the rest of England.
* Citibank (www.citibank.com) offers services specifically for individuals requiring access to multiple currencies.

For a local currency account, the major banks offer essentially the same services. Therefore you will probably choose the bank with which your firm has a business relationship, or the bank located nearest to your home or office. Although personal references may be required, your passport will be the main requirement for identity purposes. A letter of introduction from your firm helps and if you require immediate 'credit' facilities, copies of your US bank statements or a letter of introduction from your US bank will also speed the process.

## Banking Services

The UK banks offer two basic types of accounts: 'current accounts' (checking accounts) and 'deposit accounts' (savings accounts) although there are variations of each type of account. Building Societies (similar to the US savings and loans associations) also offer current accounts. Most British banks now offer interest on current accounts. Most banks will provide *'sweep accounts'*. This means the bank will automatically transfer excess funds from your current account to your deposit account. In reverse, the bank will move funds from your deposit account to your current account to maintain the agreed credit balance. You should obtain a 'direct debit/cheque guarantee card' for your current account (see cheques and cards). At the request of the customer, statements are sent quarterly or monthly. Cancelled cheques are returned only if requested and a fee is charged. Free banking is currently offered by most banks as long as you maintain a credit balance. There are no longer any restrictions on the amount of sterling that expatriates may deposit and withdraw from their bank accounts in the UK.

Monthly or quarterly bills, (telephone, electricity, gas, water, council tax) may be paid at your bank by two methods. One method is to use the *giro slips* attached to most bills. The slips can be grouped together and all paid with a single cheque. The bank stamps your bill providing a record of payment, proving beneficial as cheques are not normally returned by the bank. Other methods of payment, and perhaps the easiest, are the use of a *standing order* or *direct debit*. With a standing order you instruct your bank to pay a fixed amount to a specified payee at regular intervals, usually on a certain day each month (e.g. £1,000 rent on the 15th of every month to the estate office). With a direct debit, you authorise your bank to pay on demand varying amounts as specified by a particular supplier (e.g. whatever the electricity company *states is your quarterly bill). For additional information on paying utilities, see page – in Chapter Five: Utilities.

## Bank Hours

Regular banking hours are 9.00 – 16.30, Monday through Friday, however, they are closed on holidays. Please refer to Chapter Sixteen: Annual Events for a listing of Bank Holidays in the UK. Many banks will close at 12.00 on Christmas Eve. All major banks have cash machines which operate 24 hours a day at most of their branches and increasingly, elsewhere. You must apply to your bank for a suitable cash card. Saturday hours (09.30 to 12.00) are currently being offered by some of the UK clearing banks, mainly in their suburban locations.

> **Did you know...** ATM's in the UK do not accept deposits.

## Cheques and Cards

Writing a sterling cheque differs slightly from writing a US dollar cheque. When writing a cheque there are two important points to remember.

1. The date is written with the day, the month and then the year. For example, 5 March 1999 or 5-3-99. Do remember to either put the day first or spell out the month.

2. To write the amount, you must write 'pounds' and 'p' or 'pence'. For example, £10.62 is written 'Ten pounds and 62p' or 'Ten pounds and sixty-two pence'.

Sterling cheques are usually 'crossed', meaning that they have two vertical lines running down the middle. A crossed cheque is for deposit only and cannot be cashed by a third party. Hence, the endorsing of cheques for cash is not done in the UK.

All UK banks are now on a three and a half ($3^1/_2$) day clearing cycle with the banks discretion. Cash deposits, however, are credited immediately. Although you may cash a cheque for any amount at your own branch, cashing a cheque at either another branch of your bank, or at another bank requires your cheque card, and if over the value of your card (£50 or £100, as denoted on the back of your card), it also requires prior arrangement with your own branch. With a cheque guarantee/direct debit card you can normally cash up to £100 daily at other branches and banks; sometimes a small fee is charged.

Cheque guarantee cards can now also incorporate a credit card and/or a direct debit card facility, whereby you can use the card on its own, without writing out a cheque. A well-known direct debit card is 'Switch' (a black and white 'S' within a green square sign found on your cheque guarantee card). The advantage is that you have a clear audit trail on your statement of account (service provider or retailer's name appears on your bank statement). These will allow the retailer to directly debit your account and are limited to available funds.

> **Did You Know...**Switch is often accepted at retail stores as well when purchasing items over the phone.

## Bank Credit Cards

There are numerous bank credit cards in the UK, Barclaycard (Visa) and the Access card (MasterCard) being the best-known names. These cards can be used throughout the UK and in Europe where the appropriate sign is displayed. Similar US cards are also accepted. Initially getting one of these cards can be difficult, if you don't already have a credit record in the UK. A letter or phone call from your company can speed the process.

## Travellers Cheques

Travellers cheques and foreign currency can be purchased from all the major UK banks; however, it is usually necessary to give a few days' notice. Travellers cheques can also be obtained from Thomas Cook and American Express offices located throughout the UK. Cashing dollar travellers cheques often incurs a large fee if the bank does not have a relationship with the travellers cheque company.

## Transferring Money

If you want to transfer money from your US checking account to your UK current account, you purchase sterling from your UK bank with a cheque in dollars drawn on your US bank account. Normally the bank negotiates your small dollar cheques and credits your sterling account immediately. In the case of larger dollar amounts, the bank may collect your dollars before crediting your account or a facility for immediate credit may be agreed.

The process of transferring large amounts of money may take 10 to 14 days to complete by post. Transfer by telex may be completed in 48 hours.

If you wish to remit money to the US, ask your UK bank to draw a dollar cheque (draft) on your behalf against the sterling in your current account. The bank will either issue a cheque in dollars or, for a nominal charge, transfer amounts to your US bank by mail, cable or telex.

> **Did You Know...**As an ex-pat living in the UK, you pay UK taxes on any money you bring into the country.

**MONEY, BANKING AND TAXATION**

## Safety Deposit Boxes

Safety deposit boxes are privately run safety deposit centres. Harrod's rent Safety Deposit Boxes for an annual fee. For more information, look under Services on the Harrod's web site: www.harrods.com. Local commercial banks do not have facilities for individual safety deposit boxes. The banks do provide 'strong rooms' for their customers' valuables to be stored in; they may be in a cash or 'deed' metal box.

## Offshore Banking

Several banks provide an offshore banking option in addition to local services. Rationale for obtaining and utilising an offshore account vary according to your individual situation. They may include tax savings, shelter from monetary instability, or investment opportunity.

As a UK resident, offshore banking may provide a tax benefit as any income earned while physically located in another country is not subject to UK tax provided that these monies are deposited into an offshore account and do not make it back to the UK. For example, if you spend two months working in France for your company, you would not be liable to pay UK income tax on those two months of wages provided that the wages were deposited in an offshore account and are not brought into the UK. For more details on this and other benefits of an offshore account, contact your financial advisor.

## Taxation

When you leave the US to live in Great Britain, your tax status changes. Because you live in the United Kingdom the Inland Revenue (the UK's tax office, similar to the Internal Revenue Service in the US) has primary jurisdiction over your income; but you also have an obligation based on your American citizenship to report and pay US income tax to the IRS.

## United Kingdom Taxes

The system of taxation in the UK differs from the US system, in that the UK tax year runs from 6 April to the following 5 April. Under the "Self Assessment" system in the UK, many taxpayers calculate their own income and capital gains tax liabilities. Individuals who are correctly taxed at source on their income (e.g. their earnings are taxed via the Pay-As-You-Earn "PAYE" system) do not need to file a tax return each year. Others with more complicated affairs will often need to make an account payment for the current year based on the previous year's liability, before making a balancing payment by 31 January following the end of the tax year.

Interest will be charged on tax not paid by its due date, and penalties will be levied for tax returns filed late. Returns should be filed by 30 September following the end of the tax year if you want the Inland Revenue to work out your liability and by 31 January following the end of the tax year if you work out your own liability, interest will be charged on tax not paid by its due date.

Publication IR20, *Residents and Non-residents: Liability to Tax in the United Kingdom*, which is published by the Inland Revenue, discusses the taxation of individuals in the United Kingdom. For detailed information, visit the Inland Reveune's web site at www.inlandrevenue.gov.uk.

UK taxes are administered through the Inland Revenue, and local offices are listed in the telephone directory. If you are employed in the UK, PAYE (Pay-As-You-Earn) will be deducted from your salary. If you are self-employed your accountant will normally advise you, or you may report to your nearest Inland Revenue office, which is listed in the local telephone directory. Each person is entitled to a tax-free personal allowance which at the time of this printing (current year $^{1}/_{2}$) is £4,535. Prior to the 2000-2001 tax year, each married couple was entitled to an additional allowance. As of the 2000-2001 tax year, the married couple allowance was aboloished unless the age of one spouse was 65 or over on 5 April, 2000.

If you intend to reside in the UK for a temporary period only (temporary can mean a number of years), you normally will not be considered to be domiciled here. In this situation, if the source of your investment income is in the UK, or if such income from your investments outside the UK is remitted to you in the UK, you will be taxed on it in the UK.

Social security taxes (FICA in the US and National Insurance in the UK) are payable in the UK just as they are in America – withheld from your pay if you are an employee, and payable with your income tax and by direct debit if you are self employed. Under the totalisation agreement between the US and the UK, Americans working in the UK generally will be required to pay social security tax either in the UK or in the US but not in both countries. Which country you pay to is determined by the length of your anticipated stay in the UK.

*VAT* (Value Added Tax) is similar to a sales tax. Currently 17.5 per cent VAT is included in all your purchases, except groceries, children's clothes and certain other items. It is not deductible against either US or UK income taxes, but if you have your own business, you may pass the VAT you pay in connection with that business on to the ultimate consumer of your goods or services, provided your gross turnover is above a certain amount of your goods and services and your business is registered for VAT.

## Council Tax

The council tax is a local tax set by local councils to help pay for local services. There will be one bill per dwelling to be paid by the resident or by the owner where the property has no residents. The amount paid will be based on the value of the dwelling.

---

*Did you know...*Single occupants receive a 25% discount on council tax.

---

Capital gains tax, inheritance tax and other UK taxes and duties on your property may significantly affect the way you wish to set up your estate. American lawyers in the UK are usually skilled in adapting your will to protect your estate.

## American Taxes

American citizens are taxed by the US on their world-wide income with a tax credit, subject to credit limitations, for foreign income taxes paid.

*Filing requirements*: In general American citizens wherever they live in the world, must file a tax return if their income exceeds a certain amount. Men and women, single or married, are equally responsible. Filing dates are automatically extended for Americans abroad from 15 April to 15 June, but interest is applied from 15 April to any tax due.

Publication 54, *Tax Guide for US Citizens and Resident Aliens Abroad*, is available at the IRS office of the US Embassy, 24 Grosvenor Square, W1A 1AE (Marble Arch, Bond Street tube); (020) 7408 8076, or you may write to Forms Distribution Center, P.O. Box 25866, Richmond, VA 23260, USA, or visit the web site at www.irs.gov.

Taxpayers are entitled to elect to use a $78,000 exclusion (for the 2001 tax year) to reduce their foreign source earned (employment) income, if they meet one of two tests, the bona fide residence test or the physical presence test. A bona fide resident has lived in a foreign country for an uninterrupted period that includes an entire tax year. The physical presence test is met by being physically present in a foreign country for at least 330 full days in any 365 day period. In the first year of foreign residence, if a taxpayer wishes to elect the exclusions but does not yet qualify when the tax return is due, he may file an extension to a date after he meets the qualification.

1. *Foreign Earned Income Exclusion:* If your tax home is a foreign country and you qualify under either the bona fide residence test or the physical presence test, you can exclude the actual amount of foreign income earned during the year, up to a maximum of $78,000. If husband and wife both work they are each entitled to the exclusion. The foreign earned income exclusion is set to increase to $80,000 for the 2002 tax year.

2. *Housing Cost Amount Exclusion:* A taxpayer may also choose to exclude from gross income certain housing costs that have been provided by the employer in excess of a specified base amount.

After these deductions, any remaining earned income and all unearned income is taxed as if it were the only income and, therefore, will generally be taxed at a much lower effective tax rate. If both husband and wife work, the foreign earned income exclusion is computed separately, even if they file jointly.

*Moving and Replacement of Personal Residence.* If you moved because of your job or business, you may be able to deduct your moving expenses. Any other amounts reimbursed to an employee are taxable income.

*Foreign Tax Credit.* As you are generally subject to tax both in the UK and the US, a foreign tax credit for foreign income taxes paid may be used, to some extent, to offset US taxes due on foreign income.

*Social Security Taxes.* FICA continues to be payable by most Americans who are employed by a US company in the UK, or certain affiliates, and from the onset do not intend to stay for more than five years in the UK. In most other situations UK National Insurance contributions are payable.

*State and Local Taxes.* You may not be liable for state or local income taxes if you live abroad, although this depends on the state from which you have moved. However, you remain liable for any taxes on property (real estate or personal property) that generates income in the US.

## Canadian Taxes

In general, if you can establish that you are no longer a resident of Canada you do not have to pay taxes in Canada on income earned outside Canada. Specific questions can be directed to the International Tax Office, 2540 Lancaster Road, Ottawa, Ontario K1A 1A8, Canada; (613) 952-3741. Information may also be accessed on the Canada Customs and Revenue Agency web site at www.ccra-adrc.gc.ca.

## Tax Assistance

For further information on your UK or US tax obligations, you may contact the Inland Revenue, your UK or US accountant or lawyer, or your company's personnel or expatriate employee departments. For UK tax enquiries, there are various local enquiry offices in London listed under 'Inland Revenue' in the telephone directory. The IRS office in the US Embassy can assist you, at no cost, in filing your US returns and the Consular Office of the US Embassy has lists of American accountants and lawyers who can assist you for a fee.

There are a few small UK firms who specialise in US expatriates residing in the UK. Two suggestions are:

*Buzzacott & Livingstone*, 12 New Fetter Lane London EC4A 1AG (020) 7233 5177.

*Expatriate Tax Management*, Unit 502, 16 Brune Street, E1; (020) 7721 7993.

*Expatriate Tax Solutions*, 64 Woodbridge Road, Guildford, Surrey GU1 4RD, (01483) 306 530 (www. Expatiratetaxsolutions.com)

*MacIntyre Hudson*, Greenwood House, 4/7 Salisbury Court, EC4Y, (020) 7583 7575 (www.macintyrehudson.co.uk)

# Chapter Four:
# Working in London

Job hunting is a creative task that often requires considerable effort from the individual. Listed below are some resources that can help start your career search in London.

## GENERAL INFORMATION

*FOCUS Information Services*

FOCUS is a not for profit, volunteer-run organisation, that provides its members with programmes on working in the UK and operates a resource centre with information useful to a job seeker.

FOCUS also publishes a book, the *FOCUS Job Guide: Launching Your Career in the UK*, which is designed particularly for partners of expatriate employees. Topics include British CV Preparation, job websites, resource lists, networking groups and tips, interviewing strategies, and much more. The publication is free to members of FOCUS (limit 1 per member) and a nominal fee for non-members.

FOCUS Information Services, 13 Prince of Wales Terrace, London W8 5PG; (020) 7937 7799; Fax: (020) 7937 9482; (www.focus-info.org or e-mail: office@focus-info.org)

## Online Job Postings

A few of the larger UK job search websites include:

www.efinancialcareers.com

www.gojobsite.co.uk

www.jobserve.com

www.monster.co.uk

www.newmonday.co.uk

www.reed.co.uk

www.topjobs.co.uk

www.workthing.com

# British Newspaper Appointments Schedule

| Job Category | Monday | Tuesday | Wednesday | Thursday | Friday | Saturday | Sunday |
|---|---|---|---|---|---|---|---|
| **Accountancy** | Evening Standard, Financial Times | | Independent | Financial Times | | | |
| **Charities/Volunteers** | Evening Standard, | | Guardian | | | | |
| **Creative Media** | Guardian | Evening Standard | Evening Standard | | | | |
| **Education** | Times | Evening Standard, Guardian | | Independent, Times | | | |
| **Finance/Banking** | Evening Standard | Evening Standard | Guardian Independent | Daily Mail, Financial Times | | Guardian | |
| **General** | Evening Standard | Evening Standard | Guardian | Daily Express, Daily Mail, Daily Telegraph, Evening Standard, Times | | | Express, Independent, Observer, Sunday Telegraph, Sunday Times |
| **Hotel/Catering** | | Evening Standard | | Evening Standard | | | |
| **IT** | | Daily Telegraph | Evening Standard | Daily Telegraph, Guardian | | | |
| **Legal** | | Times | Independent | | | | |
| **Medical/Health** | Evening Standard | | Guardian | Daily Telegraph | | | |
| **Sales/Marketing** | Evening Standard Guardian | Evening Standard | | Daily Mail, Daily Telegraph, Evening Standard | | | |
| **Science/Technology** | | | | Daily Telegraph | | | |

## Newspapers

Classified job advertisements can be found in most major UK newspapers. Public libraries keep many local and national papers, which is worth considering as the cost of buying newspapers can add up.

### Newspaper job posting websites

Job advertisements can also be found on the websites of many newspapers:

- www.thisislondon.co.uk/jobs – *Evening Standard*

- http://ftcareerpoint.ft.com/ftcareerpoint – *Financial Times*

- www.jobs.guardian.co.uk – *Guardian*

- www.londoncareers.net/index2.html – *Independent*

- www.jobs.telegraph.co.uk – *Daily Telegraph*

- www.thetimes-appointments.co.uk – *Times/Sunday Times*

## Recruitment Consultants

*The Executive Grapevine: The UK Directory of Recruitment Consultants* (Executive Grapevine Publishers) is an annual publication that will help you identify the top recruitment consultants in the UK by salary range, function, industry, and location. This book can often be found at major libraries in the career section, as well as can be purchased directly from the publisher:

*Executive Grapevine International Limited*; New Barnes Mill, Cottonmill Lane, St Albans, AL1 2HA, UK; (01727) 844 335; fax: (01727) 844 779; (www.askgrapevine.com or email: *info@executive-grapevine.co.uk*)

*The London Professional Recruitment Guide* assesses the performance of recruitment consultancies across six main sectors: Accountancy, Banking & Finance, Commerce & Industry, Human Resources, Law, and Information & Communications Technology. (www.recruitment500.com)

The distinctions between different types of recruitment firms may not always be clear to a job searcher. Recruitment consultants often work in at least one of the following ways:

### Executive Search (often referred to as headhunting)

Executive search firms are retained by a corporate client on a fee basis to find an appropriate candidate to fill a particular role. This type of search is typically for senior-level positions in which the pool of suitable candidates is smaller. Executive search targets the best candidates for a position, whether or not they are actively looking for a new job.

## Advertised Selection

Recruitment firms are retained by a corporate client to advertise in the press to find candidates for a particular role. The approach relies on job candidates actively searching newspapers and trade publications to find job listings that may be of interest to them. Usually, the recruitment firm will review all cover letters and resumes/CVs received, and then interview the most relevant candidates. A short list of interviewed candidates is then presented to the client for the next stage of the interview process. Advertised selection is most frequently used for hiring middle management positions.

## Contingent Recruitment

Fees charged by a recruitment firm for this type of recruitment is contingent on a job placement being made. This type of recruitment relies on job searchers registering their resumes/CVs with the recruitment firm, and/or job searchers responding to an advertised position. Typically, corporate clients will select more than one contingent recruitment firm for a particular search to find the best pool of candidates at a given time. This type of recruitment is most common with lower salary bands, as well as temporary and contract positions. Contingent recruitment also is used for more senior roles in markets where there is a large supply of suitable candidates.

Other than ascertaining the type of a given recruitment firm, it is important to understand how the firm will likely use any personal information that you provide. It is a good idea to make sure your details are not passed on to a potential employer without your approval.

## Libraries

A visit to a larger reference library can be helpful to find more information on companies, industries, and recruitment firms. Libraries can be a great resource for trade journals, newspapers, and other periodicals. Listed below are two of the best reference libraries in London for a job search.

*City Business Library:* 1 Brewers' Hall Garden (off Aldermanbury Square), London EC2V; (020) 7332 1812; (www.cityoflondon.gov.uk). Opening hours: Monday to Friday 9.30 to 17.00.

*Westminster Reference Library Business Information:* 35 St. Martin's Street, London WC2H; (020) 7641 4634; (www.westminster.gov.uk/libraries/findalibrary.cfm). Opening hours: Monday to Friday 10.00 to 20.00, Saturday 10.00 to 17.00

## Company Information Websites

The following websites provide profiles of some UK companies and industry sectors:

www.hoovers.co.uk.

www.wetfeet.com

www.vault.com

## Networking

Networking is often a key aspect of any job search. The majority of jobs are never advertised and are filled by word of mouth and personal recommendation. Friends, relatives, former employers, former colleagues, members of professional organisations, and neighbours are all potential networking contacts. Every place you go, you could run in to a person that might be helpful in your search. This includes waiting in a line, attending a cocktail party, exercising at the gym, etc. Therefore, it is particularly important to act and look your best while looking for a job. It also is helpful to have business/social cards printed with your name, phone number(s), and e-mail address to pass out to networking contacts.

Alumni associations and alumni clubs in London can often be good for networking. There are also numerous networking groups in the UK that welcome newcomers. The FOCUS Resource Centre (listed at the beginning of this chapter) maintains an extensive list of networking organisations for its members.

Maintaining a good network is demanding work and needs constant development. Acquaintances that do not have employment information today may tomorrow. Key networking tips:

✔ Keep good records of all networking contacts in one place

✔ Keep in touch with networking contacts regularly, but not obtrusively

## Volunteering

Volunteering for an organisation can be a temporary to long-term alternative to full-time paid employment. Volunteering offers a great way to build on your CV while you look for paid employment, as well as another source for networking contacts.

The following organisations can help you identify an appropriate volunteer position for your needs and interests:

*TimeBank:* (0845) 601 4008; (www.timebank.org.uk)

*The National Centre for Volunteering:* (020) 7520 8900; (www.volunteering.org.uk)

*Reach:* enables voluntary organisations benefit from the business, managerial, technical and professional expertise of people who want to offer their career skills, working as volunteers. (020) 7582 6543; (www.volwork.org.uk)

*The National Association of Volunteer Bureaux* – can advise you where to find your local volunteer bureau. (0121) 633 4555; (www.do-it.org.uk)

## WORK PERMITS, VISAS, AND EMPLOYEE RIGHTS

Most citizens living in the European Economic Area (EEA) are entitled to take employment in the UK without a work permit. However, if they have non-EEA dependants or are intending to apply for permanent UK residency or a British passport, they do need to apply for a residence permit. If you do not fall in this EEA category, there is still a possibility to work in the UK.

Originally, work permits were established to ensure that non-EEA residents did not compete with the UK's local labour force. Today, UK labour policy has relaxed some to enable British industry to strengthen its position, particularly in sectors that suffer labour shortages. However, all foreign candidates still have to prove they are the best for the job when the post has not been filled locally.

If you are from a Commonwealth country (such as Canada, Australia, New Zealand, and South Africa) and aged between 17 and 27, you are eligible for a two-year working holiday visa. This visa must be applied for from a British embassy outside the UK. The visa is issued with the restrictions that the visa holder must not work for more than 52 weeks (full time) of their two-year stay and must not directly further their career while in Britain. You may not be able to work in the industry that you are experienced in.

Commonwealth citizens, who can prove that a parent or grandparent was born in Britain, are entitled to a residency visa for up to four years. This residency visa can be applied from the British High Commission. After four years, these visa holders, as well as any non-UK resident who has lived in the UK for four years, can apply for permanent UK residency.

If you are not entitled for the above types of visas, then an employer needs to apply for a work permit on your behalf. The permit will apply to a specific role and is not transferable to other positions within the company. The employer has the responsibility to prove it has gone to all reasonable lengths to find an EEA worker before looking elsewhere.

The application process for a work permit is fairly rigorous. The employer will need to provide work references from you, evidence of your education (copies of diplomas and/or transcripts), career history, and professional qualifications, as well as the company's annual reports and accounts. The company will only have to provide their annual reports and accounts the first time they apply for a work permit. Further applications only require the individual's documents. The employer will also need to provide a job description, information about the recruitment advertising, and other efforts made to fill the position. Work permits are rarely granted for salaries of less than £20,000 a year, and for manual, secretarial, and domestic positions.

More information on details and conditions for work permits and visas for the UK, contact:

*The UK Home Office Immigration and Nationality Directorate*: Block C, Whitgift Centre, Wellesley Road, Croydon CR9; (www.ind.homeoffice.gov.uk)

Recorded information:
| | |
|---|---|
| General | (0870) 606 7766 |
| Overseas visitors | (020) 8760 1600 |
| Overseas students | (020) 8760 1622 |
| Work permit holders | (020) 8760 1644 |
| Employers | (020) 8649 7878 |
| To order copies information brochures | (020) 8649 7878 |
| To request an application form | (0870) 241 0645 |

Phone lines are open Monday-Thursday, 9.00 to 16.45; Friday, 9.30 to 16.30.

*The Overseas Labour Service of the Department for Education and Employment:* (www.dfee.gov.uk/ols)

*The Foreign and Commonwealth Office:* (www.visa.fco.gov.uk)

## Employment Rights

All UK employers need to provide a statement of employment to the employee, which clearly indicates the following information:

✔ The Names of the employer and employee.

✔ The job title and a job description.

✔ Where the employee is expected to work.

✔ The date the employment started.

✔ Details of salary and when the payment will be made – weekly or monthly

✔ Hours of work, and any related issues such as overtime. Am employee may be expected to work beyond the contractual hours for no additional pay if more work is required.

✔ Holiday entitlement – most UK workers receive between 20 to 25 days per year.

✔ Sickness entitlement and procedures.

✔ Notice period – standard notice is one month, but this can vary from industry and position within a company.

✔ Pension scheme details.

✔ The length of the contract if the employee is working for a fixed time period.

More information on Employment Rights can be found from:

*Department of Trade and Industry: Employment Relations division:* (www.dti.gov.uk/er/)

*Department for Education and Employment:* (www.dfee.gov.uk)

# Chapter Five:
# Post Office, Telephone and Utilities

### The Post Office

The Post Office is a public corporation owned, but not managed by the UK government. The Post Office is made up of four separate businesses: Post Office Counters Ltd., Royal Mail, Parcelforce Worldwide, and Subscription Services Ltd.

***Post Office Counters Ltd.*** Post Office Counters Ltd. has a nationwide network of about 19,000 post offices. Post Offices are often stand alone offices, but can also be managed by agents and situated within shops, village halls, and even sometimes pubs in rural areas. Payments may be made at Counter Services in either cash or cheque. Post Offices in the UK provide a wider range of functions than most other countries, offering over 170 products and services that include:

✓ *Paying Household Bills* – including: phone, cable, gas, electricity, water, Council Tax, mail order, and many others

✓ *Banking* – through Alliance and Leicester Giro, a full range of banking services and payment schemes

✓ *Savings* – a range of saving and investment services including instant access Ordinary Account, the Investment Account, and fixed interest Capital Bonds

✓ *Travel Services* – foreign exchange readily available at over 600 counters and pre-order currency service at the other offices, American Express Traveller's Cheques, travel insurance, and passport validation service at 1,500 offices

✓ *Motor Vehicle Licenses* – available at around 4,000 post offices

✓ *T.V. Licenses* – available at all post offices

✓ *Lottery Products* – installed terminals for the National Lottery at over 4,000 post offices, Lottery 'Instants' at almost 10,000 post offices, and Littlewood's scratch cards at most post offices

✓ *Mobile Telephones* – mobile phones and telephone usage time can be purchased at some post offices

✓ *Postal Orders* – available at all post offices for paying household bills, paying people that do not have cheque accounts, and sending money overseas (and across country). The postal orders are valid for up to six months. Note: not all foreign countries will cash British postal orders.

✓ *Transferring Money Overseas* – available at over 1,500 post offices, Moneygram enables a fast and safe way to send and receive money around the world in minutes.

✓ *Post Shops* – stationery and special stamps are available at some post offices as well as boxes in a variety of sizes.

✓ *Photo booths* – available at 430 post offices to use for travel cards, drivers licenses, and passport.

✓ *Outdoor Activity Licenses* – gaming and fishing licenses are available at certain offices that serve particular areas.

*Note:* Not every service is provided at every post office.

Most Post Office counters are open Monday to Friday from 09.00 to 17.30 and on Saturday from 09.00 to 12.00. Neighbourhood Post Office hours vary. The Post Office at 24/28 William IV Street, WC2N 4DL; (020) 7484 9307 (near Trafalgar Square) is open from 08.00 to 20.00, Monday to Friday, and 09.00 to 20.00 on Saturday.

National Helpline: (0845) 722 3344 (calls charged at local rates) – The line is open between 8:15 and 18.00 on weekdays, and 8:30 and 19.00 on Saturday. (www.consignia-online.com)

**Royal Mail.** Royal Mail collects, sorts, and delivers the mail every day. Royal Mail provides a wide range of services, including signature on delivery, guaranteed next working day delivery, and extra compensation cover for loss, damage or delay. Royal Mail National Enquiry Number: (0845) 774 0740 (calls charged at local rates) Royal Mail Postcode Enquiry Line: (0845) 711 1222 (calls charged at local rates) (www.royalmail.com)

**Parcelforce Worldwide.** Parcelforce Worlwide provides a worldwide parcel delivery service to over 200 countries. Parcelforce Worldwide National Enquiry Centre: (0800) 224 466 (Freephone). (www.parcelforce.com)

**Subscription Services Ltd. (SSL)** SSL is one of the UK's top data management and telebusiness organisations. Subscription Services: (0117) 923 0130

You can get leaflets that provide more details about these services at your local Post Office, or by calling the above customer service numbers and visiting the above website addresses.

### Sending Mail (All costs accurate at the time of publication.)

Postage stamps can be bought at post offices, grocery stores, newsagents, and even some petrol stations. A pre-paid envelope can be recognised by two thick horizontal bars it has on the top right hand side.

## Sending Mail within the UK

Two rates apply for sending letters in the UK:

*First Class* postage stamp costs 27 pence for up to 60g. First Class post will usually arrive the next business day within the UK. The earlier in the day you post an item, the more confident you can be that it will be deliver the next day.

*Second Class* postage stamp costs 19 pence for up to 60g. Second Class is for sending less urgent items and usually takes about 3 business days for delivery.

*Recorded Mail* provides additional reassurance by allowing for confirmation of delivery of important (but not valuable) items. You can check if an item has been delivered by visiting www.royalmail.com or calling (08459) 272 100. A Proof of Delivery, which is a copy of the recipients signature, is available by calling (08457) 740 740. This costs an extra £2.20.

*Special Delivery* is recommended for valuable and time critical items. This service provides:

✓ Up-to-date delivery tracking

✓ Record of time and signature upon delivery (not necessarily the addressee's)

✓ Confirmation of delivery by visiting www.royalmail.com or calling 0845 700 1200

✓ *While you were out* card for the recipient if no one was able to accept the package. The recipient then can collect it from the Royal Mail address on the card, or have the item delivered on another day or to another address.

## Sending Mail Abroad

*Letters and Postcards* – The maximum weight you can send is 2kg and all post goes by air.

*Small Packets* – A convenient way and economical way to send goods and gifts. When using this service, write SMALL PACKET in the top left corner on the front of the item. Except for most European Union destinations, a Customs declaration must also be attached. The maximum weight you can send it 2 kg, except for Saudi Arabia, which only accepts small packages of 1kg or less.

*Printed Papers* – A cost-effective way to send pamphlets, books, magazines, and newspapers abroad. When using this service, write PRINTED PAPERS in the top left corner on the front of the item. You can't include personal correspondence. The maximum weight for most places is 2 kg, or 5kg for books and pamphlets.

*Parcels* – A variety of services offered depending on how fast you want the package to be delivered. A Customs declaration must be attached to the parcel, with the exception of most European Union destinations. Contact Parcelforce listed above for more information.

Post Office Delivery Goals:

|  | **Airmail** | **Surface Mail** |
|---|---|---|
| Western Europe | 2 Days | 2 Weeks |
| Eastern Europe | 3 Days | 4 Weeks |
| Outside Europe | 4 Days | 8 Weeks |

Airmail items need an Airmail sticker, or "By Airmail – Par Avion" written in the top left corner on front of the item.

### International Signature Services and Swiftair

*International Recorded* – For items that are low in value but require a signature on delivery. International Recorded costs £2.60 per item plus postage.

*International Registered* – For signature on delivery and compensation for loss or damage to valuable items. International Registered costs £3.15 for up to £500 compensation and £4.20 for up to £2,200 compensation. This service is not available for all countries and maximum compensation lower for some countries.

*Advice of Delivery* – For receiving a confirmation of delivery when using International Recorded and International Registered. This service costs 40 pence per item.

*Swiftair* – For express Airmail where your mail goes on the next available flight to the destination. Swiftair does not guarantee delivery times as postal standards vary in countries. Swiftair costs £2.85 per item plus Airmail postage. Swiftair can be combined with International Recorded and International Registered services.

### Shipment of Goods into the UK

Care should be taken regarding shipment of goods into the UK. Customs Services may stop incoming shipments and levy VAT charges on the value of the incoming shipment. See Chapter One: Moving for more details.

### Other Post Office Services

*Mail Redirection Service Advice of Delivery* – The Post Office enables you to have mail redirected for one, three, six, or 12 months. This service is renewable for up to two years. Mail can be redirected to a permanent or temporary address, either within the UK or abroad. Fill out a Forwarding Form at the post office at least a couple of weeks in advance of your move.

*Keepsafe* – The Post Office can hold your household's mail safely while you are away for up to two months, and then deliver it on a day that you specify. The Post Office requires at least one week's notice for this service.

*P.O. Box* – As an alternative to receiving mail at home, you can set up a P.O. Box. Renting a P.O. Box costs £42 for 6 months and £52 for 12 months. You can apply for a P.O. Box and find about the full terms and conditions of the service by contacting your local Sales Centre on (0845) 7950 950.

*Poste Restante (Holding of Mail)* – Mail can be received free of charge via the main post office of any town in Britain for a maximum of three months. However, the mail will be returned to the sender if you do not collect it within 14 days (one month if sent from abroad). Photo identification is necessary when you collect the mail. This service can be quite useful if you are going to be living at a certain address for a short amount of time. Letters should be addressed as follows:

Your Name
Poste Restante
Address of Post Office, including postcode

Several American Express offices, including the branch at 30-31 Haymarket, SW1Y (020) 7484 9610, also provide poste restante services for its customers' letters for up to 30 days. The service is free to American Express cardholders and traveler's check holders; all others pay a small fee.

## Public Call Boxes

Call boxes (public telephones) can be found in larger shops, pubs and along the street. The minimum charge is 20 pence. Coin-operated telephones generally take 10 pence, 20 pence, 50 pence and £1 coins, and/or phonecards. Most new phones require you to insert the coin before dialling. When using the older phones, dial the number and wait for the bleeping sound before inserting coins. If an additional coin will be required, ample warning is given by another bleeping sound. Do not ask someone to ring you at the pay phone unless you are certain that it will accept incoming calls.

Many new public telephones operate on phonecards available from most newsagents and Post Offices. These phonecards are composed of units of 10p and come in values of £3, £5, £10, and £20. It is useful to buy and carry a phonecard with you, as coin operated phones are being phased out, and often have longer queues than phonecard operated phones.

## Telephone Companies

You can choose from a large variety of fixed line telephone service providers include:

✓ BT (0800) 800 150, www.BT.com

✓ NTL (0800) 183 1234, www.ntl.com

✓ PowerGen (0800) 015 2029, www.powergen.co.uk

✓ British Gas (0845) 600 6311, www.house.co.uk

*Note:* You must have a BT line to use Powergen's and British Gas' telephone services.

For help and advice on telephone companies and services, the UK's Office of Telecommunications has a useful website: www.oftel.gov.uk. Also, the Industry Forum, which consists of the main fixed line phone companies, publishes a guide to quality of service, called the *Comparative Performance Indicators (CPI)*. You can get a copy of CPI by e-mailing cpi@cpi.org.uk or visiting www.cpi.org.uk.

It is fairly easy to switch phone companies. In the UK, if you change your fixed phone line and stay at the same address, you can keep your phone number. However, phone companies may make a reasonable charge for this "number portability."

Before making any final decisions, it is recommended you check with the individual telephone companies for their latest prices, and other factors such as services offered and quality of service. Bundling telephone services with another utility service provider, such as cable, TV, or gas, might enable you to take advantage of some special discounts.

Figuring out the cost of various phone services can be complicated because you need to consider:

✓ Line rental

✓ Cost of calls

✓ Discount packages

✓ How many calls you make and when

✓ What type of calls you mostly make (local, national, international, Internet)

Currently, most calls, including local calls, are charged. Telephone charges are based on metered units. The unit charge varies according to the time the call is made for local, national and international calls. Calls tend to be less expensive between 18.00 and 8.00.

Some free numbers include those with prefixes of 0800 (BT), 0500 (Mercury) and 0321 (Vodafone). Numbers with a prefix 0345 (BT), 0645 (Mercury), and 0845 are charged at local rates. Numbers with the prefix 0990 (BT), 05415 (Mercury), and 0870 are charged at the national rate even if you make a local call.

International calls can often be expensive from your main telephone company. The following companies offer discounted international rates:

*AT&T:* Offer two long distance services – The AT&T Card that is available to be billed to a US address, and *USA Direct Service*. Both offer operator assisted international rates. A variety of custom calling plans exist. For an AT&T operator call (0800) 890 011, (www.att.com).

*MCI:* Also offer long distance phone service. *MCI CALL USA* offers a toll-free call to an MCI operator who will complete your call anywhere in the US. An MCI card is also available to those living overseas. For an MCI WorldPhone operator dial (0800) 890 222, (www.mci.com).

*OneTel:* (0800) 957 0000, (www.onetel.net.uk)

*SmartTalk from Tiscali:* (0800) 954 2223; (www.tiscali.co.uk/services/smarttalk)

*SwiftCall:* (0800) 769 8000; (www.swiftcall.co.uk)

New telephone equipment is available at a local BT shop, or any High Street electronics retailer such as Dixons. New telephone equipment can also be rented from several of the telephone service suppliers, including BT. You may also purchase a phone adapter that will enable you to use a US telephone in the UK.

Telephone directories and Yellow Pages are published for London and the other cities and towns in Great Britain. The dialling codes for all other cities and towns outside of London are listed in the front of each directory.

## Mobile Telephones

Mobile phones (commonly referred to as "mobiles" with a long "i" – don't say cell phone!) are very popular in Britain. The service tends to be less expensive here than it is in the US; for instance, mobile users are not charged for incoming national calls.

Common providers include *Vodafone, O2, T-Mobile, Orange* and *Virgin*. Most of these companies offer services that will work throughout Continental Europe, however currently far fewer will also work in the US. To help decide on the right provider and plan, consider: how often and where you will use your mobile (UK, Europe, International), how long of a service contract you want, and the ease of ending any contract.

High-street electronics and telephone stores offer a wide range of phone and service choices. Popular shops include *The Carphone Warehouse* (0808 100 9250, www.carphonewarehouse.com) and *The Link* (0500 222 666, www.thelink.co.uk). Many of the mobile providers also have stand-alone stores.

It is usually possible to keep your mobile number if you change companies. However, this is based on agreements between mobile phone companies. You do not have a legal right to keep the same number.

## Internet

**ISPS.** A large selection of Internet Service Providers (ISPs) is available in the UK. ISPs offer a wide spectrum of packages, including unmetered access, pay-as-you-go, and metered access. Currently, most unmetered access plans require the customer to have a BT residential line. Some of the major ISPs in the UK include:

✓ www.aol.co.uk (0800 376 5599)

✓ www.btopenworld.com (0845 601 5190)

✓ www.demon.net (0800 027 9200)

✓ www.freeserve.com (0870 872 0099)

✓ www.onetel.net.uk (0800 957 0000)

✓ www.virgin.net (0845 650 1000)

**Broadband.** If you (or your family) use the Internet and send e-mail a lot from home, it may be worth the extra cost of setting up an ADSL broadband connection that offers internet connect at 10 times the speed of an of an ordinary 56 KBPS modem. Some of the advantages of ADSL broadband include:

✓ Connection is permanently on – you do not need to dial into your ISP and wait for it to connect.

✓ No hefty phone bills – you pay only a monthly subscription fee.

✓ Connection will not affect your existing phone line – so you can talk on the phone and be online at the same time.

✓ Access to more multimedia content – such as news, music videos, games, and film previews.

The monthly fee for ADSL broadband is typically £25 to £40. Sometimes, additional equipment and set-up charges are added on top of the monthly fee.

To get an ADSL broadband connection, you must have a BT phone line and be in a broadband area. To find out if you are, visit www.btopenworld.com/broadband and click on "Availability" then "Line Check." Broadband providers include many of the ISPs listed above, as well as many others.

### Internet Cafés

London also has many Internet cafés. Two of the larger chains are:

*EasyInternetCafé*, (0207 241 9000, www.easyeverything.com). Cafés in Kensington High Street, Oxford Street, Tottenham Court Road, Trafalgar Square, Victoria, and King's Road (opens in 2002)

*Internet Exchange*: (0207 792 6200, www.internet-exchange.co.uk). Cafés in Baker Street, Bayswater, Covent Garden, Queensway, and Trocadero.

### UTILITIES

Because of deregulation, consumers in the London area have a great choice of utility suppliers – except for water. For electricity and gas, a wide range of services and price structures are available. Moreover, switching from one supplier to another is relatively easy.

To compare major utility prices and services in your area, visit:

✓ www.buy.co.uk

✓ www.ofgem.gov.uk

✓ www.saveonyourbills.com

✓ www.unravelit.com

✓ www.uswitch.com

## Electricity & Gas

Electricity and gas meters are generally read quarterly and bills are sent following the reading. The bill will include electricity units used and their unit price, plus a quarterly standing charge.

Gas is the least expensive method of heating. If you intend to install gas appliances, you should choose a gas fitter who is registered with CORGI (The Council of Registered Gas Installers), 1 Elmwood, Chineham Business Park, Crockford Lance, Baskingstoke, Hants RG24; (01256) 372 300 (www.corgi-gas.com). CORGI will provide the names of members in your area.

If you have individual gas and water heaters for bathrooms or kitchen, you must have them serviced every year and make sure the rooms are well ventilated. A significant number of fatal accidents have occurred because of defective gas heaters.

The electrical supply in London is 240V AC. England has several types of electrical plugs; the most common is a square shaped, three-pin plug. It requires a fuse and has a 'ground' wire. The fuse is located inside the plug itself rather than at a central box; each electrical outlet has a switch to turn electricity on and off at the individual outlet. Some appliances are sold without plugs – be sure to ask whether you need to buy a plug; the store will attach it to the appliance for you.

England has several types of light bulbs, including a screw in and a pin variety. When purchasing replacement bulbs you will need to know the type of bulb the lamp requires.

## Water

*Thames Water* supplies water for much of London (0845) 9200 888, (www.thameswater.co.uk). Detailed information and telephone numbers are found in the telephone directory. Many water bills are not based on a consumption rate, but on the value of the property plus a standing charge. Usually, you usually can improve on your water bill if your home is fitted with a water meter, which Thames Water will fit free of charge. You may not use a sprinkler to water your garden unless you have a water meter.

Water bills are sent semi-annually and include charges for water plus sewage services. The landlord sometimes pays this charge.

In most houses, the only drinkable tap water is from the tap in the kitchen. Water in other taps comes from storage tanks on the premises, rather than from the main line. Water in London is very hard so you will need to use decalcification liquid on appliances such as kettles, irons, etc. If your water looks cloudy or discoloured, taste different, or smells funny, contact your local water company or the Drinking Water Inspectorate (0207 944 5956, e-mail: dwi_enquiries@detr.gov.uk, www.dwi.gov.uk).

## Television

All users of television sets must possess an annual licence, obtainable from any Post Office. Renewals are sent automatically. One licence covers all the television sets in a household. Radios require no licence. The charge for a colour television licence for 12 months is £112, and black and white televisions are £37.50. There is no charge for a television license if you are over 75 years old. Fines for not having a TV licence can cost £1,000.

For more information about television licenses, call (0870) 241 6468 or visit www.tvlicensing.co.uk. If you leave the country before the expiry of the license, you can obtain a refund by contacting Customer Services, TV licensing, Freepost (BS6689), Bristol, BS98 ITL.

If you have a television with teletext, it will enable you to see news, weather, and future programmes. Ceefax and Oracle are the two teletext information services available in the UK.

## Cable, Digital, and Satellite

In addition to the five terrestrial channels available with your television licence (BBC 1, BBC 2, ITV, Channel 4 and Channel 5), cable or satellite television may be available in your area. Different cable companies service individual geographic regions. London area cable providers include NTL. Not all locations are cable ready at this time. Basic cable service (without any premium channels) costs approximately £15-25 per month.

Digital television is becoming increasingly available to residents in the London area. Digital suppliers include NTL and Sky Digital. Digital offers several advantages to the viewer, such as wide-screen pictures, CD-quality sound, and video-on-demand. Interactive services such as home banking, home shopping and connection to the Internet are also now available digitally through the TV in some areas. Visit www.dtg.org.uk/consumer and www.itc.org.uk/the_digital_age for more information about digital television.

In order to receive satellite communication you may either purchase or rent an individual satellite dish to be installed at your residence. You must then subscribe to a subscription plan, payable on a monthly basis. Satellite dishes are available from many local high street electronic and appliance shops. Packages are available to rent from *Boxclever* (0870 333 4140, www.boxclever.co.uk). To subscribe to the available channels such as CNN, MTV and SKY, contact Sky (0870 240 4040, www.sky.com).

---

**Did you know...**Many buildings do not allow satellite dishes. Be sure to check before purchasing this service.

---

## LOCAL COUNCILS

Each council works to meet the needs of residents and to provide various community services. These include:

✓ running some of the best schools in London

✓ maintaining the roads and pavements

✓ ensuring rubbish is promptly collected

Council contact details for Central London:

*Royal Borough of Kensington and Chelsea:* Town Hall, Hornton Street, London W8
General Number: (020) 7937 5464
Emergencies (out of hours): (020) 7361 3484
Recycling: (020) 7341 5148
Refuse Collection & Street Cleaning: (020) 7341 5284
www.rbkc.gov.uk

*London Borough of Hammersmith and Fulham:* Town Hall, King Street, Hammersmith, W6
General Number: (020) 8748 3020
Emergencies (out of hours): (020) 8748 8588
Recycling, Refuse, and Street Cleaning: (020) 8753 1100
www.lbhf.gov.uk

*Westminster City Council:* P.O. Box 240, City Hall, 64 Victoria Street, SW1
General Number: (020) 7641 6000
Recycling, Refuse Collection, and Street Cleaning: (020) 7641 2000
www.westminster.gov.uk

*London Borough of Camden:* Town Hall Extension, Judd Street, St. Pancras
General Number: (020) 7278 4444
Recycling: (020) 7485 1553
Refuse Collection and Street Cleaning: (020) 7974 6914/5
www.camden.gov.uk

*London Borough of Islington:* Islington Town Hall, Upper Street, Islington
General Number: (020) 7527 2000
Recycling: (020) 7527 4679

Refuse Collection: (020) 7527 4692
www.islington.gov.uk

*London Borough of Hackney,* Hackney Town Hall, Mare Street, Hackney, E8
General Number: (020) 8356 5000
Emergencies: (020) 8356 2300
Recycling and Refuse Collection: (020) 8985 4681
www.hackney.gov.uk

*Corporation of London,* P.O. Box 270, EC2
General Number: (020) 7606 3030
Recycling: (020) 7236 9541
Refuse Collection and Street Cleaning: (020) 7236 9541
www.cityoflondon.gov.uk

*London Borough of Southwark,* Southwark Town Hall, Peckham Road, SE5
General Number: (020) 7525 5000
Recycling: (020) 7703 8030
Refuse Collection and Street Cleaning: (020) 7525 2183/2188
www.southwark.gov.uk

*London Borough of Lambeth,* Lambeth Town Hall, Brixton Hill, SW2
General Number: (020) 7926 1000
Refuse Collection and Street Cleaning: (020) 7926 9000
www.lambeth.gov.uk

## Recycling and Waste

Recycling centres for bottles, cans, clothes, and paper products are widespread in London. Several methods of recycling are available to most London residents, including: doorstep recycling collection, blue bins, mini recycling centres, and composting.

Most residents receive two domestic waste collections each week; both of these days typically include recycling collection. Normal refuse should be put in strong plastic bags and securely tied. There are usually domestic collections on Easter, May Day, spring and Bank holidays. Most councils also operate "Too Big for the Bin" service for items that are too bulky to fit in with your normal refuse. Payment must be made in advance, and usually can be made by credit and debit card, cash, cheques, and postal orders. This service tends to be fairly popular, with waiting times of up to four weeks. For specific details on all the recycling and waste services available in your area, contact you local council.

## Disposing of Bulky Items of Household Waste

At the following sites, residences can dispose of up to five black bags of waste or five bulky items (Furniture, carpets, etc.). Residents, who need to dispose of more than five bags, must complete a C.A1 form and provide proof of residence.

*Cremorne Wharf Recycling Centre,* 27 Lots Road, London SW10, (020) 7376 4527 Open: Monday to Friday 7.30 to 16.30 and Saturday 8.00 to 12.00. This site also has collection facilities for books, clothes, oil, and household electrical goods.

*Western Riverside Waste Authority,* Smugglers Way, Wandsworth, London SW18, (020) 8871 2788. Open: 7.30 to 18.00, seven days a week. Car batteries can be taken to this site where the sulphuric acid is drained and the metal sent for recycling. *Cringle Dock,* Cringle Street, Battersea, London SW8, (020) 7622 6233. Open: 8.00 to 20.00, seven days a week.

**Motor Oil.** It is illegal to pour motor oil down the drain. For information on safe disposal, contact the Oil Bank Line, 0800 663 366

**Old Cars.** If you want to dispose of your vehicle, or report apparently abandoned vehicles, contact your local council.

**Recovery of Lost Items in Gullies/Storm Drains.** Lost items (such as jewellery or keys), can be recovered from gullies/storm drains at a cost. Contact your local council to get referred to the appropriate water refuse contractor for your area.

## USEFUL TELEPHONE NUMBERS

| | |
|---|---:|
| Fire, Police, Ambulance | 999 |
| Electricity Emergency | (0800) 096 9000 |
| Gas Emergency | (0800) 111 999 |
| Directory Enquiries | 192 |
| Directory Enquiries, International | 153 |
| Operator Assistance, UK | 100 |
| Operator Assistance, International | 155 |
| Fax Directory Enquiries | 153 |
| Telephone Repairs | 151 |
| Time (From 0207/0208) | 123 |
| Direct Dial, US | 001 |
| Transport within London | |
|     London Underground | (020) 7222 1234 |
|       (tell them where and when you are going and they will suggest how to get there) | |
| Transport outside London | |
|     National Rail Enquiries | (0345) 484 950 |
|     National Bus Service | (0990) 808 080 |

# Chapter Six: Transportation

The best way to get to know London is on foot. Buy a good street guide (such as London A-Z, available in any bookshop) and off you go! Just remember the traffic will be coming from the opposite direction and pedestrians do not have the right of way except at a zebra crossing. Zebra crossings are marked with black and white stripes across the road and a flashing yellow light. Always look both ways but particularly to the right.

## PUBLIC TRANSPORTATION

For speedier travel, the bus and underground (commonly called the Tube) systems can take you almost anywhere you want to go. Free maps of the underground and bus routes are available at all ticket offices of London Transport. The routes of both are clearly marked with a colour coding system. The number for general enquiries is (020) 7222 1234.

Currently a 'travel card' can be purchased weekly, monthly, quarterly, biannually and annually at newsagents displaying a red "Pass Agent" sign and at underground ticket windows. In addition, a one-day travel card is available after 09.30 weekdays and all day Saturday and Sunday (not valid on night buses). All travel cards can be used on buses, trains and tubes in the London area. The underground, buses and trains do not operate on Christmas Day. If you take the bus, train or underground regularly, check with London Transport for the most economical ticket scheme. For an update on underground, light-rail, train and bus travel, call Travelcheck at (020) 7222 1200.

*Did you know...* You can plan your journey online before you head out the door. At www.thetube.com you can plan your journey using the tube and Docklands Light Railway (DLR). If you want to plan a journey online, to include buses, tramlink, DLR, or river bus services visit www.transportforlondon.gov.uk. This site includes both a journey planner and real time travel updates.

### Underground (Tube)

In order to purchase an underground ticket, you can go to the ticket window in underground stations and ask for a ticket to your destination. You can avoid possible delays at the ticket booth by using the ticket machines that exist in many stations. Signs are posted over the machines, listing fares. Some older machines require coins rather than notes, and occasionally exact change is required. Remember, you must keep the ticket in order to exit at your destination so if you are travelling with children be sure to hang on to their tickets as well.

Fares are based on the distance travelled. London is divided into six bands called travel zones for both bus and tube fares. The more zones you cross, the higher the fare. Children under five ride for free and children under 16 and adults over 60 are entitled to reduced fares.

The underground operates from 05.30 until approximately midnight daily with reduced schedules on Sunday and holidays. Rush hours are 08.00 to 09.30 and 16.30 to 19.00. Smoking is not allowed on the underground trains or in the stations. Dogs are allowed to travel on the underground. Often stations close due to construction so it is wise to check before you begin your journey. These are often listed on a board in the station. A pocket map of the entire tube network is available free from most underground ticket windows.

For 24 hour information on all London Underground services, please call London Travel Information on (020) 7222 1234. And, for all the online tube information that you'd ever need - and then some - visit www.thetube.com, where in addition to a journey planner and information on strikes, you can have your say about tube etiquette.

---

**Did you know...**One of the best kept Tube secrets is the Carnet pass. For £10.50, you can purchase 10 tickets that are good for zone one. Unlike a regular ticket, they can be used anytime up to one year from the date of purchase.

---

## Buses

Buses are less expensive than the underground but can be slower in heavy traffic. Most buses run until 23.00, with different timetables on Sunday and holidays; in addition, several night bus routes operate after 23.00. Most bus stops have placards indicating which buses stop there and the route. Some stops are 'request' stops and these are marked with red signs. At a 'request' stop, you must signal the driver to stop the bus by holding out your hand. On the older 'Routemaster' buses you board from the back, take your seat and the bus conductor will come to you for your fare. Many buses are now 'one man buses' where you pay the driver as you enter. Be warned that some fare collectors can get angry if you pay with a large bill. To make your journey more pleasant, try to use change. 'Hoppa' buses are smaller minibuses that cover short hops throughout London. Keep your ticket during your ride, as inspectors occasionally conduct checks.

---

**Did you know...**The Bus 'Saver' Ticket is a book of six tickets, costing £3.90 for adults or £2.10 for children. The ticket that can save you money if you currently pay cash single fares. It is a book of 6 single bus tickets, which can be bought in advance, for travel on buses, including N-prefixed Night buses. They are not valid on route 726 or on certain special bus services and excursions, but they can be used by you or bye anyone you wish to give them to. Each ticket is for a single bus journey only.

---

*The Red Arrow* buses offer a limited stop or express service between Victoria, Waterloo, London Bridge and Liverpool Street stations and major shopping and business areas. Red Arrow buses require exact fare.

*Green Line* coaches serve communities within a 40-mile radius of Central London, as well as coaches to Luton Airport. There are stops within London, indicated by green bus stop signs. For information, call (0870) 608 7261 or visit www.greenline.co.uk.

*National Express Coaches* and *Euroline* link London with other cities in the United Kingdom, Ireland and Continental Europe: bookings and enquiries call (08705) 808 080 or visit www.gobycoach.com.

## Trains

The major cities in Britain are linked by modern, high speed trains. There are also commuter lines between towns and outlying areas. Tickets can be purchased at the ticket office of any train station and at most travel agencies. There are various ticket schemes, such as cheap day return (round trip), excursion, season, family rail card, etc. You should ask about the most economical way to get to your destination before purchasing a ticket. Hold on to your ticket throughout your journey.

The 24 hour telephone number for all national train times and fares is (08457) 484 950.

Trains for various destinations depart from different London stations as follows:

| | |
|---|---|
| *The North & Central Britain*: | Euston<br>King's Cross<br>St. Pancras |
| *The South*: | Charing Cross<br>London Bridge<br>Victoria<br>Waterloo |
| *The West Country, Wales<br>& South Midlands*: | Paddington<br>Waterloo |
| *The East, East Anglia & Essex:* | Liverpool Street<br>Victoria<br>Fenchurch Street |

Trains to Gatwick Airport depart from Victoria and London Bridge, for information call (0870) 5301 530 or visit www.gatwickexpress.co.uk. The Heathrow Express runs every 15 minutes from Paddington, for more information call (0845) 600 1515 or visit www.heathrowexpress.co.uk.

## Taxis

The familiar black London taxi, now often in other colours, is the most expensive but often the most convenient and reliable form of transportation. Taxis are controlled strictly by law and all areas within London are regulated by meters.

During periods of fare increases and before meters are adjusted, your fare may be higher than the meter indicates but new fares will be explained and posted inside the cab. It is customary to tip by rounding up the charge (e.g. pay £6 for a £5.50 fare) or by giving approximately 10%.

Taxis are limited by law to carrying five adults (two children are counted as one adult). One can hail a taxi which has its 'for hire' sign lighted on the roof, queue (line-up) at an appointed taxi stand or ring one of the taxi companies (listed in the Yellow Pages under 'taxis'). London also has 'mini-cabs' (also listed under 'taxis') that are unlicensed and cannot be hailed in the street. It is important to negotiate a mini-cab price when you book and it is helpful to have a good idea of where you are going, as mini-cab drivers are not required to know London streets and directions. Standards and prices vary, so it is advisable to use a mini-cab service recommended by a friend.

If you use a reputable taxi company, and become comfortable with them, not only will they offer a courier service (pick up and delivery of goods, packages and food), but they will also take your children to and from school and home or wherever necessary. Personal and corporate accounts can be set up.

For a few minicab recommendations, see Chapter Eleven: Services.

## DRIVING IN BRITAIN

Owning a car is not essential in Central London because of the excellent public transportation. If you prefer the convenience of a car, you can buy, lease or rent a vehicle easily. It is strongly recommended that you purchase and read *The Highway Code* (available in most bookshops) which outlines the British driving regulations before beginning to drive in Britain. The differences do not end with driving on the left-hand side of the road!

Traffic and congestion are problems, as in any other major city, and petrol is expensive. Parking is limited to car parks or meters for non-residents in certain areas, and street parking in these restricted areas is only possible for residents with permits. Parking violations may result in fines, towing or the 'Denver clamp', all of which involve considerable expense and inconvenience. On the other hand, having a car makes picking up groceries and other bulky items easier and getting out of the city for a weekend much more convenient.

For traffic information in London, call AA Roadwatch at (09003) 401 100 or for national traffice information call the Royal Automobile Club traffic line at (0906) 470 1740. For car problems, call the Automobile Association (AA) 24 hour Breakdown line on (0800) 887 766, or the Royal Automobile Club (RAC) 24 hour Rescue Service linkline on (0800) 828 282. For European breakdown service, contact the AA at (0800) 085 2840. You need to be a member of these organisations to enjoy their service, so before you head out on the roads please refer to the section following on Automobile Associations.

## Driving Licences

It is important to obtain a proper driver's licence, as driving without one is illegal and will affect your insurance. *The Department of Transport's Driver and Vehicle Licensing Centre*; (0870) 240 0009, is open for calls Monday to Friday 08.15 to 16.30.

Generally, if you hold a valid driving licence or International Driving Permit (and are not barred from driving in Great Britain) you may drive those vehicles covered by your licence here for 12 months. If you are here as a visitor the 12 months begins on the date that you last entered Great Britain. If you are a new resident, the 12 months begins on the date you took up residence.

At the end of the 12 months you must hold a valid British driving licence if you wish to continue driving here. You should allow at least three weeks for the licence to be issued. If you are entitled to apply for a full Great Britain licence you should send proof of your entitlement with the application form. If you wish to exchange an EC licence, you must apply within one year of coming to live here.

You may take a driving test before or after the 12-month time limit has expired providing you hold a driving licence that entitles you to drive here. There are often delays in scheduling a test appointment.

If you wish to expedite the application process, you might state that you are willing to take the test at any time and at any location.

There are many firms offering driving lessons. The best known is the *British School of Motoring* (BSM), which can be reached on (08457) 276 276 or at www.bsm.co.uk. Motoring schools can advise you on the requirements, handle applications and instruct you in techniques required to pass the British driving test. See the phone book for additional schools of motoring in your area or try:

International Drivers Service - Suite No 10, Noel Court, Bath Road, Hounslow, Middlesex TW4 7DD, (020) 8570 9190, (www.internationaldriversservice.com). Provides overseas licence holders (expatriates) driver training courses and preparation for the obtaining of a UK drivers license. Our services are tailor made and designed to avoid the stresses and strains of driving in the UK.

*The Driving Test* published by the Department of Transport is also a useful tool. It lists available driving instructors and test centres, and breaks down the driving test components. The driving test begins with a written theory test on *The Highway Code* and *The Complete Theory Test for Cars and Motorcycles*. Both of these publications are available at most bookstores. The written theory test is followed by an eye test and 20 to 30 minute driving test. There is no limit to the number of times that these tests can be taken.

If you wish, the driving school instructor will accompany you to the test and acquaint you with the test route. It is important to remember that if you take the test on a car with automatic transmission, your licence will be restricted to automatic transmissions. If, however, you take the test on a manual transmission car, your licence will be valid for both manual and automatic automobiles. Once you have obtained a British driving licence it does not have to be renewed until you reach the age of 70.

### Insurance

Third party insurance is compulsory and it is advisable to have comprehensive insurance as well. 'No claim' reductions and other options are available. You might bring a letter from your previous insurance agency stating that you are entitled to 'no claim' insurance for the past five years. It is recommended that you contact several insurance companies regarding types of coverage and cost. You should also have a clear understanding with your insurance company regarding claims and the kind of licence you possess.

### Purchasing a Car

Purchasing a car in Britain is expensive but there is a good market for second-hand cars. The London evening papers, Sunday papers, specialised car magazines, *The Auto Trader, Loot, The American* and the American School in London monthly newsletter are all good sources. There is also a monthly magazine called the *Motorist's Guide to New and Used Car Prices*. Both the AA and the RAC will thoroughly inspect and value second-hand cars for their members for a fee.

If you plan to return to the US within a year, there can be tax advantages and other savings in buying a car made to American safety and environmental specifications. If you plan to bring your American car to Britain, you must consider the safety and environmental specifications that may require you to make substantial alterations to your automobile here.

### Road Tax

A compulsory Road Tax must be paid each year for each car. Upon paying your Road Tax, you will receive a round sticker ("tax disc") which is to be displayed inside your windscreen. If you are buying a car through a dealer, they will generally take care of this detail as part of the sales procedure but it is up to you to renew subsequent years. If you have brought a car with you to the UK, forms are available at your local Post Office branch. Annual renewal forms will be sent to you.

## M.O.T.

If your car is over three years old, you must have an M.O.T. test each year to prove its 'roadworthiness'. Garages licensed by the Ministry of Transport to conduct this test can perform the test within 24 hours, or while-you-wait. There is a fee for this service. You must present this certificate along with proof of insurance when paying your Road Tax.

## Leasing and Renting Cars

Leasing of cars by companies is a common practice in Britain and dealers can supply details of the various lengths of time and conditions. Car rental firms provide the usual services. Cars with manual transmission are most common and less expensive than automatics. Car rental companies are listed in the Yellow Pages of the phone directory under "Car Hire - Self Drive". Hertz, Avis, Budget, Enterprise, Europcar, Kenning and Thrifty are well-known rental agencies.

## Automobile Associations

You may consider joining the AA (Automobile Association) or the RAC (Royal Automobile Club) for emergency services (see the Driving in Britain section for their emergency phone numbers), as there is no other way of ensuring service in an emergency. These organisations also offer breakdown insurance for trips to the Continent and can even provide legal service in court.

*The Automobile Association*, Fanum House, Basing View, Basingstoke, Hants. RG21 2EA; (0870) 600 0371; (www.theaa.com).

*The Royal Automobile Club Motoring Services*, P.O. Box 700, Bristol BS99 1RB; (0800) 029 029; (www.rac.co.uk).

> **Did you know...**If you are a member of AAA in the United States, your membership can be transferred to the AA and the RAC here in the UK.

## Garages

While all garages are different, do not be surprised if you have to book weeks in advance in order to get your car serviced or repaired.

## Resident's Parking

In many boroughs you are entitled to purchase a Resident's Parking Permit (check with your council or at your town hall for eligibility). Residents' areas are patrolled regularly by traffic wardens and fines are given if you are in a restricted area without the proper parking permit. Resident parking regulations are usually in effect Monday through Friday from 08.30 to 18.30 and Saturday from 08.30 to 13.30. The times vary from borough to borough and within the borough. To obtain a permit, check with your local town hall.

## Car Parks

If you are not fortunate enough to locate a parking meter on the street, you may opt for a car park. Blue signs with a white 'P' direct you to public parking in unfamiliar surroundings. They can be expensive but are usually quite safe and reliable if you must travel by car. Three of the most central are:

✓ Drury Lane Car Park, Parker Street, WC2; (020) 7242 8611

✓ Selfridges Ltd., Edwards Mews off, Duke Street, W1; (020) 7629 1234

✓ Barbican Centre Garage, Silk Street, EC2; (020) 7638 4141

Car park procedures can be confusing. A sticker purchased from the machine must be attached to the windscreen in a 'Pay and Display' car park. Some car parks operate on a two-ticket system. Before returning to the car, insert the entry ticket (received at the entrance barrier) into the meter, pay the amount due, and receive an exit ticket to be inserted at the exit barrier. Many car parks are not attended, so have change on hand to operate the systems.

## Clamping

In the unfortunate case of 'getting clamped', you can call *Clampbusters* at (020) 7735 7253. For an annual fee plus a service charge they will unclamp your car, deliver it to your home and handle the paperwork.

## Petrol Stations

Petrol stations in Britain will <u>not</u> honour US gasoline company credit cards. They will accept Visa, Access and sometimes Diners Club and American Express. Some stations offer personal accounts, payable monthly. BP/Mobil offer a BP Charge Card as does Shell.

# Chapter Seven: Healthcare

## BRITISH HEALTH SYSTEM

### The National Health Service

Great Britain has a government subsidised National Health Service (NHS) and as a resident of the UK, by the deduction of National Insurance from your salary, you are entitled to medical coverage at little or no additional cost. This service includes:

- Doctor care - with home visits if necessary
- Dentistry and orthodontia
- Specialist and hospital care
- Eye tests and glasses
- Child-care clinics for under fives
- Family planning services

This service is also available to foreign visitors on an emergency basis. British taxes paid by you or your employer go towards these services so eligibility should be verified. Advice about eligibility is available from the *Department of Health and Social Security (DHSS)*. The head office is located in Richmond House, 79 Whitehall, London SW1A 2NL, telephone (020) 7210 3000. Health enquiries telephone (020) 7210 4850. Social security enquiries telephone (020) 7712 2171. The web site address for the Department of Health, Social Services, and Public Safety is www.dhsspsni.gov.uk and for the Department of Health is www. doh.gov.uk. In addition there are offices located in all London boroughs and telephone numbers are listed in the telephone directory under 'Health and Social Security, Department of'. *The Citizens' Advice Bureau* provides free information and advice about the NHS. Check the telephone directory for the nearest office location, ask at a local library or see the National Association of Citizens' Advice Bureau's web site at www.nacab.org.uk and also www.adviceguide.org.uk.

The NHS produces several leaflets explaining its different services. They are available from social security offices, family doctors and through the *Department of Health Publications*, PO Box 777, London SE1, email: doh@prolog.uk.com, fax: (01623) 724 524. In addition, for information on your local NHS services see www.nhs.uk.

### NHS Registration

All permanent UK residents are eligible to register with the NHS. Eligibility for temporary residents depends on whether you or your spouse is paying British income tax and National Insurance. For an expatriate and his/her family, the individual's company will often obtain a NI (National Insurance) number that is needed in order to apply for NHS registration. If this is not the case, you may obtain a NI number by applying in person at one of the DHSS offices. Bring your passport to the office (and marriage certificate if the name on the passport differs from that of spouse) and the necessary tax payer identification paperwork from you or your spouse's employer. The DHSS will in turn issue you a NI number.

To obtain an NHS number, you must register with a local doctor (known as a G.P. for general practitioner) who has vacancies for NHS patients. (Note: not all G.P.s handle NHS patients, some handle strictly private patients). It is up to the discretion of the G.P. to register temporary residents with the NHS. If the G.P. decides to accept you as a patient, he will take your personal details including your NI number and length of stay in the UK, and then apply to the local Family Health Service Authority (FHSA) for your NHS number.

Call your borough's FHSA for the names, addresses, and telephone numbers of G.P.s in your area. Lists of doctors are available at local libraries, main post offices, Community Health Councils, and Citizens' Advice Bureaux. Local chemists (drugstores) may have a list, but they are not officially permitted to make specific recommendations. For a complete and searchable directory of GP's surgeries (offices) which will provide address, phone number, map and whether or not the GP is accepting new NHS patients, see www.nhs.uk/localnhsservices/default.asp.

There are often waiting lists for many NHS doctors. As some doctors see their quota of NHS patients and then take on others on a private basis, the doctor may suggest you see him privately and go on his NHS waiting list. Within the NHS, for medical attention other than general family care, you must be referred by your G.P. to see a specialist. Known in the UK as a consultant, this doctor is anyone other than a G.P. Most specialists practice under the NHS and on a private basis.

A drawback of the NHS is that if your complaint is not an emergency, you may be required to wait before receiving attention (this includes non-emergency operations). In these instances, consulting a private doctor may be an advantage as there would be no waiting list. Under certain circumstances, both NHS and private doctors are willing to make house calls.

---

**Did you know...**In the UK, specialists and general practitioners are addressed as 'doctor'. Surgeons, however, including dental surgeons, obstetricians and gynaecologists, are referred to as 'Mister', 'Mrs.' or 'Miss'. The "surgery" or "operating room" in a hospital is called a "theatre", and the office of a medical professional is called a "surgery". In some instances the surgery is located in a home instead of a clinic or office building.

---

## PRIVATE MEDICAL CARE

An option to NHS medical care is private treatment. Although much more costly, it allows you to have control over when treatment should take place and who should perform it. The Consular Section at the US Embassy has a list of doctors available (www.usembassy.org.uk), and although the Embassy cannot make specific recommendations, it can be a starting point. The best references are personal recommendations from business colleagues, friends and neighbours.

Additionally, there are several privately staffed and run hospitals in the London area. These facilities are available to private care patients only. These hospitals are usually modern, offer private rooms, and overall good facilities. They may not be, however, as fully staffed or offer the wide spread emergency care of the NHS hospitals and are not subject to the same regulation as NHS hospitals. All NHS hospitals offer private wards, where limited amenities and private rooms are available for private patients.

Employee sponsored group health plans issued in the US may be extended to the UK with employer consent. Any questions regarding extent of coverage should be directed to the Personnel Office of your employer. You may wish to consider subscribing to an English form of medical insurance. BUPA, PPP and Standard Life are three of the most popular plans. The *Which Report*, a consumer magazine published by the Consumers Association, gives a factual comparison of each plan. This report is obtainable by contacting the Consumers Association at (08453) 010-010. Also see *Which*'s web site at www.which.net.

## NHS AND PRIVATE SERVICES

While the choice of private or NHS treatment for major operations is not to be taken lightly, for many minor concerns or maintenance type examinations, NHS clinics are reliable and close to home.

It is a very good idea to visit your local NHS health centre to become familiar with the facilities and services available to you. These will include ante-natal clinics and classes, baby clinics, under-5 clinics, health visitor programmes, family planning, marriage guidance counsellors, well-woman clinics, well-man clinics, travel vaccinations, physiotherapy, dietetic advice, chiropody, and social workers.

For information on NHS services, doctors, dentists, hospitals or self-help groups contact NHS Direct 0845 4647 24 hours a day / 7 days a week (www.nhsdirect.nhs.uk). NHS Direct also provides confidential health advice and information.

### Counselling

It is not always easy to get information about where to go for counselling locally. Approach your G.P., local library, the *Citizens' Advice Bureau* (www.nacab.org.uk), *the Council for Voluntary Service* (www.nacvs.org.uk) and the local *Marriage Guidance Council* (RELATE) (www.relate.org.uk).

Nationally, the *British Association for Counselling and Psychotherapy* can supply some information about counselling services and specialist organisations (www.bac.co.uk to search for a counsellor in your local area). The association also publishes a nation-wide directory of counselling and psychotherapy resources.

Some useful addresses and telephone numbers:

*British Association for Counselling and Psychotherapy*, 1 Regent Place, Rugby, Warwickshire CV21 2PJ; (0870) 443 5252, (www.bac.co.uk). They will be able to supply you with a comprehensive list of counsellors in your general area.

*RELATE (National Marriage Guidance)*, Herbert Gray College, Little Church Street, Rugby, Warwickshire CV21 3AP; (01788) 573 241; (020) 7837 4004, (www.relate.org.uk).

*American Church in London (ACL)*, 79 Tottenham Court Road, W1; (020) 7580 2791, (www.amchurchuk.com).

*American Psychotherapy Associates, Ltd.*, 39A Welbeck Street, London W1G, (020) 7486 9255 (www.ameripsych.co.uk). U.S. trained and licensed psychotherapists, who serve the international expat community. They provide services for adults, children, couples and families.

*CRUSE* (Bereavement), 126 Sheen Road, Richmond, Surrey, TW9, (020) 8940 4818.

*Alcoholics Anonymous*, P.O. Box 1, Stonebow House, Stonebow, York YO1, London telephone helpline: (020) 7352 3001, (0845) 769 7555, (www.alcoholics-anonymous.org.uk).

*Al Anon/Alateen*, (020) 7403 0888 for a 24 hour telephone service to help relatives and friends of problem drinkers.

*Child and Family Department, Tavistock Clinic*, 120 Belsize Lane, NW3, (020) 435 7111.

*London Marriage Guidance Council*, A non-profit organisation that is very compassionate and highly trained. They frequently deal with ex-pat issues and American clients.

*Westminster Pastoral Foundation*, 23 Kensington Square, W8, (020) 7361 4800, (www.wpf.org.uk).

The following organisations have been recommended:

*Narcotics Anonymous*, helpline (020) 7730 0009, (www.ukna.org).

*Samaritans, Central London helpline*, (020) 7734 2800; (08457) 909 090, (www.samaritans.org.uk).

*American Counselling Centre*, 85 Wimpole Street, W1M 8AJ; (020) 7935 1606.

## Dentistry

Lists of NHS dentists are posted in the same fashion as NHS doctors (see also www.nhs.uk/localnhsservices/dental/dentistry_leaflet.asp). As an NHS dental patient you are expected to pay a percentage of the cost of the work done. There is an upper limit set on the contribution you will be asked to make for one course of treatment. Expect to be asked to pay all or part of the charge in advance. Before each and every visit you must ascertain that the dentist will treat you as an NHS patient, otherwise you could be treated as a private patient and asked to pay the full cost of the treatment. The majority of patients see dentists on a private basis.

You are automatically entitled to FREE dental health care if you:

1. Are under 16 years of age, or a student under 19 years of age and still in full-time education.

2. Are expecting a baby and were pregnant when the dentist accepted you for treatment.

3. Have had a baby during the 12 months before your treatment began.

For further information, consult *NHS leaflet HC.11*, Benefits enquiry line (0800) 882 200, (www.doh.gov.uk/nhscharges/hc11.htm).

---

*Did you know...*Tap water in London is not fluorinated.

---

## Family Planning

A full range of family planning services is available through your G.P. or local clinic as well as specific family planning clinics run by the NHS. The larger clinics will offer all types of birth control for both men and women, well-women clinics, psycho-sexual counselling, termination referrals and follow up, and post-natal examinations. All services are available free of charge, on a walk-in basis. For further information contact;

*The Family Planning Association*, 2-12 Pentonville Road, N1 9FP; (020) 7837 5432, (www.fpa.org.uk).

## Maternity Services

It is necessary to become a patient of an obstetrician promptly. Your G.P. can recommend an obstetrician. You must decide to go with the NHS or privately.

If you decide to go with the NHS, you will have free care throughout your pregnancy and delivery. In the case of a normal delivery, the NHS provides a midwife to attend your birth along with an obstetrician and full medical support staff on call at the hospital in case of complications. You will have a private birthing room, but during recovery you will be on an NHS ward which usually has 4 to 8 beds. Do not expect a private or semi-private room unless you have made arrangements in advance to pay an extra fee for a private room if one is available at the time of your delivery.

A midwife is a specialist in normal pregnancy, birth, and the post-natal period. As well as doing the ante-natal checks, she can deliver your baby, perform ultrasound scans, and care for you once you have had your baby. She may work in the hospital or be based in the community. In some areas, you can book directly with a midwife instead of your G.P. Telephone the Director of Midwifery at your local hospital and ask if there is a midwives clinic or a G.P./ midwives clinic in the community.

Traditionally, you are booked under a consultant at the hospital and receive your ante-natal care from members of his/her team, including midwives. You visit the clinic for all of your ante-natal care, and you are delivered by labour ward midwives or the obstetrician on duty at the time you arrive to deliver your baby. Although the consultant leads the team, unless your pregnancy is complicated, you may never actually see him or her.

There are options for delivery within the NHS. Call your local hospital or speak to your G.P. to see whether these options are available in your area:

*Shared Care* - You visit the hospital two or three times during your pregnancy and for any special ultrasounds and tests. The rest of the time you are cared for by your G.P. and/or your community midwife. When you go into the hospital to have your baby, your baby will be delivered by hospital midwives.

*Midwives Clinic* - Most of your ante-natal care is done by a team of midwives at the hospital who may work in teams under a consultant. Your baby is then delivered by the same team of midwives, who take care of you on the post-natal ward too.

*G.P./Midwife Care* - Your ante-natal care is done by your G.P. or community midwife at the surgery or local health centre. When you go into labour, you are cared for by community midwives and your G.P. is informed. If complications arise, you will be transferred to consultant care.

*Domino Scheme/Midwife Care* - Your ante-natal care may be shared between the community midwife and your G.P., or done by the community midwife at the surgery or local health centre. The midwife may visit you at home for ante-natal checks, and you may go to the hospital for any special tests. When you go to the hospital to deliver your baby, your midwife or another on her team will attend the birth and provide your post-natal care once you have returned home.

*Home Birth* - Home births are becoming more common in the UK as they are gaining support from the medical community. Your ante-natal care may be undertaken entirely by your community or independent midwife with your own G.P. or another doctor acting as back-up. The midwife will deliver your baby at home and also provide your post-natal care.

If you choose private care, you are assured that your obstetrician and a midwife will assist your delivery. In the case of an unexpected emergency situation, there is always an obstetrician on call in both private and NHS hospitals. Private doctors may use both NHS and private hospital facilities.

---

**Did you know?...**Black cabs may refuse to transport you to hospital once in labour. If you are planning to deliver at a private hospital and need transportation contact the hospital to arrange for a private ambulance. If you call 999 for an ambulance, they must take you to the nearest hospital.

---

Whether you choose NHS or private care, your choice of hospitals for your delivery will be limited to the hospital or hospitals at which your obstetrician is registered. In the case of a private hospital, accommodation must be reserved much in advance and a deposit made at that time.

In London most large hospitals offer good maternity facilities. Hospitals with exceptional maternity facilities including neonatal intensive care units are:

*AMI Portland Hospital for Women and Children*, 209 Great Portland Street, W1N, (020) 7580 4400 (private)

*Chelsea & Westminster Hospital*, 369 Fulham Road, SW10, (020) 8746 8000 (has excellent childbirth facilities including birthing pools and a new private maternity wing) (NHS/private).

*Hammersmith Hospital*, 150 Du Cane Road, W12, (020) 8743 2030 (NHS/private)

*Humana Hospital Wellington*, Wellington Place, NW8, (020) 7586 5959 (private)

*Queen Charlotte's Maternity Hospital*, 330 Goldhawk Road, W6, (020) 8748 4666 (NHS/private)

*St John & St Elizabeth*, 60 Grove End Road, NW8, (020) 7806 4000 (NHS/private)

*St. Mary's Hospital*, Praed Street, W2, (020) 7886 6666 (NHS/private – Lindo wing)

*St. Thomas' Hospital*, Lambeth Palace Road, SE1, (020) 7928 9292 (NHS/private)

The NHS offers preparatory 'parent classes' at local hospitals and clinics. A listing of independent ante-natal courses and refresher courses for repeat mums is available through your G.P. An additional organisation involved in natural birth preparation classes nation-wide, is *The National Childbirth Trust* (NCT), Alexandra House, Oldham Terrace, Acton, W3, (020) 8992 8637, (www.nationalchildbirthtrust@lineone.net) or (www.nctpregnancyandbabycare.com). The NCT is a non-profit organisation formed expressly for the purpose of education for pregnancy, birth and parenthood. They have over 40,000 members nation-wide. Contact them for information on what courses are offered in your area. You must contact them early in your pregnancy if you are interested in ante-natal classes in London.

If you are delivering at a private hospital, ante-natal preparatory classes run by hospital midwives are also available. In addition, see Chapter Eight: Children for a further listing of privately run ante-natal preparatory classes.

## Ophthalmics

Your sight can be tested only by a registered ophthalmic optician (optometrist) or an ophthalmic medical practitioner. If you want to find an optician, go to your local library for a list of registered opticians in your area, ask at your local Citizens' Advice Bureau or look in the Yellow Pages under "Opticians".

Free eye tests are available to people under 16 years of age or under 19 years of age and still in full-time education.

The optician MUST give you a prescription (or a certificate that you do not need glasses), even if your sight has not changed. You cannot be asked to pay for your eye test until you have been given your prescription. You are under no obligation to buy your eye glasses from the same optician who gave you the test. Your prescription is valid for 2 years.

All charges for sight tests can be found in *NHS leaflet HC.12*, Benefits enquiry line (0800) 882 200 (www.doh.gov.uk/nhscharges/hc12.htm).

For further information, consult *NHS leaflet HC.12*.

## Paediatrics

Your local health clinic or G.P. offers a full service of paediatrics, as well as *Child Health Clinics*, which specialise in children only. Check with your local FHSA for one close to you. The following services are available:

1. Immunisations and boosters.

2. Developmental checks (i.e. hearing, vision, weight, height) at 6 weeks, 8 months, 18 months, three years and 4 years (pre-school). The service then continues via the school system.

3. Child psychotherapy, educational psychology for learning and behaviour problems, speech therapy and orthopaedics.

4. Health Visitors who make house calls to answer any questions you may have, discuss problems, remind you of injection dates, and help orient you to local play groups, and registered childminders in the area.

All clinics have emergency numbers to be used after hours. G.P.s or their deputies will make house calls in emergency situations.

## REGISTRATION OF BIRTHS

### UK Registration

All births taking place in the UK must be registered. The hospital where the birth occurs will notify the local Registrar of Births with details of the birth. The parents (mother or father, if the parents are legally married) must register the child at the local office within 42 days of the birth. Either a short or long form of birth certificate is available. The long form is more detailed (and is the only one that the US will accept as proof of the birth). There is a small fee for the birth certificates.

### US Registration

Babies born to US citizens must be registered at the United States Embassy within five years of their birth. Parents should contact the US Embassy on (020) 7499 9000 (www.usembassy.org.uk) to obtain the forms required for registration. The personal documents required are the UK long form birth certificate, the US passports of both parents, and a certified copy of the parents' marriage certificate. Divorce decrees or death certificates of all previous marriages, if any, are also required.

Once all the appropriate documentation has been submitted, in person, to the Consul at the US Embassy, the child will be issued with a *Consular Report of Birth Abroad of a Citizen of the United States of America*, and a *Certificate of Birth Abroad*. Parents may then apply for a US passport and a Social Security number for the child. There is a fee, payable by cash only, for all the above mentioned services. The entire process requires two to three hours at the Embassy; however, the baby does not need to accompany the parent.

### Obtaining British Nationality for a Child

In certain circumstances, it will also be possible to register a child born in the UK as a UK national, and to obtain a British passport for the child. (This will in no way affect the child's US citizenship). Parents interested in this possibility should contact the *Immigration and Nationality Division*, (08706) 067 766.

### Obtaining Child Benefit

If your child is born in the UK you are eligible to claim for a weekly Child Benefit Allowance until your child leaves school. Child Benefit is a tax-free Social Security benefit that does not depend on how much money you earn or on how much savings you have. For information regarding the Child Benefit Allowance call your local Social Security office. The phone number and address are in the telephone book under Social Security or Benefits Agency. Your local baby clinic usually has information as well.

## IMMUNISATIONS AND VACCINATIONS

In order to enter certain countries, when travelling on business or pleasure, immunisations are necessary (see the Department of Health's health advice for travellers at www.doh.gov.uk/traveladvice/index.htm). Under the NHS, some immunisations and vaccinations may be carried out by your G.P. free of charge. The doctor may, however, charge for signing the certificate that proves that the immunisation/vaccination has been administered.

An alternative way to proceed is by using an immunisation clinic. Appointments can easily be made and the clinics are familiar with the necessary injections. Many large travel agents such as *Thomas Cook* (Berkeley Square, W1; www.thomascook.co.uk) and *Trailfinders* (Kensington High Street, W8, www.trailfinders.co.uk) have immunisation clinics as well as the main international airlines. A particularly good service is:

*British Airways, Travel Clinic*, 156 Regent Street, W1; (020) 7439 9584, (www.britishairways.com)

For immunisation for babies, please see either Paediatrics or Chapter Eight: Children.

**EMERGENCY FACILITIES AND CASUALTY UNITS**

If an emergency situation does arise, proceed immediately to a hospital with a casualty unit. It is most important to know the nearest casualty hospital in your area. **IN A SERIOUS EMERGENCY, DIAL 999** and ask for ambulance service. Emergency service to a resident is provided free of charge by the NHS and is available to anyone, including tourists. It is interesting to note, however, that in the case of most road traffic accidents, the victim must pay for the ambulance service.

NHS Walk in Centers provide treatment for minor injuries and illnesses seven days a week. You don't need an appointment and will be seen by an experienced NHS nurse. To locate the walk in center nearest you (located in Soho, Fulham, Whitechapel, Parsons Green, Tooting and Charing Cross.) see www.nhs.uk/localnhsservices/wicenters/default.asp.

Each police station keeps a list of emergency doctors and chemists who are available on a 24-hour basis.

Almost all London NHS hospitals have a 24-hour casualty unit. Listed below are some of the largest in different areas.

**London Hospitals with 24-Hour Casualty Units** (Partial List)

**SE1**

*Guy's Hospital*, St. Thomas Street, SE1, (020) 7955 5000

*St. Thomas' Hospital*, Lambeth Palace Road, SE1, (020) 7928 9292

**W2, W9, W10**

*St. Mary's Hospital*, Praed Street, W2, (020) 7886 6666

## W1, NW1, WC1, N1
*University College Hospital*, Gower Street, WC1, (020) 7387 9300

## SW1, SW3, SW7, SW10
*Chelsea & Westminster Hospital*, 369 Fulham Road, SW10, (020) 8746 8000

## SW6, W14, W6, W12
*Charing Cross Hospital*, Fulham Palace Road, W6, (020) 8846 1234

*Hammersmith Hospital*, Du Cane Road, W12, (020) 8743 2030

## NW3, NW4, NW6, NW8, NW11
*Royal Free Hospital*, Pond Street, NW3, (020) 7794 0500

---

**Did you know?...**There are several 'Medicentres' throughout London, including locations at Victoria Station and Euston Station. These are privately run walk-in clinics, many of which are open seven days a week. They are an excellent resource for conditions that are not quite 'emergency room' emergencies. They are also useful to visitors who might need a doctor's aid. For a list of locations and services ring (0870) 600 0870, (www.medicentre.co.uk).

---

### Eye Emergencies Only
*Moorfields Eye Hospital*, 162 City Road, EC1, (020) 7253 3411

### Children's Emergencies Only
*Chelsea & Westminster Children's Hospital*, 369 Fulham Road, SW10, (020) 8746 8000

### Dental Emergencies Only
NHS Direct on 0845 4647 is a 24 hour information line and can refer you to a surgery open for treatment – private or NHS. In addition, the NHS web site search function includes an option to search by opening hours. Visit www.nhs.uk for more details.

### Animal Emergencies
*The Blue Cross Animal Hospital*, 1-5 Hugh Street, SW1; (020) 7834 4224 for 24-hour emergency veterinary service. (See Chapter Eleven: Services under 'Veterinarians' for veterinarians with 24-hour emergency service.)

### AMBULANCE SERVICES
*London Ambulance Service* (NHS); 999

*St. John's Ambulance Service*, NW1 non-emergency (private); (020) 7258 3456

## LATE NIGHT CHEMISTS

*Bliss Chemists*, 50-56 Willesden Lane, Kilburn, NW6; (020) 7624 8000 (09.00 to 23.00, 365 days a year)

*Bliss Chemists*, 5 Marble Arch, W1, (020) 7723 6116, (09.00 to 24.00, 365 days a year)

*Dajani*, 92 Old Brompton Road, SW7, (020) 7589 8600 (09.00 to 22.00, Monday to Friday; 09.00 to 20.00, Saturday; 10.00 to 20.00, Sunday)

*I. Warman Freed*, 45 Golders Green, NW11, (020) 8455 4351, (08:30 until midnight)

*Boots The Chemist*, West Concourse, Victoria Station; (020) 7834 0676, (07.30 to 21.00, Monday to Friday; 09.00 to 19.00, Saturday)

*Tesco Metro*, 311 Oxford Street (opposite John Lewis), W1, (020) 7530 8449 (08.00 to 22.00, Monday to Saturday; Noon to 18.00, Sunday)

## ALTERNATIVE MEDICINE

Your local health food store or chemist can be a good resource for alternative medicine services and products in your area.

*Bioenergetic Medical Centre*, Drs. Tatyana and Damir Shakamber; 23 Manchester St, W1, (020) 7935 6866. Alternative health specialists, combining Shiatsu, acupuncture, aromatherapy, psychoanalysis, overall philosophy that mind and body must be in tune.

*Eden Medical Center*, for excellent chiropractor and holistic health practitioners in the city.

*Hale Clinic*, 7 Park Crescent, W1, (020) 7631 0156. Integrates conventional and complementary medicine under one roof; (www.haleclinic.com).

*Neal's Yard Therapy Rooms*, 2 Neal's Yard, WC2, (020) 7379 7662; (www.nealsyardremedies.com).

## HOMEOPATHIC PRODUCTS

*Cory Pharmacy*, 168 High Road, East Finchley, N2, (020) 8444 9966 David Needleman, Homeopath.

*Sloane Health Shop*, 27 King's Road, SW3 4RT; (020) 7730 7046. Vitamins, nutritional supplements, homeopathic remedies, aromatherapy products and natural cosmetics.

*Sloane Health Clinic*, 27 King's Road, SW3, (020) 7730 1328.

## BIOLOGICAL/NON-BIOLOGICAL DETERGENTS

Biological washing detergents (laundry detergents) contain more enzymes and are harder on clothes, skin and the environment. The non-biological detergents have fewer added chemical agents and are less harmful to the environment, better for sensitive skin, and are readily available in all supermarkets. A particularly gentle detergent for baby laundry is Filetti that is available in most supermarkets.

## AIR QUALITY

To check the air quality in your area phone the Air Pollution Bulletin Service operated by the Department of the Environment, Food and Rural Affairs on (0800) 556 677, (www.defra.gov.uk). Information is updated hourly.

*National Asthma Campaign*, Providence House, Providence Place, N1, (020) 7226 2260, (www.asthma.org.uk).

## DEATH OF AN AMERICAN IN THE UK

If an American dies in the UK, the *American Citizens' Service Branch*, Consular Section of the US Embassy; (020) 7499 9000 (www.usembassy.org.uk), can advise on all procedures, including the undertaker, coroner, and shipment of the body back to the US. The Consular Section of the US Embassy in London has jurisdiction over England and Wales. For Scotland, contact the *Consular Section*, 3 Regent Terrace, Edinburgh, Scotland EH7 5BW; (0131) 556 8315 (www.usembassy.org.uk/scotland/). For Northern Ireland, contact the *American Consul General*, Queen's House, 14 Queen Street, Belfast, N. Ireland BT1, (0) 28 9032 8239.

# Chapter Eight: Children

Moving overseas when you have children can be a complicated task. Fortunately, London has plenty of offerings for the younger set – it's just a matter of becoming familiar with all the options! The following information has been shared by London "mums" who have successfully survived the experience.

## BEFORE YOU ARRIVE

Many popular US brands are widely available in the UK; however, you will find that the selection can vary depending on the store or chemist, which often means you'll have to visit a few different places in order to find everything you're looking for.

### Nappies/Babycare Items:

Pampers and Huggies brands are carried by most supermarket and chemist chains in the UK. Baby wipes by Pampers and Johnson & Johnson are also widely available; in addition, chains such as Boots, Tesco, and Sainsburys carry their own lines of wipes and nappies.

Vaseline and A&D ointment are sold in the UK. There are also several British-made nappy rash ointments such as Sudocrem and Kamillosan that work very well.

Johnson & Johnson baby bath, powder and lotion products are very popular in the UK, but there are also many other choices available.

### Formula/Breastfeeding:

Ready to feed or powder infant formulas are commonly offered in the following brands: SMA, Cow and Gate, Wysoy (a Soya milk formula), and Hipp Organic. It is also possible to find brands such as Aptamil and Enfamil and specialised formulas, such as hypoallergenic – you will just have to search a bit more, as these items are generally not carried in most chemists or markets.

The most popular and widely distributed brand of feeding accessories is Avent, offering everything from bottles and nipples to breast pumps, shields, and storage bags. Medela breast pumps, a well-regarded brand, can be ordered through select chemists or through the UK Medela distributor at (01538) 399 541. Johnson & Johnson nursing pads are sold at most chemists and supermarkets.

In addition, the Mamm, Maws and Nuk brands all have breastfeeding accessories, bottles, and pacifiers.

### Baby Food/Feeding Items:

Beechnut baby food (fruits, vegetables and juices only) is available at select outlets.

Other popular UK brands include Heinz, BabyNat, and Hipp Organic, which is made with fresh, organic ingredients, free from all pesticides and chemical fertilisers. It has a full line of cereals, vegetables, desserts, juices, snacks and toddler meals

Sippy cups, bibs, feeding bowls and accessories made by Avent, Tommee Tippee and Maws are readily available.

## Detergents:

Ivory Snow is not sold in the UK, but a good substitute is Filetti, a very gentle detergent. There is also a product called Napisan that is great for safely removing germs and stains from children's clothes.

Biological washing detergents (laundry detergents) contain more enzymes and are harder on clothes, skin and the environment. The non-biological detergents have fewer added chemical agents and are less harmful to the environment, better for sensitive skin, and are readily available in all supermarkets. A particularly gentle detergent for baby laundry is Filetti that is available in most supermarkets.

**Quick Glossary of Terms** (See Glossary for an expanded list.)

| English | American |
|---------|----------|
| Cot | Crib |
| Dummy | Pacifier |
| Nappies | Diapers |
| Pushchair | Stroller |
| Teet | Nipple |

---

**Did you know...** All US linens, including cot linens, are slightly different sizes than their UK counterparts.

---

**Did you know?...** Electrical outlets are different so monitors will not work without an adapter and transformer (Tomy and Safe'n'Sound are good UK brands).

## MEDICAL NEEDS

### HealthCare/Illness

You can see a National Health Service (NHS) doctor or a private G.P. for emergency or routine medical care. (See Chapter Seven: Healthcare) Paediatricians are considered specialists and generally are seen annually or when referred by a G.P. However, you can make an appointment directly if you wish.

Immunisations for babies and regular health checks are available free of charge through your local NHS "well-baby" clinic. The current immunisation schedule for babies in the UK is very similar to the schedule in the US. (See Chapter Seven: Healthcare for more information on NHS, Paediatrics Services, and late night chemists).

### Medicines

Benylin (cough medicine) is available at chemists but Benydryl (antihistamine) is not. Infant and children's products that contain 'paracetamol' (fever and pain relief; the UK equivalent to Tylenol) are available in liquid or tablet form as 'Junior disprol', 'Panadol', or 'Calpol'. 'Karvol' can be purchased for children and is a natural decongestant that is inhaled. The British equivalent to 'Pedialyte' is 'Dioralyte' that comes in a packet and is mixed with water.

Some other children's medicines and products:

| | |
|---|---|
| Calpol | – aspirin substitute containing paracetamol |
| Gripe Water | – colic and hiccups |
| Infacol | – colic (similar to the US product Mylicon) |
| Junifen | – fever relief containing ibuprofen |
| Phenergan | – antihistamine causes drowsiness |
| Sudacrem | – nappy rash |
| Zinc and Castor oil lotion | – nappy rash |
| E45 creme | – dry skin |
| Aqueous creme | – dry skin |
| Dentinox | – teething pain |
| Oilatum | – cradle cap, eczema |

## PREGNANCY

One of the first decisions you will have to make once you become pregnant is whether or not you plan to use private or NHS healthcare. (See Chapter Seven: Healthcare and specifically Maternity Services for more details). Most American insurance policies cover private care. British policies such as 'BUPA' do not consider pregnancy a medical condition and will not cover private healthcare costs unless you have a scheduled C-section or other high-risk condition. Whether using private or NHS healthcare, a Health Visitor will come to your home after you have given birth to check that you and your baby are healthy and adjusting to life at home. They will schedule the visits with you for up to ten days after the birth. (See Chapter Seven: Healthcare for information on Registration of Births).

## Ante-Natal Classes

Ante-natal classes (pre-natal) are available at some hospitals. Independent of any hospital, the following offer ante-natal preparatory classes and post-natal exercise classes:

*Christine Hill Associates*, Strand End, 78 Grove Park Road, Chiswick, W4; (020) 8994 4349

*The Life Centre*, 15 Edge Street, W8; (020) 7221 4602. Offers yoga for pregnancy and post-natal. Also offers baby massage classes.

*The Kensington and Chelsea Women's Club* – for membership information (020) 7863 7562

*The National Childbirth Trust*, (0870) 444 8707, for general information and to also organise pregnancy support groups.

## Maternity Wear

Some major department stores offer a small selection of maternity clothes and a large and varied selection of baby equipment.

*Blooming Marvellous*, Mail Order through catalogue (0870 751 8944) or www.bloomingmarvellous.co.uk. Also sells children's wear and toys.

*Bumpsadaisy Maternity Style*, 43 The Market, Covent Garden, WC2E; (020) 7379 9831. Also in Putney. Range of maternity styles from casual to evening wear.

*Formes*, 313 Brompton Road, SW3, (020) 7584 3337; 33 Brook Street, W1Y, (020) 7493 2783 and 28 Henrietta Street, WC2, (020) 7240 4777. French company that offers a stylish line of maternity clothes.

*H&M*, 481-483 Oxford Street, W1 (020) 493 8557; High Street Kensington, W8 (020) 368 3920; www.hm.com. These two branches of the well-known Swedish chain carry a line of trendy, fun maternity clothes under the "Mama" label. In addition, many pregnant mothers have been known to wear H&M's regular ladies line while pregnant – in bigger sizes!

*Great Expectations*, 78 Fulham Road, SW3; (020) 7584 2451. Designer clothes and maternity underwear for the mother-to-be.

*Mothercare*, 174-176 Oxford Street, W1N; (020) 7580 1688. Many locations around London. Complete range of items for mothers-to-be and children up to size 10, including baby beds, linens and toiletries.

*Rigby & Peller*, 22 Conduit Street, W1 (020) 7491 2200; and 2 Hans Road, SW3 (020) 7589 9293. Good source for nursing bras/maternity underwear.

## Websites

There are many sites for expectant and new mums. They cover many topics including how to conceive a baby, breastfeeding, furniture and equipment-buying guides, and finding good childcare. Some of the most useful sites that we have found are listed below.

www.babyworld.co.uk, Information and tips on many aspects of pregnancy and child rearing, a monthly panel test of baby products, a section for you to pose questions to doctors and midwives. Online shopping and a discussion group for dads.

www.ukparents.co.uk, Interesting articles, good product updates, online shopping, and lively forums on a variety of subjects.

www.babycentre.co.uk, Articles and interactive tools developed by British experts in women's and children's health and development. Online shopping, plus buying guides for baby products.

## CHILD CARE

Once you arrive in the UK you may wish to take advantage of the wonderful child care that seems to be so much more readily available here than at home. Before deciding on help with the children and/or housekeeping, it is helpful to be aware of the distinctions between the following:

---

*Au Pair* – A young girl who comes to live with a family in order to learn the English language. She will help with childcare and light housework for up to 30 hours per week in exchange for her room and board and pocket money. She is usually a student and may not speak fluent English.

*Mother's Helper* – A non-professional who will do housework and care for children either full- or part-time.

*Nanny* – A certified nursery nurse who holds a Nursery Nursing Examination Board Certificate (N.N.E.B.). She does not do housework or meal preparation for the family but takes care of all needs of the children including their laundry and meal preparation. She can live in or out.

---

## Agencies

When working with an agency make sure that you have a complete understanding of the fees charged. There are membership fees, engagement fees and booking fees depending on the situation and agency. These fees vary widely. *The Good Nanny Guide* is an indispensable resource book outlining the traditional duties and pay scales of all types of help and it can be found at most bookstores. It is advisable to contact more than one agency. Finding a good match for your specific needs will depend on the sort of people a given agency has "on the books" at the time you call. Help can be found to suit most permanent and part-time requirements.

*Annie's Nannies*, (020) 7267 6432 (North London), (020) 7924 6464 (South/South East London), (020) 7924 7474 (West and Central London); Live-out Nannies, Mother's Helps, Nannyshares and Babysitters both long term and temporary.

*Childminders*, 6 Nottingham Street, W1M; (020) 7935 2049/3000; Babysitting service, also provides light domestic help such as cleaners, ironers, party staff.

*Delaney International*, Bramble Cottage, Thorncombe Street, Bramley, Surrey GU5; (01483) 894 300; Specialises in Australian Nannies and Mother's Helps plus European Au Pairs.

*Elite Nannies*, 22 Rowena Crescent, Battersea, SW11; (020) 7801 0061/0062; Permanent and temporary Nannies, Mother's Helps and Maternity Nurses.

*Kensington Nannies*, 49-53 Kensington High Street, W8; (020) 7937 3299/2333; Nannies and Mother's Helpers, both full and part-time.

*Maternally Yours*, 222 Old Brompton Road, SW5; (020) 7341 9410; Specialises in Maternity Nurses.

*Occasional and Permanent Nannies*, 2 Cromwell Place, SW7; (020) 7225 1555; Nannies, Mother's Helps, Governesses.

*Quick Help Agency*, 307A Finchley Road, NW3; (020) 7435 7671; Nannies, Mother's Helps, Au Pairs, Cleaners, Care for Elderly

*The Nanny Service*, 6 Nottingham Street, W1M; Temporary (020) 7935 3515; Live-in/Daily (020) 7935 6976; Specialises in Australian, New Zealand and British Nannies on a temporary or permanent basis -both daily and live-in.

*Universal Aunts*, P.O. Box 304, Clapham SW4 0NN; (020) 7738 8937; Nannies, Mother's Helps, Cleaners, Butlers, Cooks.

Two additional excellent sources for childminders, full or part-time are:

*"The Lady"* magazine, 39-40 Bedford Street, WC2E; (020) 7379 4717, a weekly (Tuesday) publication available at newsagents, listing situations vacant for all domestic help. One also receives a good response by placing ads listing personal requirements.

*Best Bear*, is an agency that rates and recommends nanny services. They pose as interested childcare workers and conduct interviews with services to see what type of childminders they hire. (020) 8675 3131 (www.bestbear.co.uk).

One of the top colleges for Nannies and Maternity Nurses is The Norland College. Norland maintains a College Register that will list details of a vacancy. Though it does not actively search for a Nanny, it will charge a fee if a placement occurs as a result of the listing. Norland's telephone number is (01488) 682 252. Another top college for Nannies is Princess Christian College in Manchester. Call the main number at (0161) 224 4560 for information about nanny placement.

If one employs a Nanny on a part or full-time basis, one is required by law to pay regular Tax and National Insurance Contributions to the Inland Revenue on her behalf, as well as provide her with regular payslips. There are two payroll service companies that can take care of all the details for a fee:

*Nannytax*; (01273) 626 256

*Taxing Nannies*; (020) 8882 6847

## Baby First Aid/Safety

www.childalert.co.uk. (Website only, no telephone). A comprehensive reference/ guidance web-site that focuses on addressing a variety of child safety topics and parenting concerns. There is a section on childproofing, plus the opportunity to arrange for free baby-proofing advice.

*The Parent Company*, 6 Jacob's Well Mews, W1U, (020) 7935 9635; (www.theparentcompany.co.uk). Offers classes in first aid and basic life support and can arrange private sessions in your home.

*The Portland Hospital*, Physiotherapy Department, 205-209 Great Portland Street W1; (020) 7390 8061. Offers a $2^{1}/_{2}$ hour baby/toddler first aid class taught by a midwife. Topics covered include how to make your house safer, what to do in emergencies and how to administer CPR, with practice on a dummy. Classes are held approximately every 6 weeks.

## Gym Crèches

For moms who like to get a bit of exercise, there are several London sports clubs that have crèche (nursery) facilities for children, including Holmes Place, David Lloyd, Esporta and the Harbour Club. The amenities vary between each, so be sure to telephone or visit before making your decision. (See Chapter Fourteen: Sports and Leisure for contact information.)

## Restaurants

There are a surprising number of London restaurants that positively welcome children. For starters, remember that Sunday lunch is a popular family meal, so children are usually expected anywhere. Here is a small selection of child-friendly restaurants; you may also want to look in *Zagat's* or any other London restaurant guide for more options.

*Bank*, WC2; (020) 7234 3344. Brassiere with play area and colouring books during Sunday brunch.

*Julie's*, W11; (020) 7229 8331. Low-key, with a crèche on Sundays.

*Lemonia*, NW1; (020) 7586 7454. Child-friendly Greek.

*The River Cafe*, W6; (020) 7381 8824. Gourmet Italian that welcomes children.

*Tate Modern*, SE1; (020) 7401 5020. Both restaurant and café are non-smoking and have high chairs.

## The National Childbirth Trust

For recent arrivals to the UK or anyone with young children, *The National Childbirth Trust (NCT)* is a tremendous resource.

The NCT is a non-profit organisation and a registered charity full of excellent information on all matters relating to childbirth and early parenting. They have branches all over London and these can be reached via the main branch that is at: Alexandra House, Oldham Terrace, Acton, W3; 0870 444 8707; www.nct-online.org. Many of the neighbourhood branches of the NCT have produced wonderful information packs on having a baby in London that can be a great help to a pregnant expatriate.

The NCT branches have also published many helpful books about children in London such as: *Clapham for Kids* and *Chiswick for Kids*. *'Under Fives Welcome in and around Westminster'* can be obtained from the Social Services Department, Westminster City Hall, Victoria Street, SW1E.

Out of the NCT have sprung many very interesting and helpful groups including: *Parents at Work*, 45 Beech Street, EC2Y; (020) 7628 3565; www.parentsatwork.org.uk. This group's goal is to help working parents find a better balance between home and work responsibilities. They have a free helpline and fact sheets on issues such as maternity rights; legal and practical advice for returning to work; establishing a flexible work schedule; and helping working parents with a disabled child.

In addition, they publish the *Working Mothers' Handbook*, an excellent book on the various types of care one can expect to get for children here in London and the costs, interviewing techniques, standard of training and authoritative bodies which oversee these employees.

## SHOPPING

### Books

The large bookstores such as Waterstone's (see Chapter Twelve: Shopping under 'Bookstores') have an extensive children's book area. Also stores such as *Daisy & Tom*, *Harrods*, and *Mothercare* have a good selection of children's books. www.amazon.co.uk is a convenient way to purchase books for children.

*The Children's Book Centre*, 237 Kensington High Street, W8; (020) 7937 7497. Also has toys and gifts.

### Children's Wear

Most department stores have children's departments – *Harrods*, *Peter Jones* and *Selfridges* probably have the largest selection. Stores such as *Marks & Spencer* and *BHS* are excellent for competitively priced, unfussy clothes for boys and girls from 0-14 years of age.

*Barneys Wimbledon*, 6 Church Road, Wimbledon Village, SW19; (020) 8944 2915. Cute range of clothes and shoes for babies and children.

*Benetton*, 129-131 Kensington High Street, W8; (020) 7937 3034; additional branches throughout London. Colour co-ordinated trousers, shirts and sweaters for boys and girls.

*Bonpoint*, 35b Sloane Street, SW1; (020) 7235 1441; 17 Victoria Grove, W8 (020) 7583 5131. Exclusive French children's wear.

*Daisy & Tom*, 181 King's Road, SW3; (020) 7352 5000. Large store with clothes, toys, books and nursery furniture and equipment. They also have a carousel, a small puppet theatre, children's café and children's haircutters.

*Gap Kids*, 122 King's Road, SW3; (020) 7581 9720. Also 146 Kensington High Street, W8; (020) 7937-1909 and other branches throughout London.

*H&M*, 123b Kensington High Street, W8; (020) 7937 3329. Other branches throughout London. Swedish chain with well priced contemporary children's wear.

*Little Treasures*, 10 Braemar Crescent, Leigh on Sea, Essex SS9 3RL; (01702) 559 005. Traditional English clothes such as smocked dresses, fairisle sweaters, round collar shirts, classic shorts, breeches and trousers. By mail order only.

*Mini Boden*, Elliott House, Victoria Road, NW10; (020) 8453 1535; (www.boden.co.uk). Fun, playful clothes, shoes and accessories for babies through teens. Order through catalogue or website.

*Mothercare*, 461 Oxford Street, W1; (020) 7580 1688. Other branches throughout London. Absolutely everything can be bought from Mothercare including children's clothing from 0-8 years, maternity clothes, pushchairs, nursery furniture, and home and car safety equipment.

*Patrizia Wigan Designs Ltd.*, 19 Walton Street, SW3; (020) 7823 7080. Other branches at 72 New King's Road, SW6; (020) 7736 3336 and 61 Barnes High Street, SW13; (020) 8876 4540. Modern classics from birth to pre-teens.

*Rachel Riley*, 14 Pont Street, SW1X; (020) 7259 5969. Traditional English clothes with a French influence designed by Rachel. Also has a mail order catalogue.

*Trotters*, 34 King's Road, SW3; (020) 7259 9620 and 127 Kensington High Street, W8; (020) 7937 9373. Wide range of clothing and shoes. Also, children's haircuts.

*Young England*, 47 Elizabeth Street, SW1; (020) 7259 9003. Traditional English clothes such as smocked dresses and tailored coats for children from birth to seven years.

---

**Did you know...**When shopping for baby clothes, it's helpful to remember that in general American sizes are generously cut, British sizes are fairly accurate and French sizes are very small. For example, an average sized 3-month-old baby will usually fit American and British clothes marked as 3 months, but will fit French clothes marked 6 months. A good rule of thumb with French baby clothes is to double the age of the baby.

---

## Equipment Hire/Nappy and Household Goods Delivery

*Chelsea Baby Equipment Hire*, 108 Dorset Road, SW19; (020) 8946 9172

*The Food Ferry*, (020) 7498 0827; (www.foodferry.com). A home delivery supermarket with a good selection of baby products, including Beechnut baby foods.

*Nappy Express*; (020) 8361 4040. Next day delivery service for baby products (toiletries, food).

(See Chapter Eleven: Services for a more complete list of Delivery Services).

If you are looking to acquire gently used baby items, such as strollers, highchairs, furniture and clothing, the NCT runs a series of "Nearly New" sales throughout the country. For dates and schedules, contact the NCT through the main number listed earlier in this section. Also, the Kensington Chelsea Women's Club holds an annual Children's Jumble Sale each autumn, a good source for second-hand items. Contact the Kensington Chelsea Women's Club (KCWC) at (020) 7863 7562 for more information.

## Nursery Equipment and Furniture

*Peter Jones, John Lewis Stores, Harrods, Selfridges* and *Marks & Spencer* have good baby/children departments. *Mothercare* (see Children's Wear) and *The Early Learning Centre* (see Toys) specialise in baby/children items. Other stores that specialise in nursery items include:

*Baby List*, 50 Sullivan Road, SW6; (020) 7371 5145. Large variety of brand name items. For a fee, will help put together a list of complete nursery needs.

*Daisy & Tom* (see Children's Wear).

*Dragon's of Walton Street*, 23 Walton Street, SW3; (020) 7589 3795. Specialises in hand-painted furniture.

*Lilliput*, 255-259 Queenstown Road, Battersea, SW8; (020) 7720 5554; 278 Upper Richmond Road, Putney, SW15; (020) 8780 1682; and 100 Haydons Road, Wimbledon, SW19; (020) 8542 3542. Large variety of brand name items.

*Little Bridge*, 56 Battersea Bridge Road, SW11; (020) 7978 5522. Bureaus, beds, desks, chairs, bookshelves and toy chests made of sturdy pine that can be painted in a large range of colours and any design of your choosing.

*The Nursery Window*, 81 Walton Street, SW3; (020) 7581 3358. Specialises in layettes and items for new-borns made from their own fabric.

*Simon Horn*, 117-121 Wandsworth Bridge Road, SW6; (020) 7731 1279. Custom made cots and beds.

## Toys

Most major department stores such as *Harrods* and *Peter Jones* have large toy departments and *Hamley's* has everything!

*Cheeky Monkeys*, 202 Kensington Park Road, W11; (020) 7792 9022.

*Daisy & Tom* (see Children's Wear).

*Early Learning Centre*, 36 King's Road, SW3; (020) 7581 5764. Other branches throughout London including Hammersmith (020) 8741 2469. Specialises in educational toys for young children.

*Great Little Trading Company*, (08702) 414 080, (www.gltc.co.uk). Practical, innovative products for children and parents. By mail order only.

*Hamley's*, 188-196 Regent Street, W1, (020) 7494 2000. World's largest toy shop!

*J. J. Toys*, 138 St. John's Wood High Street, NW8, (020) 7722 4855.

*The Toy Box*, 12 Gloucester Road, SW7, (020) 7591 6400. Toys for 0-9 year olds. Also mail order; (0700) 222 9227.

*Toys 'R' Us*, Tilling Road, Brent Cross Shopping Centre, NW2; (020) 8209 0019; and 12-14 Church Street West, Woking, Surrey GU21; (01483) 726 449. Other locations.

*Toys, Toys, Toys*, 10-11 Northways Parade, Finchley Road, Swiss Cottage, NW3; (020) 7722 9821. Toys for 0-14 year olds.

*Traditional Toys*, 53 Godfrey Street, SW3; (020) 7352 1718.

*Tridias*, 25 Bute Street, SW7; (020) 7584 2330. Also mail order.

## Videos

Before you purchase any videos, it is worth ascertaining whether you have an American, UK or multi-system VCR.

*Harrods, Daisy and Tom* and www.amazon.co.uk have a good selection of children's videos, including favourites such as Sesame Street, Barney, Disney and Teletubbies. You can also find the Baby Einstein series at Harrods or by special order at the Children's Book Centre on Kensington High Street.

Shows such as Teletubbies, Sesame Street, Barney and Blue's Clues are broadcast daily on UK television. If you have cable, you can arrange for access to channels such as Nickelodeon and the Cartoon Network.

## ENTERTAINING YOUR CHILD

### Active Movement and Music

*Crêchendo*, (020) 8772 8120, (www.crechendo.com). Centres across London. Active learning classes for children 4 months to 7 years. Classes offer movement, music, sight and sound experiences.

*Gymboree Play & Music*, several locations including Putney, Swiss Cottage, Bayswater, Brighton and Cambridge; call (0800) 092 0911 or visit www.GymboreePlayUK.com. Activity and music classes from birth to 5 years.

*Latchmere Leisure Centre*, Burns Road, Battersea SW11; (020) 7207 8004; Runs musical movement classes for children 8 months to 4 years.

*The Life Centre*, 8 Edge Street, W8; (020) 7221 4602; Offers baby massage class from birth – 6 months, and a baby gym/activity class from 6 months – 1 year.

*Tumble Tots*, many locations; (020) 8959 4261 (North); (020) 8944 8818 (South West). Organised work on ladders, tunnels, mats, etc., with music and songs. Age 9 months to 6 years

## Adventure (Multi-Activity Play Areas)

*Bramley's Big Adventure*, 136 Bramley Road, W10; (020) 8960 1515, (www.bramleysbig.co.uk). 3-level indoor playground for children 0 to 11 years old. Will also host children's parties.

*ClownTown*, 222 Green Lanes, Palmers Green, N13; (020) 8886 7520. Children's indoor adventure centre with Tarzan ropes, slides, ball ponds, etc. for children under 5 feet tall; separate play area for toddlers.

*Fantasy Island*, Vale Farm, Watford Road, Wembley, Middlesex HA0; (020) 8904 9044. An 'island' themed play arena for children up to 5 feet tall and/or under 12 years of age. Separate 'adventure' play area for children under 5.

*Legoland Windsor*, Winkfield, Berkshire SL4; (0870) 562 6375; (www.legoland.co.uk). Open late March through November. Over 50 rides and attractions, plus seasonal special events.

*Play Dome*, Woodside Leisure Park, Kingsway, Garston, Watford, Herts WD2; (01923) 894 801. Massive, well-equipped play environment for children under 12 with a separate under 5's area.

*Snakes and Ladders*, Syon Park, Brentford, Middlesex TW8; (020) 8847 0946; Vast building housing three separate play areas for toddlers, intermediate and older children under 12. Also has a café and garden, and can host children's parties.

*Tiger's Eye*, 42 Station Road, Merton Abbey Mills, SW19; (020) 8543 1655. Large indoor adventure centre for toddlers to 10 year olds.

## Art

*The Art Workshop*, 5 London branches in Chiswick, Notting Hill, Muswell Hill, Mill Hill and West Hampstead; (020) 7431 5696, (www.art4fun.com). Themed American art activity centre. Home of "The Art Party". Birthday parties, holiday courses and classes.

*The Pottery Cafe*, 735 Fulham Road, SW6; (020) 7736 2157. Decorate a variety of pottery. Available for children's parties.

*London Brass Rubbing Centre*, The Crypt, St. Martin's in the Fields, Trafalgar Square, WC2N; (020) 7930 9306. Brass rubbing.

*Paint Pots*, The Chelsea Christian Centre, Edith Grove, Chelsea SW10; (020) 7376 4571. Art classes for children, 18 months to 5 years. (See Music also).

## Boat Trips

*Canal Cruises*, 250 Camden High Street, NW1; (020) 7485 4433. Canal trips on Regent's Canal and Camden Lock; the *Jenny Wren* (operates March to October) and the *My Fair Lady* (year round).

*Guildford Boat House*, Millbrook, Guildford, Surrey, GU1; (01483) 504 494. $1^1/2$ hour boat trip from Town Wharf to St. Catherine's Lock, rowing boats for daily hire, and canal boats for holiday hire (four days minimum). Open Easter to October.

*Jason's Trips*, Jason's Wharf, opposite 60 Blomfield Road, Little Venice, W9; (020) 7286 3428; Boat trips (one way 45 minutes, return $1^1/2$ hours) leaving from Little Venice to Camden Lock. March to September.

*London Water Bus Company*, Camden Place, Camden Town, NW1 and Little Venice, NW1; (020) 7482 2550 (Office); (020) 7482 2660 (Information). Boat trips (one way 45 minutes, return $1^1/2$ hours) leaving from either Camden Lock or Little Venice via the zoo. Open daily April to October and weekends in winter.

*Westminster Passenger Services Association Up River*, Westminster Pier, Victoria Embankment, SW1; (020) 7930 2062. Boat trips on the Thames to Richmond, the Tower of London, Greenwich, Kew Gardens, and Hampton Court. Round trip or one way, returning by public transportation.

Paddle boat rides in Hyde Park, Regent's Park and Battersea Park. Some parks offer rowing and sailing also.

## Cookery

*Books for Cooks*, 4 Blenheim Crescent, W11; (020) 7221 1992; (www.booksforcooks.com). Special workshops for children ages 5-14.

*Cookie Crumbles*, 64 St. Leonards Road, SW14; (020) 8876 9912; (www.cookiecrumbles.net). Monthly themed cookery workshops for ages 5-15.

*Divertimenti Cookery School*, 34 Marylebone High Street, W1U; (020) 7486 8020; (www.divertimenti.co.uk). Offers Saturday classes for little ones, covering themes such as "Italian Day" and "Party Food."

*Kids Cookery School*, 107 Gunnersbury Lane, Acton W3; (020) 8992 8882; (www.kidscookeryschool.co.uk). Offers holiday and half-term classes and workshops for ages 3 and up.

## Dance

*Cherry Childe School of Dancing*, Trinity Hall, Hodford Road, NW11; (020) 8458 6962. Ballet, modern and tap for both boys and girls.

*English National Ballet School*, Carlyle Buildings, Hortensia Road, SW10; (020) 7376 7076. Two-year full-time classical ballet training for the serious student beginning at age 16. Caters to both boys and girls.

*Royal Academy of Dance*, 36 Battersea Square, SW11; (020) 7326 8000; (www.rad.org.uk). Ballet, jazz and contemporary dance for all ages and abilities for both boys and girls.

*Royal Ballet School*, 153 Talgarth Road, W14; (020) 8876 5547 (Lower School), (020) 8748 6335 (Upper School). Classical ballet classes for the serious student beginning at age 11. Upper School by audition only. Boys and girls.

*Stella Mann School of Dancing*, 343a Finchley Road, NW3; (020) 7435 9317. Ages 3 and up for ballet, 5 plus for modern and tap. Boys and girls.

*Vacani School of Dancing*, St. Michael's House, 2 Elizabeth Street, SW1W 9RB; (020) 7823-5461. Also at Bayswater, Clapham, Fulham, Richmond and East Sheen. Classical ballet. Two years plus. Boys and girls.

*West London School of Dance*, 16 Balderton Street, W1; (020) 8743 3856 (Office). Locations also in Kensington and Notting Hill. Classes in ballet, tap and jazz. Boys and girls from $2^1/_2$ to 18 years.

## Drama

*Albert and Friends*, Riverside Studios, Crisp Road, W6 9RL (mailing address); (020) 8237 1170; (www.albertandfriendsinstantcircus.co.uk). Workshops for circus skills, dance, drama and music.

*Allsorts Drama*; (020) 8969 3249/(020) 8871 4987. Locations in South Kensington, Fulham and throughout London. Drama courses for ages 3 to 16 years. Includes music and movement, improvisation, mime, characterisation, costume and stage make-up.

*Battersea Arts Centre*, Lavender Hill, SW11; (020) 7223 6557/7326 8213. Drama, mask and model-making, puppetry, photography and music. Classes range from 6 months to 15 years old.

*Stagecoach*, Locations in Battersea (020) 7207 1817; Wimbledon (020) 8979 7795; and Putney (01932) 254 333; (www.stagecoach.co.uk). Drama, dance and singing classes for 4-16 year olds.

*Westminster School of Performing Arts*, SW1; (020) 7222 8873. Drama, music, gymnastics, singing and dance for 2 to 18 year olds.

## Entertainers/Party Venues

Magicians, clowns and mimes will organise children's parties (complete with prizes and favours) or just entertain at your direction. Be sure to book these popular entertainers well in advance (three to four months prior to event) to avoid disappointment.

There are several terrific websites to help with birthday planning, offering tips on everything from party venues to themes, food, entertainment and party bags. Visit (www.familiesonline.co.uk/topics/parties) for helpful hints and links to other party websites; (www.nonstopparty.co.uk) for tableware, balloons and party products; www.parenthub.com for party venue ideas, checklists, birthday cakes and links to other birthday sites; and (www.birthdayexpress.com) for party themes, cakes, games and costumes.

*Albert and Friends*, Riverside Studios, Crisp Road, W6 (mailing address); (020) 8237 1170. Runs largest children's circus. Also does workshop parties, clown-based parties.

*Arda Halls*; (020) 8969 0154; puppet shows.

*Blueberry Playsongs*, (020) 8677 6871. Guitar, songs and puppets for children's parties.

*Bob Thingummybob*, 48 Tenby Avenue, Kenton, Harrow, Middlesex HA3; (020) 8907 4606. Puppet shows, guitar and magic for children 3 years and upwards.

*Crechendo*; (020) 8772 8120. Themed parties and entertainers.

*Gymboree*; (020) 7229 9294. Parties with climbers, slides, balls and hoops, plus games, activities and music with a Gymboree teacher.

*Joey the Clown and Mr. Nutty*; (020) 8668 7228.

*Marmaduke* (Impian Productions); (01992) 446 211.

*Merlin Entertainment*, 29 Norwood Drive, N. Harrow HA2; (020) 8866 6327. Has 30 entertainers with a range of different magic and circus skills.

*Oscar's Den*, 127-129 Abbey Road, NW6; (020) 7328 6683. Party and balloon shop, bouncy castles and other play equipment for hire, tables, chairs, highchairs for hire, entertainers.

*Children's Entertainment*; 101B Slough Road, Datchet, SL3; (01753) 548 822. Magicians, bouncy castles, kiddie fun fairs, party bus, kiddie discos. Entertainment for 4 to 12 year olds.

*Peter Cass – Patchy Peter Clown*, 4 Ash Grove, Hemel Hempstead, Hertfordshire HP3; (01442) 261 767. Entertainers for children 3 years old and upward. Balloon modelling, magic, ventriloquism, puppet shows and games. Two hour party.

*Rhubarb the Clown*, 72 Hillside Road, N15; (020) 8800 5009. Clown act for all ages that is 45 minutes to one hour. Includes mime, magic, juggling and unicycles.

*Smartie Artie*, 2 Piggottshill Lane, Harpenden, Herts AL5; (01582) 483 977. Does one hour party that includes puppets, games, comedy magic, and balloon making. For 3 years and up.

*Splodge Education*, Box 31368, SW11 3GG; (020) 7350 1477; (www.planetsplodge.com). Helps plan interactive, themed parties that incorporate art, drama and music for ages 2-12. Also offers half-term clubs and special school workshops.

*Twizzle Entertainment*, 20 Mortlake Street, SW14; (020) 8392 6788; Mobile (07774) 606 814. Party entertainment that includes clown, games, competitions and magic. Also does theme parties, mini-discos, puppet shows and sing-alongs with musical instruments for all ages.

## Halloween

One popular and fun-filled Halloween event is a party hosted each year by the Kensington Chelsea Women's Club. Registration is usually at least a month in advance; contact the KCWC at (020) 7863 7562 (www.kcwc.org.uk) for more information.

## Libraries

Your local library in London is well worth an investigative trip. In addition to excellent collections of children's books, many have record and cassette lending programmes and organised activities for children. Many libraries have story reading for younger children during term time or school holidays. The library is also a prime source of information on other local happenings for children, especially during the school holidays. Children receive their own lending cards by providing proof of local residence. The Information Service based at the Library Association, 7 Ridgmount Street, WC1E; (020) 7636 7543, has a directory of all branches in the London area and will gladly assist you in finding the branch nearest your home.

## Museums

There are countless museums in and around London of interest to children of all ages. The major museums in London have special activities, exhibits and quizzes during school holidays. Ring for information or consult weekly events magazines. The Science Museum in Exhibition Road is exceptionally good for entertaining young children on rainy days.

## Music

*Bea's Baby Music School*; (020) 7228 0904; (www.babymusic.co.uk). Music classes held in Chelsea, Battersea, Barnes and Putney for children from 6 months to 6 years old.

*Blueberry Playsongs*; (020) 8677 6871; (www.blueberry.clara.co.uk). Locations in Chelsea, Clapham, Notting Hill, Putney, Hammersmith and Richmond. Music classes for children from 9 months to 6 years old.

*Colourstrings*; (020) 8948 2066; (www.colourstrings.co.uk). Music classes for young children where they learn to sing and play instruments, even some well-disguised music theory.

*London Suzuki Group*, 96 Farm Lane, SW6; (020) 7386 8006; (www.suzukimusic.net). Teaches the Suzuki method for string instruments and piano to children from the age of four and up. Annual concert at Queen Elizabeth Hall in March. Summer school course in Dorset also available for 4 to 17 year olds.

*Mini Music*, (020) 8767 1352/8776 8180; (www.minimusic.co.uk). Locations in Balham, Southfields, Wandsworth, Hammersmith, Fulham, Kensington and Notting Hill. Creative musical workshops for under 5's.

*Monkey Music*; (01582) 766464; (www.monkeymusic.co.uk) Music and movement classes for children from 6 months to 5 years old; has multiple London locations.

*Muzsika*, (020) 7794 3048. Lively music workshops for children aged 6 months to 5 years. Classes are held in Notting Hill and St. John's Wood.

*Paint Pots*, The Chelsea Christian Centre, Edith Grove, Chelsea, SW10; (020) 7376 4571. Musical activities classes from 18 months to 6 years old. (See Art also).

*The Royal College of Music*, Junior Department, Prince Consort Road, SW7; (020) 7591 4334. Instruction and recommended teachers.

*Tafelmusik*; (020) 7794 3048/7431 9115. Locations in Notting Hill and St. John's Wood. Creative music workshop for children 8 months to 6 years old.

## Parks/Playgrounds

There are over 80 parks within a seven-mile radius of Hyde Park Corner. Most parks are open dawn until dusk. (See Chapter Fourteen: Sports and Leisure)

There are several parks that are especially good for children, including:

*Holland Park*, Ilchester Place,W8; (020) 7471 9813. Lovely children's play area on the southwestern side of the park has sand, swings and other equipment for under 5s. There is also a new adventure play park under construction for older children.

*Primrose Hill*, Prince Albert Road, NW8. Has a gated children's play area on the southern end of the park, bordering Prince Albert Road.

*Diana Princess of Wales Memorial Playground*, Orme Gate, Hyde Park, W2; (020) 7978 7060. Large new gated play area on the north side of Hyde Park with sand, swings, slides, and lots of wooden play pieces, including a pirate ship, for children to climb on.

*Regent's Park*, NW1; (020) 7486 4216. Has 2 gated children's play areas – one on the northeast side of the park close to the London Zoo; the other is on the southeast end, adjacent to the broad walk in good proximity to Marylebone.

*St. Luke's Gardens*, Sydney Street, SW3; (020) 7978 7060. Popular children's play area convenient to Chelsea and South Kensington.

For more information on children's facilities, contact the Royal Borough of Kensington & Chelsea on (020) 7471 9813, (www.rbkc.gov.uk/ParksAndGardens).

### Playgroups
*The National Childbirth Trust, The Kensington and Chelsea Women's Club, Hampstead Women's Club* (see Chapter Seventeen: Organisations for contact information), your local library and your local Health Centre or Clinic are excellent sources for playgroups in your neighbourhood.

### Riding
London has several equestrian schools. Most of the schools will expect their students to be properly attired and equipped; check with the school. Both lessons and hacking are offered. (See Chapter Fourteen: Sports and Leisure for details.)

### Scouts
American Boy Scouts and Girl Scouts are alive and well and living in London. Contact the American School in London; (020) 7449 1200. However, you may choose to have your children participate in English scouting instead since this is where it all began. Contact:

*Girl Guides/Girl Scouts Association*, World Bureau, Olave Centre, Lyndhurst Road, NW3; (020) 7794 1181.

*The Scout Association*, Baden-Powell House, 65 Queens Gate, SW7 5JS; (020) 7584 7030.

### Skating
*Alexandra Palace Ice Rink*, Wood Green, N22; (020) 8365 2121. Open skating lessons, cafe.

*Firstbowl Queensway*, 17 Queensway, W2; (020) 7229 0172. Two to three hour skating sessions, seven days a week.

## Sports

The website www.londonsports.com is jointly run by the London Baseball Association (Little League), the London Basketball Association and the London Football (Soccer) Association. Each of these groups offers sports programs for children who live in London. Visit the site for more information or to register.

*The Baseball Association* has 7 different leagues, (T-ball, Coach-pitch, Minor League, Major League, Juniors Baseball, and Jr. and Sr. girls' softball). Practices and games take place at Wormwood Scrubs in Hammersmith during the spring.

*The Basketball Association* has a winter basketball program for girls and boys aged 8-14. Many of the games are played at the American School, London in St. Johns Wood.

*The Football Association* runs an autumn program beginning in September. There are 6 different leagues to accommodate boys and girls from kindergarten through ages 12/13. Games are all played at Regents Park playing fields.

*The Chelsea Estates Youth Club* runs a football club for 12-18 year olds. For more information, call (020) 7351 9478.

In addition, several health clubs offer excellent children's programmes. (See Chapter Fourteen: Sports and Leisure.)

## Swimming

Swimming pools offer lessons and regular activities for children as well as special programmes during school holidays. Many facilities have a separate shallow teaching pool for very small children, separate diving areas and wave machines. (See Chapter Fourteen: Sports and Leisure under 'Swimming' for more information.)

*Aquababies*; (020) 7702 4888; (www.aquababiesltd.co.uk). Swimming pools located throughout London. Swimming classes for ages 3 months to 4 years.

*Aqua Tots Baby Swimming*; (020) 8688 6488; (www.aquatots.com). Several pools in London, Surrey and Kent. Underwater swimming classes for ages 0 to 4 years.

*Little Dippers*; (01273) 328 275. Locations in London, Sussex and Kent. Infant water safety training classes for ages 0 to 1 year.

*Swimming Nature*; 0870 900 8002; (www.swimmingnature.co.uk). Classes in Pimlico/Victoria, Chelsea, Notting Hill and Regents Park for babies 6 months and older.

## Theatres for Children

Guildford's *Yvonne Arnaud Theatre*, (01483) 440 000 for performances and *Youth Theatre* (01483) 565 191 for summer workshops will sometimes have special children's activities on weekends and holidays. Many of the following offer not only performances but also excellent children's workshops.

*Battersea Arts Centre*, Lavender Hill, SW11; (020) 7223 6557/7326 8213. Films and mime shows on Saturdays.

*The Colour House Theatre*, Merton Abbey Mills, SW19; (020) 8542 6644. Children's shows for ages 3 and up.

*The Little Angel Theatre*, 14 Dagmar Passage (between Dagmar Terrace and Cross Street), Islington, N1; (020) 7226 1787. Puppet shows for ages 3 years and up.

*Polka Theatre*, 240 The Broadway, Wimbledon, SW19; (020) 8543 4888; (www.polkatheatre.com). Theatre for children 3 years and up.

*Puppet Theatre Barge* (floating theatre on Thames barge), Little Venice, (opposite 37 Blomfield Road), W9; (020) 7249 6876; (www.puppetbarge.com). Marionette and puppet shows for children 4 years and up. November-June at this location. Summer months have various locations along the Thames; call or visit website for details.

*Riverside Studios*, Crisp Road, W6 (mailing address); (020) 8237 1170. Runs largest children's circus.

*Tricycle Cinema and Theatre*, 269 Kilburn High Road, NW6; (020) 7328 1000; (www.tricycle.co.uk). Theatre productions and cinema screenings on Saturdays for children under five, plus half-term workshops.

*Unicorn Theatre for Children*, theatre location varies, call for details; (020) 7700 0702; www.unicorntheatre.com. Theatre for children ages 4 to 12 years. Family show at Christmas.

*Warehouse Theatre*, 62 Dingwall Road, Croydon CR0; (020) 8680 4060; (www.warehousetheatre.co.uk). Plays and shows on Saturday morning for children ages 4 to 9 years.

## Zoos

Visit the Good Zoo Online (www.goodzoos.com), which has a complete listing of all the zoos and wildlife parks in the UK.

*Battersea Park Children's Zoo*, Battersea Park; (020) 8871 7540.

*Chessington World of Adventure*, Chessington, Surrey; 0870 444 7777; (www.chessington.com).

*London Zoo*, Regent's Park, NW1 4RY; (020) 7722 3333; www.londonzoo.com.

*The London Butterfly House*, Syon Park, Brentford, Middlesex; (020) 8560 7272/0378; (www.butterflies.org.uk). A live butterfly zoo.

*Whipsnade Wild Animal Park*, Dunstable, Bedfordshire; (01582) 872 171; (www.whipsnade.co.uk). Walk or drive over 600 acres; animals are enclosed in very large spaces.

*Woburn Wild Animal Kingdom*, Woburn Abbey, Woburn, Bedfordshire; (01525) 290 246. Drive through animal reserve; animals are free to roam. Separate area has animal demonstrations, exhibits and children's playground.

## GUIDEBOOKS AND MAGAZINES FOR PARENTS

*Children's London, Evening Standard*; (www.thisislondon.com). Comprehensive listings of all sorts of children's activities. Check out the "6 of the best" section, listing everything from ice cream parlours to pottery cafes to bowling lanes and adventure playgrounds.

*Families*; (020) 8696 9680; (www.familiesonline.co.uk). Useful magazine for families with young children in six London areas: SW, SE, W, N, NW and E. Available free in many children's stores or by paid subscription. The website is a great resource, covering issues such as health, childcare, schools, birthday parties and the monthly "Out and About" section that lists events, activities and entertainment.

*Harden's London Baby Book*, by Kate Calvert; (www.hardens.com). Detailed reference book, with information on birthing options, shops and mail order suppliers, support groups, books, websites and a directory of practitioners who specialise in treating pregnant women and children.

*The London Baby Directory, An A-Z of everything for pregnant women, babies and under fives*, edited by Karen Liebreid; www.babydirectory.com. Useful resource book available in various children's stores or by writing to Cuneix Interactive, 10 Grove Park Terrace, London W4 3QG. Updated annually.

*Parents' Directory*, Needwood, West Lavant, Chichester, West Sussex, PO18 9AH; (01243) 527605 (Jan Sullivan). Directories available for South West London, South East London and North West London. Summer and winter editions by subscription.

*Time Out*. Weekly magazine found at newsagents; look for section on Children, Kids' London. Also publishes a *Kids Out* which is a monthly magazine for families available at newsagents.

## FURTHER INFORMATION

*London Tourist Board*; (020) 7932 2000; (www.londontouristboard.com). A good starting point for any information. There is a special London line for children's information – (09068) 663 344, but note that you will be charged a premium rate for use of this number. Also check out the special Kid's London section on the website.

*The Royal Borough of Kensington and Chelsea*, Kensington Town Hall, Horton Street, W8; (020) 7937 5464. Produces *Directory of Services for Children Under Eight in Kensington and Chelsea*. For more information call the Social Services Department (020) 7937 5464 or visit (www.rbkc.org). There is a children's information service section on the website that addresses early education, childcare, library services, parks and homework clubs.

# Chapter Nine: Schools

A primary concern for any family moving to London is how to educate the children. The decision must be based on a number of considerations that might not be relevant in other situations. For example, you must consider how long you plan to reside in England, how old and how adaptable your children are, and whether a change from the American system to the English system would be disruptive or beneficial to your child.

Before you make any decision, you should talk to friends and colleagues with children of similar ages to your own children and visit as many different schools as possible. There are so many excellent alternatives that you should be able to find the best school for your child without too much difficulty.

The first thing that one should know is that there are three systems available:

State or voluntary aided or grant maintained schools

Independent or private (fee-paying) schools

American and international (fee-paying) schools

At all British schools, pupils take exams. It might be helpful to know that GCSE (General Certificate of Secondary Education) exams in numerous subjects are taken at about age 15 and 'A' (for 'advanced') level exams are taken in three, or occasionally four, subjects at age 17 and 18. The 'A' level results are crucial to the British University admissions process. Recently, another set of 'AS' exams was introduced, to be taken in the year preceding 'A' levels, but these have been controversial and are scheduled to be phased out.

All of these exam results, school by school, are published annually as the 'league tables' most of the major British newspapers publish and discuss them in some detail. They can be useful but, as their critics point out, are only one measure of a school's success. The *Good Schools Guide* (see below) has a good discussion of their limitations.

## STATE OR VOLUNTARY AIDED OR GRANT MAINTAINED SCHOOLS

Full-time education is compulsory for children between the ages of five and 16 and is provided free by the government. Children generally enter primary school at the beginning of the term in which the child's fifth birthday occurs. They transfer into a *middle school* or *secondary school* (depending on location) at eight, nine or eleven, then complete their work in the *sixth form* of their secondary schools or in separate *sixth form colleges*. The system is quite confusing to a newcomer and may differ from location to location.

To obtain more detailed information, contact:

*The British Council*, 10 Spring Gardens, SW1, (020) 7389 4383, Education Information Service.

*The Department for Education*, Library and Information Resource Centre, (public enquiry unit), Sanctuary Buildings, Great Smith Street, SW1, (08700) 002 288, (www.dfee.gov.uk). Overall policy setting government department; they will supply the telephone number for your local education authority.

Useful information can be found in a book entitled *"The Education System in England and Wales"* published by Longmann, and in the publications listed below.

To enrol your child in a London government-run school, you should contact your local education authority (the Education or Social Services Department of your borough or council), or make inquiries at the school directly.

## INDEPENDENT OR PRIVATE SCHOOLS

Although all independent schools are required to register with the Department of Education, private schools vary in size, facilities and most important of all, philosophy towards education. Entrance into many schools is determined by examination and/or personal interview. Some require long advance notice for admission; many parents register their children at birth. Do not be put off by this; nor should you be totally discouraged by being told that there is no place for your child in a particular school. *Gracious* determination has paid off more than once in the past.

Although a very small percentage of students in England attend independent schools, there are over 2,000 to choose from, including local day schools and boarding schools. The boarding school tradition, in fact, is far stronger here than elsewhere and it is not uncommon for boys to be sent away at eight and girls at eleven. Many good schools, both primary and secondary, are single-sex. To help you select a day or boarding school there are publications and consulting services, both free and fee-paying, that might be of help.

> **Did you know...**Independent schools in England are referred to as 'public' schools. This goes back to the time when only wealthy families could afford to send their children to school.

### Publications

*The ISC Guide to Accredited Independent School*, annual publication available from Independent Schools Council Information Service (ISCIS), 35-37 Grosvenor Gardens, SW1W 0BS; (020) 7798 1550.

*Gabbitas Guide to Independent Schools*: Available from bookshops or Gabbitas Educational Consultants, 126-130 Regent Street, W1, (020) 7734 0161. A comprehensive directory of independent schools (pre-prep to senior) with a geographical directory and advertisements.

*The Good Schools Guide,* 7th ed. 2001, Lucas Publications. Information on over 350 top private and state schools in the UK (junior and senior, day and boarding).

*Good Nursery Guide,* Sue Woodford and Anne de Zoysa, Ebury Press. Information on day care and education for babies and children under five in Great Britain and Northern Ireland.

*Independent Schools Yearbook,* Gillian E. B. Harries, editor, A&C Black. Information on almost 1,500 schools for pupils of 3 to 18 years arranged by type of school and location.

Your local borough council will send a list of schools in the borough on request. Call the Department for Education (see above) or the local council offices.

## Consulting Services

*Gabbitas Educational Consultants,* 126-130 Regent Street, W1, (020) 7734 0161. Offers a free advisory service on the selection of independent schools and colleges in the UK. A counselling service for parents and students concerned with any aspect of education including further and higher education is also available.

*Independent Schools Council Information Service* (ISCIS), 35-37 Grosvenor Gardens, SW1, (020) 7798 1550. ISCIS has a very helpful advisory service specifically for foreigners entering the British school system.

*The Good Schools Guide Advisory Service,* (020) 733 7861 or (020) 828 1052, e-mail: editor@goodschoolsguide.co.uk. The editors of The Good Schools Guide run an advisory service on all aspects of choosing a school for your child.

*School Choice International, Inc.,* 1600 Harrison Avenue, Suite 208, Mamaroneck, NY 10543, USA, (USA) (914) 381 1788, (UK) (020) 7830 9632, (www.SCIcchools.com). This is an educational advisory service that helps families moving to London find schools for their children. They can walk a family through the entire UK educational process.

## Some Schools We Know

We have listed below a number of private or independent schools known to Junior League of London members. The schools are divided into groups: nursery schools (children to the age of four or five); junior or preparatory schools (boys to the age of eight) and prep schools (boys to the age of 13 and girls to the age of 11); and senior schools (boys 13 to 18 and girls 11 to 18). Ages given are approximate' some 'nursery' schools go up to age 7; some junior schools have nursery department; and a number of schools have both junior and senior departments.

Examinations and interviews for entry into private secondary schools are given at different ages for boys and girls: boys take an exam for prep school at 7 or 8 and take the Common Entrance Exam at 13 and girls take the "11+" or Common Entrance Exam at 11, 12 or 13. Many schools have organised 'open days' when groups of prospective parents (and their children) are shown around the school, with opportunities to meet the staff.

Our list is by no means exhaustive; there are many more good schools than are listed here. These are simply schools recommended by at least one of our members.

**Nursery Schools in London** (boys and girls under five)

Note that in many cases, it is wise to register a child for nursery school as soon as possible, even at birth. Many nursery schools take children at age two and a half.

*Acorn Nursery School*, 2 Lansdowne Crescent, W11, (020) 7727 2122, (ages 2½ to 5, 56 places).

*Broadhurst School*, 19 Greencroft Gardens, NW6, (020) 7328 4280, (ages 2½ to 5).

*The Chelsea Kindergarten*, St. Andrew's Church Hall, Park Walk, Chelsea, SW10, (020) 7352 4856, (ages 2½ to 5, 40 places).

*Chelsea Open Air Nursery School*, 51 Glebe Place, SW3, (020) 7352 8374, (ages 3 to 5).

*Dr. Rolfe's Montessori School*, 10 Pembridge Square, W2, (020) 7727 8300, (ages 2½ to 5, 60 places).

*Eaton Square Nursery and Pre-preparatory School*, 30 Eccleston Street, SW1, (020) 7823 6217, (ages 2½ - 5, 25 places).

*Falkner House*, 19 Brechin Place, SW7, (020) 7373 4501, (ages 2½ to 4, 20 places).

*Garden House School*, 53 Sloane Gardens, SW1, (020) 7730 1652, (boys 3 to 8, girls 3 to 11).

*Great Beginnings Montessori Nursery School*, 82A Chiltern Street, W1, (020) 7486 2276, (ages 2½ to 6).

*The Hampshire Schools, The Knightsbridge Under School*, 5 Wetherby Place, SW7, (020) 7370 7081, (starts at 2).

*Holland Park Nursery School*, The Undercroft, St. John's Church, Landsdown Crescent, W11, (020) 7221 2194.

*The Knightsbridge Kindergarten*, 67 Old Church Street, SW3, (020) 7581 4242, (ages 2 to 5, 40 places).

*Ladbroke Square Montessori School*, 43 Ladbroke Square, W11, (020) 7229 0125, (ages 2½ to 5½, 60 places).

*The Maria Montessori School Hampstead*, 26 Lyndhurst Gardens, NW3, (020) 7435 3646, (ages 2½ to 6).

*Miss Morley's Nursery School*, Fountain Court Club Room, Ebury Square, SW1; (020) 7730 5797.

*Miss Willcocks Nursery School*, Holy Trinity Church Hall, Prince Consort Road, SW7, (020) 7937 2027, (ages 2½ to 5, 32 places).

*North Bridge House*, 33 Fitzjohn's Avenue, NW3, (020) 7435 9641 (ages 2½ to 6).

*Pooh Corner Nursery*, 48 Emperor's Gate, SW7, (020) 8772 0181, (ages 2 to 5, 28 places).

*The Phoenix School*, 36 College Crescent, NW3, (020) 7722 4601.

*Rainbow Montessori School*, Pond Square, N6, (020) 8348 2434, (ages 2½ to 7).

*St. Christina's School*, 25 St. Edmund's Terrace, NW8, (020) 7722 8784, (boys 3 to 7, girls 3 to 11).

*St. Nicholas Preparatory School with Montessori Nursery*, 23-24 Prince's Gate, SW7, (020) 7225 1277, (ages 2¾ to 13, 250 places).

*Thomas's Kindergarten*, 14 Ranelagh Grove, SW1, (020) 7730 3596. (ages 2½ to 5, 65 places).

*Thomas's Kindergarten*, The Crypt, St. Mary's Church, Battersea Church Road, SW11, (020) 7738 0400, (ages 2½ to 5, 50 places).

*Young England Kindergarten*, St. Saviour's Hall, St. George's Square, SW1, (020) 7834 3171, (ages 2½ to 5, 50 places).

*Zebedee Nursery School*, St. Paul's Church Hall, Onslow Square, SW7, (020) 7584 7660.

Further information on nursery schools from:

*Pre-school Playgroups Association*, Greater London Regional Office, 314-316 Vauxhall Bridge Road, SW1; (020) 7828 2417.

## Boys' Junior and Preparatory Schools

*Colet Court* (St. Paul's Preparatory School), Lonsdale Road, SW13, (020) 8748 3461, (ages 7/8 to 13, 432 boys).

*Dulwich College Junior School* (see under Boys' Senior Schools)

*Eaton House The Manor*, 58 Clapham Common Northside, SW4, (020) 7924 6000 (130 boys 8 to 13; also pre-prep, 4 to 8, 255 boys and girls).

*The Falcons Pre-Preparatory School*, 2 Burnaby Gardens, Chiswick, W4, (020) 8747 8393, (ages 3 to 8, 183 boys).

*Garden House School*, 28 Pont Street, SW1, (020) 7589 7708, (ages 3 to 8, 100 boys). (See Nursery Schools.)

*The Hall*, 23 Crossfield Road, NW3, (020) 7722 1700, (ages 5 to 13, 375 boys).

*Highgate Junior School*, 3 Bishopswood Road, N6, (020) 8340 9193, (ages 7 to 13, 370 boys; also pre-prep, 3 to 7, 150 boys and girls).

*St. Philip's School*, 6 Wetherby Place, SW7, (020) 7373 3944, (ages 7 to 13, 100 boys).

*Sussex House*, 68 Cadogan Square, SW1, (020) 7584 1741, (ages 8 to 13, 180 boys).

*Westminster Under School*, Adrian House, 27 Vincent Square, SW1, (020) 7821 5788, (ages 8 to 13, 260 boys).

*Wetherby School*, 11 Pembridge Square, W2, (020) 7727 9581, (ages 4 to 8, 150 boys).

**Boys' Senior Schools** (ages 13 to 18 unless noted).
*City of London School*, Queen Victoria Street, EC4, (020) 7489 0291, (10 to 18, 870 boys).

*Dulwich College*, Dulwich Common, SE21, (020) 8693 3601. (Total 1400 pupils, divided into Junior School, 7 to 11; Lower School 11 to 13; Middle School, 13 to 16; Upper School, 16 to 18).

*Highgate School*, North Road, N6, (020) 8340 1524, (13 to 18, 600 boys). See Boys' Junior Schools, Highgate.

*St. Paul's School*, Lonsdale Road, SW13, (020) 8748 8135, (770 boys). See boys' Junior Schools, Colet Court.

*University College School (UCS)*, Frognal, Hampstead, NW3, (020) 7435 221, (ages 11 to 18, 730 boys; also has a Junior School, 7 to 11)

*Westminster School*, Little Dean's Yard, SW1, (020) 7963 1003, (13 to 18, 650 pupils). (See Boys' Junior Schools, Westminster Under.)

**Boarding Schools for Boys**
*Church of England affiliated*

| | | |
|---|---|---|
| Charterhouse | Eton | Harrow |
| Marlborough | Millfield | Radley |
| Rugby | Stowe | Winchester |

*Roman Catholic administered*

| | | |
|---|---|---|
| Ampleforth | Downside | The Oratory |

For additional information on Catholic schools contact:

*Catholic Education Service for England and Wales*, 39 Eccleston Square, SW1, (020) 7828 7604.

**Girls' Junior and Preparatory Schools**

*Bute House Preparatory School for Girls*, Bute House, Luxemburg Gardens, W6, (020) 7603 7381 (ages 4 to 11, 280 girls).

*Channing School*, Fairseat, the Junior School, Highgate, N6, (020) 8340 2328, (ages 4 to 11, 160 girls). Also has a senior school (11 to 18, 335 girls).

*City of London School for Girls*, Barbican, EC2Y, (020) 7628 0841, (Junior Department, ages 7 to 11, also has a Senior School, 11 to 18; total 670 girls).

*Falkner House*, 19 Brechin Place, SW7, (020) 7373 4501, (ages 4 to 11, 140 girls). (See Nursery Schools).

*Francis Holland (Sloane Square)*, 39 Graham Terrace, SW1, (020) 7730 2971, (Junior School, 4 to 11 and Senior School, 11 to 18, total of 365 girls).

*Garden House School*, 53 Sloane Gardens, SW1, (020) 7730 1652, (ages 3 to 11, 260 girls). (See Nursery Schools).

*Glendower Preparatory School*, 87 Queen's Gate, SW7, (020) 7370 1927, (ages 4 to 12, 179 girls).

*Kensington Preparatory School*, 596 Fulham Road, SW6, (020) 7731 9300, (ages 4 to 11, 230 girls).

*Pembridge Hall School*, 18 Pembridge Square, W2, (020) 7229 0121, (ages 4½ to 11, 250 girls).

*Putney High School*, 35 Putney Hill, SW15, (020) 8788 4886, (Junior Department, ages 4 to 11, 270 girls; Senior School, 11 to 18, 580 girls).

*Queen's College Preparatory School*, 61 Portland Place, W1

*Queen's Gate School*, 131-133 Queen's Gate, SW7, (020) 7589 3587, (Junior School, ages 4 to 11; Senior School, 11 to 18, 380 girls).

*Sarum Hall*, 15 Eton Avenue, NW3, (020) 7794 2261, (ages 3 to 11, 165 girls).

*St. Christopher's School*, 32 Belsize Lane, NW3, (020) 7435 1521, (ages 4/5 to 11, 230 girls).

### Girls Senior Schools

*Channing School* (see Girls Junior)

*City of London School for Girls* (see Girls Junior).

*Francis Holland (Regents Park)*, Clarence Gate, NW1, (020) 7723 0176, (ages 11 to 18, 380 girls).

*The Godolphin and Latymer School*, Iffley Road, Hammersmith, W6, (020) 8741 1936, (ages 11 to 18, 700 girls).

*Kensington Preparatory School*, 596 Fulham Road, SW6, (020) 7731 9300, (ages 4 to 11, 275 girls)

*More House School*, 22-24 Pont Street, SW1X, (020) 7235 2855, (ages 11 to 18, 240 girls).

*North London Collegiate School*, Canons, Edgware, Middlesex HA8, (020) 8952 0912, (ages 11 to 18, 750 girls; also Junior School, 4 to 11).

*Putney High School* (see Girls' Junior).

*Queen's Gate School* (see Girls' Junior).

*South Hampstead High School*, 3 Maresfield Gardens, NW3 5SS; (020) 7435 2899, (ages 11 to 18, 660 girls; also Junior School, 4 to 11)

*St. Paul's Girls' School*, Brook Green, W6, (020) 7603 2288, (ages 11 to 18, 630 girls).

*Westminster School*, Little Dean's Yard, SW1, (020) 7963 1003, (girls accepted in Sixth Form, 650 pupils), (see Boys' Senior Schools).

## Boarding Schools for Girls

*Church of England affiliated*

Benenden School

Heathfield School

St. Mary's School (Calne)

Sherborne School

Cheltenham Ladies College

Roedean School

St. Mary's School (Wantage)

Wycombe Abbey

*Roman Catholic administered*

Marymount School

Woldingham School

St. Mary's School (Ascot)

For additional information on Catholic schools contact:

*Catholic Education Service for England and Wales*, 39 Eccleston Square, SW1, (020) 7828 7604.

## Co-Educational Schools

*Cameron House*, 4 The Vale, SW3, (020) 7352 4040, (ages 4½ to 11, 100 pupils).

*The Hampshire Schools*, The Knightsbridge Upper School, 63 Ennismore Gardens, SW7, (020) 7584 3297, (ages 4 to 13, 300 pupils). (See Nursery Schools).

*Hill House International Junior School*, 17 Hans Place, SW1, (020) 7584 1331, (ages 3 to 13, 250 pupils).

*Norland Place School*, 162-166 Holland Park Avenue, W11, (020) 7603 9103, (boys 4 to 8, girls 4 to 11, 240 pupils).

*North Bridge House School*, 1 Gloucester Avenue, NW1, (020) 7267 2542 (boys and girls 4 to 18, 850 pupils)

*St. Christina's School* (see Nursery schools).

*St. Joseph's Roman Catholic Primary School*, Highgate Hill, N19, (020) 7272 1270.

*Thomas's Preparatory School*, 28-40 Battersea High Street, SW11, (020) 7978 4224, (ages 4½ to 13, 450 children). Also locations in Kensington (020) 7938 1931 (ages 4½ to 11, 205 children) and in Clapham (020) 7924 5006 (ages 4½ to 11, 350 pupils).

*The Vale School*, 2 Elvaston Place, SW7, (020) 7584 9515, (boys 4 to 8/9, girls 4 to 11, 100 pupils).

More and more boys' schools are taking in girls at sixth form and lower. Please consult the publications listed earlier in this chapter for up-to-date information.

## INTERNATIONAL SCHOOLS

*International School of London*, 139 Gunnersbury Avenue, W3, (020) 8992 5823. Co-educational day school, ages 4 to 18, 220 pupils. Prepares students for GCSE exams and then offers a two-year international education in preparation for the International Baccalaureate.

*Marymount International School*, George Road, Kingston-upon-Thames, Surrey KT2, (020) 8949 0571. Girls only, day and boarding, ages 11 to 18, 340 girls. Offers International Baccalaureate in addition to American curriculum.

## NATIONAL SCHOOLS

A number of schools provide education for students of specific nationalities with classes taught in their native tongue.

### American (Kindergarten - 12th Grade)

The schools listed below provide a traditional American college preparatory curriculum. A few allow students to take GCSE and 'A' level exams as well.

*The American School in London* (known as 'ASL'), 2-8 Loudoun Road, NW8, (020) 7449 1200, (www.asl.org). Co-educational day school, ages 4 to 18, 1200 pupils. The oldest American School in London with a large modern campus. High percentage of American students.

*The American Community Schools* have 2 campuses: ACS Surrey, 'Heywood', Portsmouth Road, Cobham, Surrey KT11, (01932) 867 251. Co-educational boarding and day school, ages 3 to 19, 1350 pupils. ASC Middlesex, 'Hillingdon Court', 108 Vine Lane, Hillingdon, Uxbridge, Middlesex UB10 OBE; (01895) 259 771. Co-educational day school, ages 3 to 19, 600 pupils. The schools are 65 per cent American. The other 35 per cent represents more than 40 different nationalities.

*Southbank International School*, 36-38 Kensington Park Road, W11, (020) 7229 8230. Co-educational day school, ages 4 to 18, 250 pupils. Small progressive, 20-30% American.

*The TASIS England American School*, Coldharbour Lane, Thorpe, Surrey TW20, (01932) 565 252. Co-educational boarding and day, ages 4 to 18, 880 pupils. A branch of The American School in Switzerland. Large percentage of the students are American.

*US Forces Schools in West Ruislip*; (01895) 6166 678 (K-6th grade), and London Central High School; (01494) 455 151 (7th-12th grade). Children of civilian parents are only admitted if there is space available and must pay tuition.

*West Ruislip Elementary*, Pentland Way, Ickenham, Uxbridge, Middlesex UB10 8TS.

*London Central High School*, RAF Daws Hill, High Wycombe, Buckinghamshire HP11 1PZ

## French

*Ecole Francaise Jacques Prevert*, 59 Brook Green, W6, (020) 7602 6871. Co-educational school. (ages 4 to 10, 270 pupils.)

*Lycée Francais Charles de Gaulle*, 35 Cromwell Road, SW7, (020) 7584 6322. Co-educational day school. (ages 4 to 18/19, 2900 pupils.)

## German

*The German School*, Douglas House, Petersham Road, Richmond, Surrey TW10, (020) 8948 3410. Co-educational day school, ages 5 to 19, 615 pupils. German curriculum.

## Greek

*Hellenic College of London*, 67 Pont Street, SW1X, (020) 7581 5044. Co-educational day school, ages 2 to 18, 220 pupils.

## Japanese

*The Japanese School*, 87 Creffield Road, Acton, W3, (020) 8993 7145. Co-educational day school, ages 6 to 15, 775 pupils.

## Norwegian

*The Norwegian School*, 28 Arterberry Road, Wimbledon, SW20, (020) 8947 6617. Co-educational day school, ages 3 to 16, 104 pupils.

## Swedish

*Swedish School in London*, 82 Lonsdale Road, SW13, (020) 8741 1751. Co-educational day school, ages 3½ to 16, 120 pupils.

## REMEDIAL SCHOOLS

*Center Academy, The Developmental Centre*, 92 St. Johns Hill, Battersea, SW11, (020) 7738 2344. Day school and part-time students, ages 8 to 18. Diagnostic and remedial services for children with dyslexia and other learning disabilities. Associated with *The Developmental Centre*, St. Petersburg, Florida.

*Dyslexia Teaching Centre*, 23 Kensington Square, W8, (020) 7937 2408. Offers one-to-one tuition for adults and children and small groups.

*Fairley House*, 30 Causton Street, SW1, (020) 7976 5456. Treats children with dyslexia and other learning disabilities until they are able to return to conventional schools. Ages 6 to 12. Also gives full assessments and educational advice.

*Swiss Cottage School*, Avenue Road, NW8, (020) 7681 8080. State maintained school for physically disabled children, ages 2 to 16.

For additional information on other dyslexia centres:

*The British Dyslexia Association*, 98 London Road, Reading, Berkshire RG1 5AU, (0118) 966 2677, Helpline: (0118) 966 8271.

## APPLYING TO AMERICAN UNIVERSITIES

If your child has attended English schools through 'A' level exams and wishes to attend an American university, few English schools will have prepared him/her for the required S.A.T. exams or be able to help him/her select the best university for his/her needs. A service available in London that might be of help is the *US-UK Educational Commission* (also known as the Fulbright Commission), Educational Advisory Service, Fulbright House, 62 Doughty Street, WC1N 2LS; (020) 7404 6994 (open Monday 13.30 to 19.00 and Tuesday to Friday 10.30 to 16.00). Nearest tube: Russell Square. This organisation principally advises students concerning university study in the US. They hold an annual university day and have a comprehensive reference library of information on US colleges. Additionally, they supply information concerning American colleges in the UK. First time enquirers should send s.a.e. with a request for an information pack. Comprehensive library of US College catalogues also available.

And finally...

A note to you parents still trying to decide whether to keep your children in the American school system or to switch to the British system. After much debate, we decided that the best way to convey the differences was to ask two parents to express their own, personal feelings on the subject; one whose children are in an American school and one whose children are in an English school. We hope that their views will prove helpful.

## The American School system

*For those living in London, there are some fine American schools in the area. If your children have started in the American system, or if they plan to return to it, it may be preferable for them to continue in the American tradition. There are major curriculum differences between the American and English systems resulting in adjustments for the children when they come to London and again when they leave. The American schools eliminate this problem since they strictly adhere to the school programme in the United States as well as the calendar year.*

*The turnover in the American schools is about one third each year, about the same as the turnover of Americans living in London. The advantage of this is that a child entering the school for the first time does not feel 'new' as there are many others in the same situation. A disadvantage is that a child may have to say goodbye to some of his friends. American schools are very aware of the adjustments the children are required to make and the social programmes provided at the schools reflect an understanding of this problem.*

*As is the case in public schools in the United States, self-expression and creativity are encouraged in American schools overseas.*

*A high school student who is planning to return to the States for college will be able to take the necessary tests and receive college guidance.*

*American schools have a high percentage of Americans attending but many nationalities are represented. Consequently, there is a deeper learning adventure through shared experiences of classmates who have lived all over the world.*

## The English School System

The English school system is a traditional one and justifiably famous for its strong discipline and emphasis on the basics of education; reading, writing and maths. Proper education begins at an early age, children begin reading at four and French, and sometimes Latin, are begun well before secondary school. A highly structured approach is standard, which might strike some as a bit stifling, but one can rest assured that the child will be well equipped for handling more complex work later.

In and around London there are numerous fine English schools, some large, some small, and each has its own philosophy. One can choose a school that is predominantly English or one that caters to the needs of the international community. Some are emphatically academic, some offer a well-rounded curriculum with excellent programmes in sports and/or music. Some schools are co-educational, but many of the finest schools remain single-sex schools.

Most English schools require students to wear uniforms. While this may seem costly initially, the outfits are usually sturdy and practical. Uniforms also ensure that your child will be reasonably well 'turned out' and eliminate all competition to be 'best dressed'. Most mothers love uniforms.

Perhaps the most intangible advantage of sending your child to an English school is that of having a decidedly English experience. Your child will participate in English life and have English friends. You, as parents, will have greater exposure to English families and to 'local' life. Your child may develop exemplary manners, learn to keep a stiff upper lip in difficult situations and speak with an English accent, but most importantly, your child (and you) will gain invaluable experience of the life and culture of the community you are living in.

# Chapter Ten:
# Cooking, Food and Drink

The best way to approach cooking in a foreign country is to focus on all the marvellous new tastes and new ingredients available and not on the few ingredients that can't be easily or inexpensively obtained. Realise that while in the US we rely on measuring cups to cook, the British weigh their ingredients and an inexpensive kitchen scale will simplify cooking with British recipes.

While English cooking doesn't always have an outstanding reputation, modern British cooking is changing popular perception. It reflects the diversity of the people in London and stands up to the best restaurants in the world.

The place to start is to purchase any one of the excellent British cookbooks, such as *Delia Smith's Cookery Course*, *Mary Berry's Complete Cookbook* or *Leith's Cookery Bible* for a basic kitchen reference. There are many outstanding and well-known English chefs who have also authored cookbooks; try one of Marco Pierre White's or Gordon Ramsay's books for something a little more special. Nigella Lawson, a popular British food writer, has several good books including *Nigella Bites* and *How to Be a Domestic Goddess*.

The aim of this chapter is to familiarise the cook with the local vocabulary, the mechanics of cooking, sources for special ingredients and any items that may be worthwhile to bring with you. To begin, a calculator may be one of the most important cooking tools. Also, British ovens are often smaller than ovens in the US. Always check to see that your pans fit in the oven before you start.

| LIQUID MEASURES | | |
|---|---|---|
| | **oz.** | **ml.** |
| US/UK 1 teaspoon | $1/6$ oz. | 5 ml. |
| UK 1 dessert spoon | $1/3$ oz. | 10 ml. |
| US/UK 1 tablespoon | $1/3$ oz. | 10 ml. |
| US 1 cup | 8 oz. | 240 ml. |
| UK 1 cup | 10 oz. | 300 ml. |
| US 1 pint | 16 oz. | 470 ml. |
| UK 1 imperial pint | 20 oz. | 585 ml. |
| UK gill | 5 oz. | 150 ml. |

In measuring dry ingredients such as flour or sugar, when using a British recipe remember to weigh the items as the ingredients will be listed in ounces or grams. (Remember eight ounces of two different ingredients may have distinctly different volumes).

Once you start saving British recipes from magazines and newspapers, having a set of British measuring utensils and a scale on hand will make cooking much less time consuming.

| DRY MEASURES | | | |
|---|---|---|---|
| | **US** | **UK** | **Metric** |
| Flour | 1 cup | 5 oz. | 140 gms. |
| Sugar | 2 Tbsp. | 1 oz. | 25 gms. |
| | 1 cup | 8 oz. | 225 gms. |
| Brown Sugar | 1 cup | 6 oz. | 170 gms. |
| Breadcrumbs or Nuts | 1 cup | 4 oz. | 115 gms. |
| Yeast | 1 US pkg. | $^1/_4$ oz. | 7 gms |
| Butter | 2 rounded Tbsp. | 1 oz. | 25 gms. |
| | 1 cup (2 sticks) | 8 oz. | 225 gms. |

Butter is sold in the UK in blocks weighing 250 grams. If approximately $^3/_8$" is cut off one end of the block, the remainder will equal 2 sticks of butter in a US recipe. (One stick of US butter contains 8 US tablespoons.)

**FURTHER CONVERSIONS**

| | |
|---|---|
| Ounces to grams | Multiply by 28.35 |
| Quarts to litres | Multiply quarts by 0.95 |
| Grams to ounces | Multiply grams by 0.03527 |
| Pounds to grams | Multiply pounds by 453.6 |
| Pounds to kilograms | Multiply pounds by 0.4536 |
| Kilograms to pounds | Multiply kilograms by 2.2 |
| Centigrade to Fahrenheit | Multiply C by 1.8 and add 32 |
| Fahrenheit to Centigrade | Multiply F by 5, subtract 32 and then divide by 9 |
| Stones to pounds | Multiply by 14 |

**COOKING, FOOD AND DRINK**

## COOKING TEMPERATURES

| C | F | Gas Mark | Description |
|---|---|---|---|
| 110 | 225 | $^1/_4$ | Very Slow |
| 125 | 250 | $^1/_2$ | Very Slow |
| 140 | 275 | 1 | Slow |
| 150 | 300 | 2 | Slow |
| 165 | 325 | 3 | Moderate |
| 180 | 350 | 4 | Moderate |
| 190 | 375 | 5 | Moderate/Hot |
| 200 | 400 | 6 | Moderate/Hot |
| 220 | 425 | 7 | Hot |
| 230 | 450 | 8 | Hot |
| 240 | 475 | 9 | Very Hot |

## DRINKING WATER

The quality of tap water is regulated by EC and UK legislation. Bottled mineral waters are not required to be as thoroughly and regularly tested as tap water, however, and are more likely to contain higher levels of bacteria. London tap water, although meeting the necessary quality standards, is very hard and may be unpalatable to some. Water purifiers are a popular alternative to buying bottled water and range from small activated carbon filters attached to a jug to plumbed-in filter systems.

The evidence of hard water may be seen on the inside of your kettle, on shower heads and on other household appliances in the form of "limescale". Limescale should be removed periodically with a commercial limescale remover or with a mixture of one-half cup of white vinegar with one-half cup of water. Boil and rinse well. It is always a good idea to empty a kettle after each use to avoid re-boiling water and thereby concentrating the hardness. This practice is especially important when using boiled water to make up baby formula.

For more information on the quality of your drinking water contact your local water authority (the address is on your bill). In Central London:

*Thames Water Utilities*, P.O. Box 436, Swindon SN38; (01645) 200 800.

If you are interested in using bottled water by a company that rents water coolers and provides reusable bottles, look for a company that is a member of the British Water Cooler Association (BWCA). Some good options are:

*Culligan Water*, Culligan House, 73-74 Capitol Way, NW9; (0800) 212 353

*London Spring Limited*, 2 Hermitage Works, 7 Vale Grove, N4; (020) 8880 1218

*Nature Springs*, Arklow Road, SE14; (0800) 848 382

## BAKING PRODUCTS

### Flour

| | |
|---|---|
| *Plain Flour* | Substitute for American all-purpose flour. A soft wheat flour used as a pastry flour and for thickening sauces and gravies. |
| *Superfine Plain Flour* | Similar to American cake flour. A light white flour used in British recipes for cakes with delicate texture. |
| *Self-raising Flour* | A flour with the raising agent already included, requiring no extra baking powder. |
| *Strong Flour* | US bread flour. A white flour of a high gluten content for breads and puff pastry. |
| *Malted Wheat Flour* | A brown flour with malted wheat grains for a distinctive texture and nutty flavour. |
| *Wholemeal Flour* | Wholewheat flour for baking and breads. |

### Baking Powder

Most American baking powder is double-acting so when using an American recipe use double the amount of English baking powder. Conversely, remember to use only half the amount of US baking powder when following a British recipe. To make US baking powder use $^1/_4$ tsp Bicarbonate of Soda (Baking Soda in the US) and a scant $^3/_4$ tsp cream of tartar.

### Yeast

$^1/_4$ ounce package of dry Fleischman's is equal to $^1/_4$ ounce or 7 gram "sachet" of dry yeast available in the UK.

### Sugar

English granulated sugar is coarser than its US counterpart and is widely used but not recommended for baking.

| | |
|---|---|
| *Caster Sugar* | a finer granulated sugar that dissolves easily and is ideal for baking or desserts. Similar to US superfine or bar sugar. |

| *Demerara Sugar* | a coarse, crunchy, brown sugar. It is good in coffee or over cereals but is not a substitute for brown sugar in baking. |
| --- | --- |
| *Muscovado Sugar* | a soft and dark sugar used in cooking fruit cakes, baked bean casseroles, and barbeque sauces. |
| *Soft Light and Dark Brown Sugars* | comparable to US style brown cane sugar |
| *Vanilla Sugar* | a white sugar flavoured with vanilla and is used in custards and puddings. |

> ***Did you know...*** Vanilla extract is not widely available in the UK. You will see vanilla essence in the stores but this will not have quite the same flavour. One packet may be substituted for 1 tsp vanilla extract.

## Gelatin

Aspic Powder or 'gelatin' is closest to 'Knox Unflavoured Gelatin'. Gelatin in the UK comes powdered and in packets called sachets. The amount of gelatin in sachets varies from brand to brand. As a guideline, 1 tablespoon (15 gms) should set 16 oz. (480 ml) of liquid. The contents of 1 package of 'Knox Unflavoured Gelatin' is the equivalent of 1 tablespoon or $^1/_2$ ounce.

Flavoured gelatin called "Quick Jel" comes in sachets and is perfect for adding to fruit flans, saves having to make a full quantity of jelly and sets much quicker.

> ***Did you know...*** UK 'jello' is called 'jelly' because it comes in a concentrated gel and may not work as well in US cake recipes and other baking.

## Chocolate

| *Bitter* | not unsweetened, but a dark bittersweet covering for candy. |
| --- | --- |
| *Plain* | can be compared to the US semi-sweet. |
| *Cake Covering Chocolate* | an icing or frosting chocolate. |

> ***Did you know...*** There is no equivalent to 'Bakers Unsweetened Cooking Chocolate' in the UK. Although you can find it at Selfridges, Europa, and in the American speciality food stores it is expensive. For unsweetened chocolate, substitute $3^1/_2$ tablespoons of unsweetened cocoa plus 1 tablespoon of butter or margarine to equal 1 oz. square of chocolate.

## DAIRY PRODUCTS

### Milk

Milk can be purchased in supermarkets and grocers' shops or it can be delivered to your door in returnable glass bottles (one size only: Imperial pint, 20 ounces). Each local area has a designated milk delivery company. To arrange milk delivery in your area check the Yellow Pages for your local dairy.

All milk in the UK is pasteurised but not all types are homogenized, so check the label. For home delivered milk, the types of milk can be distinguished by the colour of the bottle top.

### Cream

Cream in England has a higher fat content than in the US

| | |
|---|---|
| *Half Cream* | used like "half and half". |
| *Single Cream* | 18% butterfat, slightly thicker than half cream. |
| *Double Cream* | 48% butterfat. Poured over fruits and desserts. If whipped too much, double cream quickly turns to butter. |
| *Sour Cream* | 18% butterfat. A little thinner than US. (Fromage Frais is a good substitute). |
| *Crème Fraiche* | 39% butterfat. Also comes in a 'half-fat' version. Similar to sour cream but slightly thicker and less acidic. |
| *Spooning Cream* | 30% butterfat. Not suitable for coffee or whipping. Spoon over fruit and desserts. |
| *Whipping Cream* | 40% butterfat. Suitable for recipes that call for heavy or whipping cream. |
| *Clotted Cream* | a speciality from the West of England, very thick, used on fruits and desserts and on scones in "cream teas". |
| *Fromage Frais* | a lightly whipped lower fat equivalent of double cream can be used when cooking. Fromage frais "fresh cheese" is a good source of calcium and is given as snacks to children. |

### Cheese

English cheeses range from Gloucester (say Gloster) which is mild, to Blue Stilton that is blue-veined and has a strong sharp flavour. In between there is Lancashire (LANKashur) which grates easily and is good in cooking and Leicester (LESter), a mild good substitute for American cheddar. English and Irish cheddars are wonderful all-purpose cheeses that range from mild to mature. Danish Havarti can be substituted for Monterey Jack and the Danish also make a mozzarella. (Monterey Jack is available at Selfridges). Cheese speciality shops include Paxton & Whitfield on Jermyn Street, Jeroboams, which has several locations, and Harrods.

## Butter and Margarine

Butter and margarine are widely available in several different varieties. Butter is supplied by different dairy regions in the UK, Ireland, and France and the difference in taste is a matter of personal preference. Margarine made from 100% polyunsaturated fats is sold in grocery stores along with butter/margarine blends.

## Eggs

Most eggs are brown and are graded according to size; size 1 is the largest while size 7, the smallest. Most British cooks prefer size 2 or 3 in baking and cooking. Free-range eggs are produced from hens that are allowed to graze naturally.

## FRUITS AND VEGETABLES

There is a wide and wonderful assortment of fresh fruits and vegetables available year round in Britain. You are likely to find a good selection available at your local supermarket, greengrocer or through a delivery service such as Greenshoot, Just Organic, or Food Ferry. In addition to the most common fruit and veggie offerings, many speciality greengrocers stock a variety of imported produce which often means you might enjoy peaches from Chile in February or find custard apples from India, for example.

## MEATS

### Beef

Most beef is English but Scotch beef is available at most butchers for a higher price and is considered to be of better quality.

A roast, on or off the bone, is called a *joint*. Ground Beef is called *mince*. Minced steak is the best quality as it is the leanest. The meat will taste slightly different as most cattle are not corn fed as they are in the US.

Steaks for grilling are *fillets* (pronounced 'fill-it') or *entrecôte* steaks which are similar to the US Sirloin. A US flank steak is called a *skirt of beef* and is similar to a US London Broil.

For a Pot Roast ask for *topside, silverside* or *brisket*.

### Lamb

British spring lamb is a real treat and unsurpassed for taste but New Zealand lamb is less expensive. Lamb is available in chops, rack, cutlets, leg roasts and shoulders.

### Pork

Pork roast as well as chops, tenderloin, and spareribs (called American or Chinese spareribs) are all cuts that are easily found in supermarkets.

*Gammon* is one of the best and most expensive of hams while York ham is also of high quality. *Bradenham and Smoked French* ham is similar to Smithfield country ham. A wide variety of bacon is available smoked or unsmoked. For the familiar breakfast slice ask for *rashers* without the rind or *streaky bacon*, streaked with fat and lean. UK sausages have a high cereal content, and each region has its own distinctive blend of pork, beef, and spices.

## Poultry

A wide variety of poultry is available including free-range chicken, corn fed chicken, French chicken, and in larger supermarkets turkey, duck and game birds may also be found. If you prefer, ask for grain-fed, free-range or organic chickens. (Chapter Eleven: Services for a list of Butchers).

*\*John Wells*, (01483) 282 524. Sells and delivers American beef and poultry. Good turkeys as well, however order early if you are planning on having a Thanksgiving or Christmas turkey delivered.

## FISH

White sea fish are divided into two types, round and flat.

*Flat fish* include plaice, skate, halibut, brill and flounder. Lemon and Dover sole are delicate white fish with quality good after April. *Round fish*: bass, cod, bream and haddock. Salmon, best in June, July, and August, can be purchased as steaks or fillets, and trout are available at fishmongers and supermarkets.

> *Did you know...*When buying fresh fish, look for brightness, prominent eyes and red gills. The fishmonger will scale, clean and fillet a fish if asked.

*Shellfish*: There is a large range of shellfish available from fish shops and specialist Food Halls whilst more and more supermarkets now have their own fish and shellfish counters. Look out for crabs, mussels, scallops, lobsters, oysters (in their season), langoustines, cockles and winkles.

## "TO MARKET, TO MARKET"

### Supermarkets

Safeway, Sainsburys, Tesco and Waitrose all have a large choice of competitively priced supermarkets throughout Britain, especially in London. They offer a wide range of products from other countries. In addition, do try your local butcher, fishmonger, baker and greengrocer where you will find a more personal service and begin to feel a part of your neighbourhood. (Chapter Eleven: Services)

> *Did you know...*Some small shops may be closed at weekends. Many shops and supermarkets are now open on Sundays. Some supermarket chains (Harts, for example) are open 24 hours on certain days. The Europa chain is usually open late, on Sundays and holidays and supplies American and international products.

Stores can be incredibly overcrowded and run out of items late in the day, before a holiday, or the Saturday before a Bank Holiday Monday. Few shops have packers or personnel to take your groceries to your car. Most stores provide plastic carrier bags, and you will often have to bag your own groceries.

To pay for your groceries by cheque you need a cheque-guarantee card (see Chapter Three: Money, Banking and Taxation). This card allows you to write a cheque for up to £50.00 or more depending on arrangements already made with your bank. Most guarantee cards are now also automatic bank debit cards and the amount of your groceries will be automatically deducted from your bank account. Look for the 'Switch' or 'Delta' symbol. Credit cards are also widely accepted.

Many chains such as Sainsbury's have Reward cards designed to give frequent shoppers special offerings and discounts.

### Department and Speciality Stores

Department stores also offer a large range of foods and products in their 'food halls'. An international assortment can be found at Harrods, Selfridges, Fortnum & Mason and The Food Hall at Harvey Nichols. Marks & Spencer is Britain's finest chain for ready prepared, high quality food. Although the food is expensive in department stores, they are an additional place to go for speciality items and American products. Additionally, several of them offer home delivery.

### Farmer's Markets

Farmer's markets provide the opportunity to purchase locally produced food at its freshest, seasonal peak. Almost all of the produce and goods you will find at a farmer's market has been produced or grown or baked or prepared by the individual stall seller, so you are always assured of the quality and freshness of the items. The selection of items available at a farmer's market will naturally vary depending on season and location, but you can usually expect to find a good assortment of fruits, vegetables, meat, eggs, dairy products, jams, bread and cakes.

The popularity of farmer's markets in this country continues to grow as a means of encouraging consumers to buy local food and thus help support British farmers. There are markets in many different areas of London; for more information or a complete list of locations and schedules, call the National Association of Farmer's Markets on 01225 787914 or visit their website www.farmersmarkets.net.

### Farms

For the freshest fruit, pick your own. There are several 'pick-your-own' farms within the confines of the M25. It is advisable to ring each farm for directions, opening times and available crops. Many times extra items like farm fresh eggs, bread and honey are also available. A day of picking your own fruits and vegetables is a great family outing. Listed below are some of our local favourites:

*E. Brill & Sons, Peterly Manor Farm*, Great Missenden; (01494) 863 566

*Aldborough Hall Farm,* Aldborough Road North, Aldborough Hatch, Essex; (020) 8597 6540

*Garson Farm,* Wintersdown Road, West End, Esher, Surrey; (01372) 464 389. "When we visited, Garson's had a great selection of fruits and vegetables out in the fields just waiting to be harvested. It was a fun way to spend an afternoon, and makes a great weekend outing, especially if you have children."

*Hewitts Farm,* Chelsfield, Orpington, Kent; (01959) 534 666

## Online Shopping/Shopping Services and Delivery

There are many companies in Britain who currently offer home delivery of foods, bringing a whole new level of convenience to busy consumers. These range from outlets like The Food Ferry (www.foodferry.com), to ones who specialize in organic foods such as Simply Organic (www.simplyorganic.net) and The Organic Delivery Company (www.organicdelivery.co.uk) to many of the well-known British supermarket chains – among them Sainsburys (www.sainsburys.co.uk), Tesco (www.tesco.com), and Waitrose (www.waitrose.com).

You can usually place your order via fax, website or phone. In addition to the range of standard grocery items, several of these sites are very broad, with offerings such as wine, flowers, music/books, recipes and gift items. Delivery procedures vary, but in some cases, you will be able to specify a particular timeframe to suit your needs, making this a very convenient way to shop.

## Organic and Health Food

More and more people are now aware of the benefits of organic farming and food – recognising not only that their own health is related to the quality of the foods they eat, but also that it is better for the environment. According to the Soil Association, three out of four households in the UK now purchase organic foods. All organic food production and processing in this country is governed by a strict set of rules and regulations.

Some of the main features of organic farming include:

*   The restricted use of chemical fertilizers and food additives that have been linked to asthma and heart disease

*   A greater commitment to the environment, encouraging the use of healthy, fertile soil and encouraging a diversity of birds, butterflies and plants on organic farms

*   Animal farming free from routine drugs and antibiotics

The Soil Association is the UK's leading campaigning and certification organisation for organic food and farming. They have an excellent website (www.soilassocation.org) that contains detailed information on all aspects of organic food and farming. The site also includes a complete list of retail outlets in London and throughout the UK that sell organic food products, organized by location.

We have listed some favorites below, but do contact the Soil Association for additional stores and delivery services.

The Soil Association
40-56 Victoria Street
Bristol BS1 6BY
Phone: 0117 929 0661
Fax: 0117 925 2504
www.soilassociation.org

The Ministry of Agriculture, Fisheries and Food (MAFF) publish a booklet called *The Balanced Approach*, on the food additives regularly used in the UK. A copy can be obtained by writing to the Ministry: *The Balanced Approach, Food Sense, MAFF Publications*, SE99 7TP. To find out more about publications available from the Ministry, you can ring (020) 8694 8862 and ask for 'Inquiries Section'. Additional organic food companies are listed in Chapter Eleven: Services under 'Butchers' and 'Deliveries'. Companies who deliver organic food are listed in the previous section under 'Organics.'

*Alara Wholefoods*, 58 Marchmont Street, WC1; (020) 7837 1172. Sells organic fruit and vegetables, with fresh shipments every Monday.

*Fresh & Wild*, 210 Westbourne Grove, W11; (020) 7229 1063. A good selection of organic and health food ingredients, including vitamins and herbs. Also has an onsite juice bar.

*The Grain Shop*, 269a Portobello Road, W11; (020) 7229 5571. Organic baker and take-away.

*Holland & Barrett.* A chain of health food stores with over 37 locations in Greater London. Consult the Yellow Pages for your nearest location.

*Neal's Yard*, Covent Garden, WC2; (020) 7379 7222. A "green" shopping complex including bakery, dairy, alternative medicines, health shop and soup and salad bar.

*Planet Organic*, 42 Westbourne Grove, W2; (020) 7221 7171. One stop supermarket selling complete range of organic produce, environmentally friendly household cleaners, body care and cosmetics. Deli, cheese and bakery counter, coffee and juice bar and fresh fish counter.

*Portobello Wholefoods*, 266 Portobello Road, W10; (020) 8968 9133. Organic fruit, vegetables, vitamins, homeopathic remedies, essential oils and fresh organic breads.

*Sheepdrove Organic Farm*, Lambourn, Berkshire RG17, (0148) 871 659. Winner of the Soil Association Organic Producer of the Year award for top quality organically produced meats. Orders are packed in insulated boxes and sent overnight.

**MEAL DELIVERY**

On the nights when you're too tired to cook, it helps to have some restaurant delivery options on hand. For those of us used to having multiple options to choose from, you may find that London lags a bit behind in this area. Many restaurants do takeaway, the British version of "takeout," but fewer offer delivery. Listed below are some exceptions to this; most deliver to multiple postcodes, so call to find out if you are in their delivery area. In addition, you might try scouting out your particular neighbourhood to discover local options or consult *Zagat's*, that has a specific section on restaurant delivery.

*Basilico*, branches in Clapham (020) 7924 4070, Fulham (020) 7384 2633, and Golders Green (080) 0316 2656. Delicious thin-crust pizza delivered to selected postal codes.

*Room Service Deliveries*, (020) 7644 6666, (www.roomservice.co.uk). Delivers to most areas of central London, offering a choice of over 40 restaurants with varied cuisines.

*Rotisserie Jules*, branches in Notting Hill Gate, (020) 7221 3331, and South Kensington (020) 7584 0600. Fresh roasted chicken, lamb, side dishes and desserts.

## INTERNATIONAL FOODS AND SPECIALITIES

There are several books available such as *The Essential Guide to London's Best Food Shops* that provide detailed listings of markets and speciality food stores located in many areas of London. It may be worth purchasing one to become acquainted with what your neighbourhood offers, or to locate a specific ingredient.

The following list contains a very small selection of these shops.

### American

*Harvey Nichols*, 5th Floor, 109 Knightsbridge, SW1; (020) 7235 5250.

*Jerry's Home Store*, Harvey Nichols; 109 Knightsbridge and Tottenham Court Road (0870) 840 6060; (www.jerryshomestore.com). They receive new shipments every one to two months; call to double-check what is in stock.

*Panzer's Delicatessen*, 13-19 Circus Road, NW8; (020) 7722 8596. Has "plenty, plenty, plenty" of American items!

*Partridges*, 132-134 Sloane Street, SW1; (020) 7730 0651 and 17-23 Gloucester Road, SW7; (020) 7581 0535.

*Rosslyn Deli*, 56 Rosslyn Hill, Hampstead, NW3; (020) 7794 9210. Has a separate American section.

*W. H. Cullen*, has many locations in Central London and also Cobham, Claygate, Esher, Leatherhead, Oxshott, Walton-on-Thames and East Horsley.

### Chinese

*Loon Fung Supermarket*, 42/44 Gerrard Street, W1; (020) 7437 7332.

*Wing Yip*, 395 Edgeware Road, NW2; (020) 8450 0422.

## French

*Bagatelle*, 44 Harrington Road, SW7; (020) 7581 1551.

*Fileric*, 12 Queenstown Road, SW8; (020) 7720 4844.

## Greek

*Athenian Grocery*, 16A Moscow Road, W2; (020) 7229 6280.

## Italian

*Fratelli Camisa*, 53 Charlotte Street, W1; (020) 7255 1240.

*La Picena*, 5 Walton Street, SW3; (020) 7584 6573.

*Lina Stores*, 18 Brewer Street, W1; (020) 7437 6482.

*Luigi's*, 349 Fulham Road, SW10; (020) 7352 7739.

*Speck*, 2 Holland Park Terrace, Portland Road, W11; (020) 7229 7005. Has a good selection of meats, cheeses and a fabulous assortment of fresh pastas, soups and other Italian specialties prepared daily; can also do catering.

## Kosher

Butchers:

*La Boucherie Kosher Ltd.*, 4 Cat Hill, East Barnet, Herts, EN4; (020) 8449 9215 and 145 High Street, Barkingside, Ilford, Essex, IG6 2AJ; (020) 8551 9215.

*Menachem's*, 15 Russell Parade, NW11 9NN; (020) 8201 8629.

Also Panzer's Delicatessen (see above) and Selfridges.

## Gourmet

*Mortimer & Bennett*, 33 Turnham Green Terrace, W4; (020) 8995 4145.

*The Pie Man Food Co.*, 16 Cale Street, SW3; (020) 7225 0587 and 20 Stratford Road, W8; (020) 7937 3385.

Also Harrods, Harvey Nichols, Fortnum & Mason and Marks & Spencer's Food Halls.

## Warehouse Club

*Costco Warehouse Club*, Watford; (01923) 213 113.

For recommended cookbook and cookware shops see Chapter Twelve: Shopping.

## PUBS, WINE BARS AND OFF-LICENCES

## Pubs

Pubs and licensed restaurants are entitled to serve drinks 'on' the premises. Pubs actually fulfil both requirements – you can have a drink there or buy a bottle to take out – a useful thing to know if you are travelling and picnicking. London pub hours vary with some pubs open all day but generally the hours are 11.00-15.00 and 17.30-23.00. Beware of shorter hours in the countryside and on Sundays in London.

## Wine Bars

Wine bars serve only wine and offer a limited menu. They also tend to offer lager and "Guest Beers". As the name suggests, "Guest Beer" is only available for a short period of time to promote a particular beer or region.

## Off-Licences

Liquor stores or wine shops are known as off-licences. These shops are licensed to sell beer, wine and spirits for consumption 'off' the premises. (See Chapter Twelve: Shopping under 'Wine' for names of chain stores.) Additionally, almost every neighbourhood has its own local off-licence incorporated within a small convenience store that sell everything from crisps to deodorant.

# FOOD GLOSSARY

| US | UK |
|---|---|
| Arugula | Rocket |
| Almond Paste | Marzipan |
| Bacon | Streaky Bacon or Rasher |
| Baking Soda | Bicarbonate of Soda |
| Beans, Green | Haricots or Runner Beans |
| Beets | Beetroot |
| Beer, dark with bitter taste | Bitter |
| Beer, golden in colour | Lager |
| Biscuit, Baking Powder | Scone |
| Bread | Cob, Split Tin, Bloomer |
| Broil | Grill |
| Cake | Gateau |
| Can | Tin |
| Candy | Sweets |
| Celery Root | Celeriac |
| Chicory | Endive |
| Chips | Crisps |
| Cheesecloth | Muslin |
| Chocolate Chips | Polka Dots |
| Cilantro | Coriander |
| Confectioners Sugar | Icing Sugar |
| Cookies | Biscuits |
| Corn Starch | Cornflour |
| Cart, grocery | Trolley |
| Dessert | Puddings |
| Dishwashing Liquid | Washing-up Liquid |
| Drug Store | Chemist |
| Eggplant | Aubergine |
| English Muffins | Crumpets |
| Fish Sticks | Fish Fingers |
| Flank Steak | Skirt of Beef |
| French Bread | Bread Stick |
| (Small Loaf) | Baguette |
| French Fries | Chips |
| Frosting | Icing |
| Fruit Pie | Fruit Tart |
| Gelatin, unflavoured | Aspic Powder or Gelatin |
| Green Onions | Salad or Spring Onions |
| Ginger Snaps | Ginger Nuts |
| Ham | Gammon |
| Hamburger Meat | Mince |
| Hamburger Buns | Baps |

| US | UK |
|---|---|
| Hotdogs | Frankfurters |
| Hominy Grits | Maize Meal |
| Kool-Aid | Squash (a concentrate) |
| Jello | Jelly |
| Lemonade | Lemon Squash |
| Liquor | Spirits |
| Liquor Store | "Off Licence" Store |
| Molasses | Black treacle |
| Napkin | Serviette or Table Napkin |
| Packet | Sachet or Sleeve |
| Peapods | Mange Tout |
| Pie, open, single crust, fruit | Flan or Tart |
| Pie Crust | Pastry Case or Flan Case |
| Pits (Cherry, Peach) | Stones, Pips |
| Popsicle | Ice Lolly |
| Potatoes, Baked | Jacket Potatoes |
| Potato Chips | Crisps |
| Pound Cake | Madeira cake |
| Raisins, golden | Sultanas |
| Roast (Beef) | Joint |
| Roll | Roulade |
| Sandwich (w/lettuce, tomato) | Roll (w/salad) |
| Sausages | Bangers |
| Seven-Up | Lemonade |
| Shrimp | Prawns |
| Shrimp, Jumbo | Crevettes |
| Sponge cake | Sponge |
| Squash | Marrow |
| Turnip, Yellow | Swede |
| Vanilla Sauce | Custard |
| White Vinegar | Distilled Malt Vinegar |
| Zucchini | Courgette |

**Other Helpful Terms – Kitchen Items**

| US | UK |
|---|---|
| Faucets | Taps |
| Stove Top Burners | Hobs |
| Oven | Cooker |
| Saran Wrap | Cling Film |
| Disposable Garbage Bags | Dustbin Liners |
| Wax Paper | Greaseproof Paper |

## Other Helpful Terms – Foods

| UK | US |
|---|---|
| "Bubble and Squeak" | A patty made from swede and mashed potatoes. Other leftover vegetables may be added. |
| "Toad in the Hole" | Sausage baked in a Yorkshire pudding |
| "Bangers and Mash" | Sausages and mashed potatoes |
| "Clotted Cream" | Thick rich cream to top scones |
| "Branston" or "Ploughman's Pickle" | A vegetable chutney |
| "Children's Tea" | Children's evening meal |
| "Top and Tail" | Snipping the top and bottom off a fruit or vegetable |
| "Pudding" | Dessert |

# Chapter Eleven: Services

It is important for people who become residents in England to realise that, generally speaking, England is not, by many standards, a particularly consumer orientated society. While services are certainly available, the attitude of the "providers" can vary enormously.

There are numerous agencies that provide a wide variety of services. In some cases, membership, engagement or booking fees can apply. As always, be careful when employing anyone in the household service section, particularly plumbers, electricians, builders or interior designers, so that you do not end up paying more than necessary. The following publications are a useful source of information:

*Talking Pages* (0800 600 900) and *Yellow Pages* (divided into different areas). For household and domestic help try *Focus* (020 7937 0050) or *The Lady*, a weekly magazine. *Jean Oddy & Co.* (020 7625 7733) is a wonderful resource for locating a wide range of reliable services free of charge. Local newspapers, shops and libraries can also be sources of useful local information.

The following list of services is not intended to be inclusive; it simply provides some suggestions. Services that are marked by an asterix * have been recently recommended for inclusion by Junior League of London members.

## ANTIQUE AND FINE FURNITURE REPAIRERS AND RESTORERS

*China Repairers*, The Coach House, Kings Mews, N2; (020) 8444 3030. Repairs all types of ceramics.

*Edwardian Antiques*, 108 Fortune Green Road, West Hampstead, NW6; (020) 7794 9820. Repairs and restoration to all styles of furniture. Also, makes replicas of furniture from Edwardian period. Sells furniture and mirrors.

*Clifford J. Tracy*, 6-40 Durnford Street, off Seven Sisters Road, N15; (020) 8800 4773. Restoration and polishing of fine antique furniture.

*Hornsby Furniture Restoration*, 35 Thurloe Place, SW7; (020) 7225 2888. Repairs and restoration of both modern and antique furniture. Also offers services such as French polishing, gilding and re-caning.

*Frank Pratt*, Baileys Close Farm, Pastor Lane, Breachwood Green, Herts, SG4 8NY; (01438) 833 988; Fax (01438) 833 989.

## ARTISTS

*Lamar Raine*, (020) 7622 6520, (www.lamarraine.com). Artist that does portraits of both people and homes in watercolour and crayon and hand-cut silhouettes.

*Portrait Commissions*, (020) 8767 8594. A company that helps to find the right artist to paint a portrait.

## ACCOUNTING SERVICES

*A C Bookwise*, "Fir Tree House", 4 The Brow, Chalfont-St-Giles, Bucks, HP8 4JD, (01494) 875 635 or (07976) 751 908. Contact: John or Celia Maguire. Computerised Bookkeeping & Accounts

## BAKERIES

*Clarke's*, 122 Kensington Church Street, W8; (020) 7229 2190; (www.sallyclarke.com). Wonderful breads, cakes and tarts. Clarke's also has a wonderful restaurant located at the same address.

*Baker & Spice*, 46 Walton Street, SW3; (020) 7589 4734. Wide selection of breads baked in an old brick oven. A selection of prepared foods available. Also offers a catering service.

*Beverly Hills Bakery*, 3 Egerton Terrace, SW3; (020) 7584 4401, (www.beverlyhillsbakery.com). Wide selection of muffins. Also have cookies and pies. Gift basket delivery service available.

*The Chelsea Cake Shop*, 66 Lower Sloane Street, SW1; (020) 7730 6277. Custom designed cakes for special occasions.

*Patisserie Valerie*, 44 Old Compton Road, W1; (020) 7437 3466; (www.patisserie-valerie.co.uk). Other locations in London. French pastries and cakes.

*Poilane*, 46 Elizabeth Street, SW1; (020) 7808 4910. One of Paris' most famous boulangerie and patisserie, particularly known for its sourdough bread.

## BEAUTY SERVICES

### Alternative and Complementary Treatments

*The Grove Complementary Health Centre*, 182 Kensington Church Street, W8. A wide selection of facials, aromatherapy, massage and treatments.

*The Harmony Clinic*, 38a George Street, Croydon, Surrey CR10 1PB; (020) 8688 2370.

*Neal's Yard Therapy Rooms*, 2 Neal's Yard, WC2; (020) 7379 7662. A well-known therapy centre offering a range of treatments from Alexander Technique, lymphatic drainage to shiatsu.

### Salons and Spas

*Aveda Spa and Hair Salon*, 174 High Holborn, WC1 (Holborn Tube stop), (020) 7759 7355. Great services and café.

*Violet Adair*, 1B Kensington Church Walk, W8; (020) 7584 8412. Waxing, lash tinting, manicures, facials, etc., in a full service salon.

*Cobella Akga Day Spa Salon*, Cobella House, 5 Kensington High Street, W8, (020) 7937 8888/1818. (www.cobella.com)

*Elizabeth Muszka*, (020) 603 8408. Professional beauty therapist, facials, manicures, pedicures, massage, reflexology, waxing, etc. Home visits.

*Elizabeth Arden Red Door*, 29 Davies Street, W1; (020) 7629 4488, (www.reddoorsalons.com).

*Philippa Benson*, 172 Fulham Road, SW10; (020) 7370 3402.

*Boots*, 127a Kensington High Street, W8; (0845) 121 9001. Reasonably priced range of services available in this and other branches.

*The Green Room*, 21 Earls Court Road, W8; (020) 7937 6595 and locations all over London. A full service salon using The Body Shop products.

*Harrods Hair and Beauty Salon*, 5th Floor, 87 Brompton Road, SW1; (020) 7893 8333.

*The Sanctuary*, 12 Floral Street, WC2; (08700) 630 630, (www.thesanctuary.co.uk). Aromatherapy, facials, massage and treatments.

*SPAce.NK*, 127-31 Westbourne Grove, W2; (020) 7727 8002, (www.spacenk.co.uk). A wide selection of facials, aromatherapy, massage and treatments.

*The Spa at the Mandarin Oriental Hotel*, 66 Knightsbridge, SW1; (020) 7838 9888.

*Unlisted London*, 9 Montpelier Mews, SW7; (020) 7589 6625. Beautiful salon near Harrods, but main focus is on providing beauty services in your home.

## Nails

*Knightsbridge Nail Centre*, 7 Park Close, Knightsbridge, SW1; (020) 7225 3695.

*Nails Inc.*, 41 South Molton Street, W1; (020) 7355 3634.

*NYNC*, 17 South Molton Street, W1 (020) 7409 3332. (www.newyorknail.co.uk).

*Scarlett*, 37 Maddox Street, W1; (020) 7499 5898.

*Super Nails of Los Angeles*, 101 Crawford Street, W1; (020) 7723 1163.

## BED AND BREAKFASTS AND HOTELS

*The Dorset Square Hotel*, 39-40 Dorset Square, NW1; (020) 7723 7874.

*The Franklin Hotel*, 28 Egerton Gardens, SW3; (020) 7584 5533.

*Harrington Hall*, 5-25 Harrington Gardens, SW7; (020) 7396 9696.

*London Hospitality*; (020) 8696 0089. Up-market bed and breakfast company

*The Pelham Hotel*, 15 Cromwell Place, SW7; (020) 7589 8288.

*Stapleford Park*, Stapleford Park, near Melton Mowbray, Leicestershire, LE14 2EF, (01572) 787 522, (www.stapleford.co.uk). Hotel, spa and sporting estate. Luxury getaway outside of London.

*The Vicarage Hotel*, 10 Vicarage Gate, W8; (020) 7229 4030.

## BURGLAR ALARMS AND LOCKSMITHS

*Banhams*, 233 Kensington High Street, W8; (020) 7622 5151.

*Chubb Electronic Security*, 96-100 Clifton Street, EC2; (020) 7247 4321.

*Tara Alarms*, 33 Ebury Bridge Road, SW1W; (020) 7730 0932. Central London only.

## BUTCHERS

*Cannonbury Butchers*, 220 St. Paul's Road, N1; (020) 7359 4311.

*J. Seal's Butchers*, 7 Barnes High Street, SW13; (020) 8876 5118.

*\*John Wells*, (01483) 282 524. Sells and delivers American beef. Good turkeys as well; however, if you want to order for Thanksgiving, order early.

### Kosher Butchers:

See Chapter Ten: Cooking, Food and Drink under 'Kosher'.

### Organic Butchers

*W. A. Lidgate*, 110 Holland Park Avenue, W11; (020) 7727 8243. Delivers throughout London.

*Mackden Brothers Limited*, 44 Turnham Green Terrace, W4; (020) 8994 2646.

*W. J. Miller*, 14 Stratford Road, W8; (020) 7937 1777.

*Natural Meat Company (Noel's)*, 23 Friar's Stile Road, Richmond, TW10; (020) 8940 0414.

*\*Randall's Butchers*, 113 Wandsworth Bridge Road, SW6; (020) 7736 3426.

*Wholefood Butchers*, 31 Paddington Street, W1; (020) 7486 1390.

## CAR CLEANING AND SERVICING

> **Did you know...**that many larger supermarkets offer quick and inexpensive car washes in the carpark while you shop?

*American Carwash Company*, 35 Great Eastern Street, EC2; (020) 7739 6345. Car Cleaning and valeting.

*\*Andrew Brock Automobile Engineer*, 31a Shawbury Road, SE22 9DH (020) 8299 0299. Efficient and trustworthy car servicing.

*Capital Car Wash*, 131-177 Belsize Road, NW6; (020) 7328 1662.

*Fly Away Car Storage*, Heathrow Airport; (020) 8759 1567 or (020) 8759 2020. A unique service for travellers who park their car in the car park at Heathrow Airport. The company will collect and return your car and also will wash and service it while you are away.

*Kleencars,* 206 Ladbroke Grove, W10; (020) 8968 5748 or on weekends (01223) 845 645; Mobile (0585) 077 882 (Mr. Michael Elkins). Car cleaner, repairs, and holiday storage.

## CARPENTERS AND PAINTERS

*Gary Curnick;* (01268) 711 523. Extremely neat and tidy carpentry work with great care and attention. High quality finish. Honest and fair prices.

*Tom Baker;* (01908) 368 445 or (07751) 596 952. Internal and external decorator. Particularly good with wallpaper and paint effects.

*\*McManhon & Rae,* (01375) 480 593. Located in Essex. Very reliable painters and decorators. Expertise in wall-papering and specialist paint finishes.

## CARPET AND UPHOLSTERY CLEANER

*\*Look New Dry cleaners & Carpet Care,* 12 Market Place, Hampstead Garden Suburb, NW11; (020) 8455 2207. Shirts, dry cleaning and carpet care with collection and delivery depending on your location.

*\*Pilgrim Payne & Co. Ltd.,* 290-294 Latimer Road, London W10; (020) 8960 5656. Carpet, upholstery and curtain cleaning with great care and attention.

*\*Servicemasters;* (0956) 271 288. High quality service.

## CATERERS

*Delectable Feasts/Fiona Dalrymple,* Unit 18, Battersea Business Centre, 103 Lavender Hill, SW11; (020) 7585 0512. Caters for brunches, lunches, hampers, afternoon teas, parties and banquets.

*Finns,* 4 Elystan Street, Chelsea Green, SW3; (020) 7225 0733. Ready prepared meals made daily.

*Four Season's Food,* 80B Albert Hall Mansions, Kensington Gore, SW7; (020) 7584 8150.

*\*G. Brothers.* (020) 7228 4081. Located in Battersea

*Gorgeous Gourmets,* Unit D, Gresham Way, Wimbledon, SW19; (020) 8944 7771; (www.gorgousgourmets.co.uk). Catering equipment and/or food for banqueting or small parties.

*\*Jackson Gilmour Ltd.,* Unit 12, The Tramsheds, Coomber Way, Croydon, CR0 4TQ; (020) 8665 1855; (www.jacksongilmour.com). Fantastic individualised service. No event is too big or too small.

*Leith's Ltd.,* The Queen Elizabeth II Conference Centre, Broad Century, SW1; (020) 7798 4288, (www.geicc.co.uk). Any type of catering.

*New Quebec Cuisine Ltd.,* 13 New Quebec Street, W1; (020) 7402 0476; (www.newquebeccuisine.co.uk). Innovative healthy cuisine. Outside caterers.

*The Pie Man Food Co.*, 16 Cale Street, SW3; (020) 7225 0587. Also 20 Stratford Road W8; (020) 7937 3385, (www,thepieman.co.uk).

*Searcy Tansley*, 124 Bolingbroke Grove, SW11; (020) 7585 0505, (www.searcys.co.uk). Event catering and hire for groups of 50 people or more.

*\*Unlisted London – Home Division*, (08702) 255 007. Offer a variety of services including event planning that caters for parties for two to fifty.

## CHARTERED ACCOUNTANTS

*\*Buzzacott Livingstone*, 12 New Fetter Lane, EC4; (020) 7556 1400. (www.ustax.co.uk).

*Grashoff & Co.*, 35 Whellock Road, W4; (020) 8995 4748; Fax (020) 8995 4749; (e-mail: infor@handbook.co.uk).

*Ross Badger*, Venn House, Venn Street, SW4; (020) 7498 1276. Prepares both US and UK taxes. Very reasonable.

*Summers & Co.*, 6 Jacob's Well Mews, W1; (020) 7935 0123.

*Willis Woods*, 505 Coppergate House, 16 Brune Street, E1; (020) 7721 7730.

## CHARITY SHOPS

Second-hand goods and clothing can be donated to local charity shops. There are many throughout London, these are just a few. Consult the Yellow Pages for one of these shops near you:

✓ Nottinghill Housing Trust

✓ Oxfam

✓ Salvation Army

✓ Sue Ryder

## CHRISTMAS TREES

*Santa Fir*, Shamley Green, Near Guildford, Surrey; (01483) 268 296.

*British Christmas Tree Growers Association*; (020) 8946 2695. Telephone for details of the nearest "chop your own" Christmas trees.

*\*Down to Earth*; (020) 7371 5999. Delivery and removal of Christmas trees.

Cut Christmas trees can be bought at nurseries, flower shops, Portobello Market, 'street corner' florists, and at New Covent Garden.

## CLEANERS AND LAUNDRIES

*\*Bemros*, 60 Lower Richmond Road, SW15, (020) 8788 0635.

*\*Elias*, 16-17 Glendower Place SW7; (020) 7584 1246.

*Jeeves of Belgravia*; (020) 8809 3232, (www.jeevesofbelgravia.co.uk). Laundry, dry-cleaning, shoe mending and clothing repair. Multiple branches around London. Collection and delivery.

*Just Shirts*, Unit C16 Charles House, Bridge Road, Southall, Middlesex UB2 4BD; (020) 8843 1887; (www.justshirtsoflondon.co.uk). Shirts and dry cleaning collected and delivered anywhere in London within 24 hours.

*\*A.F. Lustre*, 384 Kings Road, SW3; (020) 7352 9652. Delivery service and Sunday hours.

*\*Look New Dry cleaners & Carpet Care*, 12 Market Place, Hampstead Garden Suburb, NW11; (020) 8455 2207. Shirts, dry cleaning and carpet care with collection and delivery depending on your location.

*Mayfair Laundry*, Stirling Road, W3 (020) 8809 3232, Laundry, dry cleaning, shoe mending and clothing repair. Multiple branches around London. Collection and delivery.

*Montagu's*, 16 Kensington Court Place, W8; (020) 7937 2373, also 194 Fulham Palace Road, W6; (020) 7385 9065.

*Mr. Steeds*, 61 Abbeville Road, SW4; (020) 8673 1271.

*Perkins*, various locations throughout London. Laundry, dry-cleaning, alterations, collection and delivery.

*\*Shirt Masters*, Parkside Business Estate, Unit 2, Rolt Street SE8; (020) 8469 2339. Free pick up and delivery of dry-cleaning.

*Shirt Stream*, Unit 7, Gold Hawk Industrial Estate, Brackenbury Road, W6; (020) 8743 9618, (www,shirtstream.com). Dry-cleaning and shirt service done within 24 hours. Free pick up and delivery throughout Greater London.

*Smarts Drycleaning*, 104 Parkway, Regents Park, NW1; (020) 7485 3839.

*Valentino Dry Cleaners*, Unit 5, 125 Shaftsbury Avenue, WC2; (020) 7240 5879. Leather and Suede Cleaning.

## CLOTH NAPPY SERVICES

Environmentally friendly cloth nappy services:

*Nappynet Limited*, "The Snappy Nappy Service", 51 Earls Court Road, W8; (020) 8812 4032.

*Terries to You*, 36 Campden Hill Road, W8; (020) 8986 5197.

*National Association of Nappy Services*, call for nearest nappy washing service; (0121) 693 4949.

## COMPUTERS AND PHOTOCOPYING

For basic computer supplies check the Yellow Pages or, in the alternative, take a walk up Tottenham Court Road. If bringing a computer from home, make sure it has the correct power supply. A transformer is necessary for most American printers and fax machines.

For photocopying services - Kall Kwik, Prontaprint, and Kinkos have many outlets throughout London.

For computer "by the hour" and printing facilities - check with your local library. In addition, some photocopy shops (e.g. *Copy King* on Brompton Road) have computers and printers for on-site use.

*PC World*, (08705) 464 464, (www.pcworld.co.uk). A chain of computer stores that can satisfy almost every computer need. Some stores also have in-store technicians to answer questions regarding computer problems you may have.

## DELIVERIES

*Express Dairy*, (020) 7278 1185; (www.doorstepdelivery.co.uk). Delivery of milk and dairy products.

*The Food Ferry*, (020) 7498 0827; Fax: (020) 7498 8009. A home delivery supermarket, which offers same day service, including all groceries, pet foods, baby items, water and beer.

*Friendly Drinks*, (020) 8892 2612. London area delivery.

*Frys of Chelsea*, 14 Cale Street, SW3; (020) 7589 0342. Fruit and vegetables.

*Flanagan & Company*, Supermarket Direct; (020) 8877 8000. Extensive catalogue.

*Marks & Spencer*, will deliver food purchases made in their store to your home. Various locations.

*Milk Delivery - Express Dairy*, (020) 7278 1185.

*The Mineral Water Company*, (020) 8450 0888/8424. Delivery of mineral water, juices, soft drinks.

*Nappy Express*, (020) 8361 4040. Next day delivery of nappies, baby products (toiletries, food), cleaning products, laundry products, etc. Call for brochure.

*Skyco*, 10 Twynersh Ave, Chertsey, Surrey, KT16 9DE, (01932) 565 559. International food club with a lot of American Products. Deliverers directly to your door.

### Newspapers/Magazines

Many newspapers and magazines can be delivered to your home. See your local newsagent shop to make arrangements.

**Paper Delivery**

*Renown Distributors Ltd.*, 17-23 Battersea Bridge Road, SW11; (020) 7223 3199.

**Organic Foods - Home Deliveries**

*Abel & Cole*, (020) 7737 3648; (www.abel-cole.co.uk). Cartons of organic foods delivered weekly.

*Choice Organics*, (020) 7924 1744. Cartons of organic foods and eco-friendly products delivered in recyclable boxes.

*Farm-A-Round*, (020) 7627 8066; (www.farmaround.co.uk). Organic produce by the box from farms in Kent and Sussex delivered to your door.

*The Fresh Food Company*, 326 Portobello Road, W10; (020) 8969 0351; (www.freshfood.co.uk). Organic meat, fruit, vegetables, dairy, wines and beers, and confectionery. Home delivery and mail order.

*Swaddles Green Farm*; (01460) 234 387; (www.swaddles.co.uk). Organic meats, soil fertilisers, and a catalogue of eco-friendly products available, delivered weekly.

**ELECTRICIANS**

*Tony Murphy*, (0956) 396 969 (Mobile). Honest work at a fair price.

*Barry Squires*, (020) 8771 5346.

*Anthony Turner*, (0973) 518 903 (Mobile).

*Andy Travers*, (020) 8393 4225; (0831) 530 873 (Mobile).

**FISHMONGERS**

*Chalmers and Gray Fishmongers*, 67 Notting Hill Gate, W11; (020) 7221 6177.

*Cope's Seafood Company*, 700 Fulham Road, SW6; (020) 7371 7300.

**FLORISTS**

*Susie Ind*; (020) 7828 6430. Arrangements in your home.

*Vase*, 10 Clifton Road, W9; (020) 7286 7853. Floral arrangements in your own home on a regular basis.

(See Chapter Twelve: Shopping for flower shops.)

**GARDENERS**

*Adair Marsh Gardening*, (01672) 514 225. American woman permanently residing in England who is genuinely passionate about gardening. Trained at Kew Gardens.

*Marion Haythe*, (020) 7722 5222. Garden and patio design and window boxes.

*Mother Earth - Jan Guinness*, (020) 7720 2819. Reasonable rates.

*Phillipa O'Brian BSc Hort*, (020) 8743 5964. Garden design, planting, hard landscaping and window boxes.

## GENERAL CONTRACTORS

*Golden Square Maintenance*, 13-14 Golden Square, W1; (020) 7439 1076. Complete building services, competitively priced, very knowledgeable, work guaranteed.

*\*McMahon & Rae*, (01375) 480 593 or (01376) 550 438. Painting and decorating services, wallpaper hanging and small building works.

## GENERAL DOMESTIC HELP AND HOUSECLEANERS

*Abercrombies Employment Agency*, Premier House, 10 Greycoat Place, SW1; (020) 7233 0007.

*The American Cleaning Company*, (020) 7624 8788. Various locations in London.

*The Clean Team*, 3-6 Kenrick Place, W18; (020) 7625 5999. A professional team of three cleaners that use their own cleaning products and equipment.

*Home Organisers*, Unit 3, Investment House, 28 Queen's Road, Weybridge KT13 9UT; (01932) 844 321. Membership organisation - emergency help service for babysitting.

*Jet Maid*, (020) 7417 9818 or (020) 8727 9100.

*Livelihoods Agency (Mrs. Henderson)*, 54A Ebury Street, SW1; (020) 7730 0329. An agency specialising in daily domestic help including housekeepers and butlers.

*Newman Cleaning Services*; (020) 8670 9320. Windows and carpet cleaning service.

*Spic & Span*, (020) 7233 6860.

*\*Unlisted London – Home Division*, (08702) 255 007. Professional cleaners, builders, landscapers, etc.

*Workbusters*, Studio 4, 91-97 Freston Road, W11; (020) 7243 5656.

## GREEN GROCER

*Michanicou Bros.*, 2 Clarendon Road, W11; (020) 7727 5191. Daily deliveries.

## HAIRDRESSERS AND BARBERS

*Charles Worthington*, 34 Great Queen Street, WC2; (020) 7831 5303. (www.charlesworthington.co.uk). Several locations throughout London.

*\*Beauty by Nicole Fenton*, 3A Kensington Church Walk, (020) 7937 8618

*\*Elizabeth Arden*, 29 Davies Street, W1; (020) 7629 4488.

*Ellishelen*, 75 Walton Street, SW3; (020) 7589 8519.

*Gina Conway Salon and Gallery*, 612 Fulham Road, SW6; (020) 7331 7633.

*Jean Marie*, 68 Gloucester Road, SW7; (020) 7584 6888.

*Jo Hansford*, 19 Mount Street, W1; (020) 7495 7774. Colour specialists.

*John Frieda*, 75 New Cavendish Street, W1; (020) 7636 1401.

*\*L&S Hair*, (020) 8892 9955.

*\*Michael John*, 25 Albemarle Street, W1; (020) 7629 6969.

*Stannard and Slingsby*, 211-213 High Street Kensington, W8; (020) 7937 0333.

*\*Simon Lee*, 46 Abbeville Road, SW4, (020) 8772 0403.

*\*Toni & Guy*, 49 Sloane Square, SW1; (020) 7730 8113. Multiple locations throughout London.

*\*Valentino*, 1 Thackeray Street, W8; (020) 7937 8416.

**Barbers**

*Adams of London*, 12 St. George Street, W1; (020) 7499 9779.

*Flittner*, 86 Moorgate EC2; (020) 7606 4750.

*George F. Trumper*, 9 Curzon Street, W1; (020) 7499 1850.

*Truefitt & Hill*, 71 St. James Street, SW1; (020) 7493 2961.

**Children's Haircutters**

*Daisy and Tom*, 181-3 King's Road, SW3; (020) 7352 5000.

*Trotters*, 34 King's Road, SW3; (020) 7259 9620. Also at 127 Kensington High Street, W8; (020) 7937 9373.

**INSURANCE**

*\*Ellis David Limited*, (020) 7354 3881, (www.ellisdavid.com). Insurance brokers with an American accent, they offer the added benefit of car coverage in North America at no extra cost.

**INTERIOR DESIGNERS**

*Anna Bilton Designs*, 46 Cadogan Place, SW1; (020) 7235 3553.

*\*April Russell*, 148 Oakwood Court, Abbotsbury Road, W14, (020) 7348 0907, (www.aprilrussell.com). Design and makeup of curtains and upholstered furniture.

*FSI*, 117 Old Brompton Road, SW7; (020) 7244 8671.

*Fiona Campbell Ltd*, 259 New King's Road, SW6; (020) 7731 3681.

*Keever Design*, 14 Robinhood Way, Greenford, Middlesex UB6; (020) 8903 1015. Individually crafted solid wood kitchens and bedrooms.

*Kensington Design*, (Sonita Kember), 12 Stratford Road, W8; (020) 7938 4388.

*Larson Design*, (Heidi Larson); (020) 7229 8298.

*Percy Bass Ltd.*, 184-188 Walton Street, SW3; (020) 7589 4853.

*Soft Options*, (Annie Aplin), Burgess Lane, Kintbury Holt, Newbury, Berkshire, RG20 0HY; (01488) 668 335. Excellent for curtains.

### KENNELS (QUARANTINE AND BOARDING) AND PETSITTING SERVICES

The regulations governing animal quarantine are evolving and finally, easing with the arrival of pet passports. For a more complete listing of quarantine kennels and the current quarantine requirements, contact the *Ministry of Agriculture, Fisheries and Food*, Hook Rise South, Tolworth, Surbiton, Surrey KT6 7NF; (020) 8330 4411.

### Kennels

*The Animal Inn*, Dover Road, Ringwould, Near Deal CT14 8HH; (01304) 373 597; fax: (01304) 380 305. Cats and dogs. Five minutes from the white cliffs of Dover, this facility is considered state of the art as far as quarantines and boarding kennels go.

*Granary Kennels*, Hawkridge Wood, Frilsham, Newbury, Berkshire RG16 9XA; (01635) 201 489. Dogs - boarding and quarantine; cats - boarding only.

*Moss Bank Kennel and Cattery*, 6 Oxdrove, Picket Piece, Andover, Hants; (01264) 365 560. Very caring.

*Neander International Kennels Ltd*, London Road (A23), Albourne, West Sussex BN6 9BJ; (01273) 832 416 or fax: (01273) 833 612. Dogs and cats.

### Pet-sitting Services

*Animal Aunts*, Smugglers Cottage, Green Lane, Rogate, Petersfield, Hampshire GU31 5DA; (01730) 821 529. They care for your pets in your home. Petsitting service covers London, Surrey, etc.

*Pets At Home*, (01634) 580 010. They care for your pets in your home. Petsitting service covers most areas of London.

### LEATHER, LUGGAGE AND SHOE REPAIRS

*Fifth Avenue Shoe Repairs*, 230 Fortys Green Road, N10; (020) 8444 4237.

### PROBLEM SOLVERS AND LIFESTYLE MANAGEMENT

*Personal Time Saver*, 809 Howard House, SW1; (020) 7828 2977; (www.personaltimesaver.co.uk). Problem solving for busy people. Can provide a wide range of services from running errands, party organisation and access for deliveries in your absence.

## TAXIS AND MINICAB SERVICES

Unlike black cabs, which are licensed, minicabs cannot be hailed from the street and must be booked by phone. Since they are not regulated, standards may vary. Many minicab services are local, but the following taxi and minicab services have been used and recommended by League members.

*ABC*, (020) 7228 5555.

*Addison Lee*, (020) 7387 8888.

*\*Airport Transfers*, (020) 8691 3400. Can be paid in advance with a credit card.

*\*Black Cab*, (020) 7432 1432. Can be booked in advance with a credit card.

*Euro Passenger*, (020) 7923 0777.

*Gemini Cars*, (0178) 447 1111.

*Pronto Radio Cars*, (020) 7286 8888.

## MONOGRAMMING SERVICES

*Harrods* has a monogramming service in its Linen Department for items purchased at Harrods.

*Eximious Ltd.*, 10 West Halkin Street, SW1; (020) 7235 7828. Personalised items for sale.

*The Monogrammed Linen Shop*, 168 Walton Street, SW3; (020) 7589 4033. Personalised items for sale.

*W. Bennett & Co & Keith Engraving*, Unit H-14, Grays Mews Antique Market, 1-7 Davies Mews, Davies Street, W1; (020) 7408 1880. Engravers of precious metals and glass.

## MOVERS & REMOVALS

*\*Davies Turner Worldwide Movers Ltd.*, 49 Wates Way, Mitcham, CR4, (020) 7622 4393.

## OSTEOPATH

*Stephen Sandler;* (020) 8529 0815. Specialising in the aches and pains of pregnant women. Will also see men.

*\*Naval Mair, The Battersea Osteopathic Practices*, 28 Ashness Road SW11, Webbs Road Entrance; (020) 7738 9199.

## PACKAGE DELIVERY, COLLECTION AND COURIERS

*DHL Worldwide Express*, (0345) 100 300.

*Federal Express International*, (0800) 123 800. Door-to-door service.

*Mail Boxes Etc.*, 56 Gloucester Road, SW7; (020) 7581 9999. Various other locations. Will pack and ship packages world-wide using various courier services.

*Moves*, (020) 7625 0211. Courier service for London by motorbike or van.

*The Packing Shop*, 6-12 Ponton Road, SW8; (020) 7352 2021. They will collect, pack and ship packages world-wide. Speciality: fine arts and antiques.

## PARTY PLANNERS AND SUPPLIES

*Fait Accompli*, Unit 1, 39 Tadema Road, SW10; (020) 7352 2777. A service specialising in organising parties and events.

*HSS Events Hire*, 37 Cumberland Avenue, Park Royal, NW10; (020) 8961 2666. China, linen, cutlery, glassware, furniture, etc. available for hire.

*Non Stop Party Shop*, Chelsea Farmer's Market, 125 Sydney Street, SW3; (020) 7351 5771. A retail store that offers balloon decoration, party accessories and costumes. Various locations in London, including Kensington High Street.

*Oscar's Den*, 127 Abbey Road, NW6; (020) 7328 6683. Retail and delivery of party supplies.

*Party Planners*, Lady Elizabeth Anson, 56 Ladbroke Grove, W11; (020) 7229 9666. Will arrange everything for any social function.

*Party Professionals*, 33 Kensington Park Road, W11; (020) 7221 3438. Will tastefully organise everything for any event from intimate dinners to balls.

## PHOTOGRAPHERS

*\*Contre-Jour*, (020) 8670 1234. Families, children, weddings. Will travel throughout Europe and the UK.

## PICTURE FRAMING

*\*Campbell's of Walton Street*, 164 Walton Street, SW3; (020) 7584 9268. Exceptional service, picture restoration, cleaning and framing.

*\*Old Church Galleries*, 320 Kings Road, SW3, (020) 7351 4649. Antique maps, prints and framing services.

## PLUMBERS

*Tony Murphy*, (0956) 396 969 (Mobile). Honest work at a fair price.

*South of the River*, 128C Northcote Road, SW11; (020) 7228 5086.

*Ward Bros.*, (020) 8656 9851.

## RECYCLING

Most communities offer recycling for some or all of the following: glass, cans, newspapers, magazines, rags and Christmas trees, with many now providing door side pick up on designated days. For information about facilities or door side pick up in your area, contact your local borough council, town hall or public library.

## Recycling Offices

*City of Westminster*, Recycling Office, 4th Floor, Emanuel House, 10 Rochester Row, SW1; (020) 7641 7956. Call for information.

*Borough of Hammersmith and Fulham*, Recycling Office; (020) 8576 5491. Safeway, Fulham; Chelsea Harbour; Hammersmith Town Hall.

*Royal Borough of Kensington and Chelsea*, Recycling Office; (020) 7341 5148. Sainsbury's, Cromwell Road; Kensington Sports Centre; Homebase, Warwick Road; Tesco, Warwick Road.

*Merton Council (Wimbledon Area)*, Recycling Information; (020) 8545 4741. Save Centre, Colliers Wood; Garth Road, Morden (accepts garden waste); Tesco, New Malden.

*Wandsworth Borough Council*, Recycling Office; (020) 8871 8232. Western Riverside Transfer Station, Smugglers Way; Sainsbury's, Garrett Lane; Battersea Park.

> **Did you know...**Used postage stamps are collected by the charity Guide Dogs for the Blind; (020) 8464 1433.

## RENTAL (Hire)

Check the London (Central) Yellow Pages and Children's Classified for separate listings.

### Baby Equipment

See Chapter Eight: Children.

### Bicycles

*Bell Street Bikes*, 73 Bell Street, NW1; (020) 7724 0456. Sales and rentals.

*Mend-A-Bike*, 4 Effie Road, SW6; (020) 7371 5867. Sales and rentals.

### Costumes (Fancy Dress)

*Angels & Berman's*, 119 Shaftsbury, WC2; (020) 7836 5678. All types of costumes.

*Barnum's Carnival Novelties*, 67 Hammersmith Road, W14; (020) 7602 1211. As well as selling party goods, they sell Father Christmas costumes.

*The Carnival Store*, 95 Hammersmith Road, W14; (020) 7603 7824. Specialises in animal costumes, but has many other types as well.

### Do-It-Yourself Tools

*The Hire Shop*, 865 Fulham Road, SW6; (020) 7736 1769. Hire out small tools, drills, lawn mowers, carpet cleaners, etc.

## Hats

*Felicity Hat Hire*, 226 Munster Road; (020) 7381 5128, also 144 Colney Hatch Lane N10; (020) 8365 2800 and 113b North Cote Road SW11; (020) 7738 0838. All types of hats for that special occasion.

## Television and Video Equipment

See the London (Central) Yellow Pages and Chapter Twelve: Shopping.

## Wedding and Formal Attire

*Moss Bros.*, 88 Regent Street, W1; (020) 7494 0665. Gentlemen's formal wear for sale or hire.

*One Night Stand*, 44 Pimlico Road, SW1; (020) 7730 8708. Ladies formal wear for hire. Appointment required.

## SECOND-HAND CARS

*Rupert Goalen*, 19A Wilton Row, SW1; (020) 7235 6326.

## SELF STORAGE

*Abbey Self Storage*, Abbey Business Centre, Ingate Place, Battersea, SW8; (0800) 622 244. Twelve London locations.

*Safestore*, Camelford Walk, Clarendon Road, Notting Hill, W11; (020) 7792 1087. Nine London locations.

*West London Self Storage*, 165-187 Freston Road, W10; (020) 8743 4647.

## SPECIAL APPLIANCE REPAIRS

*Abbey Appliances*, 9 Lower Place Business Centre, Steele Road, Park Royal, NW10; (020) 8965 1150. Kitchen appliance repairs.

*Andrews and Company*, 26 King's Terrace, off Plender Street, NW1; (020) 7388 5952. Silver plating.

*Elizabeth Hanley*, 97 Cadogan Lane, SW1; (020) 7823 1752. Repairing and converting lamps and offering handmade lampshades.

*Honeylight Computers Ltd*, 1 Parkgate House, Broomhill Road, SW18; (020) 8871 4187 or (020) 8871 5009.

*Luxury Lamps*, 60 Upper Montagu Street, W1; (020) 7723 7381. Repairs and converts lamps.

*Waldebeck Services*, Unit 18, Abenglen Industrial Estate, Betam Road, Hayes, Middlesex UB3; (0800) 956 1409 (sales) (07831) 154 516 (service). Repair and sell all American major appliances.

## TAILORS/ALTERATIONS

*Alteration Master*, 35 Britannia Row, N1; (020) 7704 2626. Fast, efficient and friendly service.

*The Alteration Station*, 29 The Pavement, SW4; (020) 7627 0167.

*Designer Alterations*, York House, 347 York Road, Battersea, SW11, (near Wandsworth Bridge), (020) 7498 4360.

*Express Tailoring*, 3 New Burlington Place, Saville Row, W1; (020) 7437 9345. Open Saturdays for fittings.

*First Tailored Alterations Ltd.*, 85 Lower Sloane Street, SW1; (020) 7730 1400.

*Jussepe*, 39 Carnaby Street, 3rd Floor; (020) 7287 0722.

*Mariko Modes*, Earl's Court Square, SW5, (020) 7835 1689. Alterations and dressmaker. Perfectionist.

*Maurice Alteration Service*, 5 Monmouth Street, WC2; (020) 7836 9401.

*Mrs. Stirling van Buren*, 52 Palace Garden Terrace, W8; (020) 7229 0711.

*Thimble Tailoring*, 24 Thackeray Street, W8; (020) 7938 1161.

## VETERINARIANS

*Abingdon Veterinary Clinic*, 85 Earls Court Road, W8; (020) 7937 8215.

*Brompton Veterinary Clinic*, 96 Fulham Road, SW3; (020) 7225 2915. 24 hour emergency cover at clinic. In addition to regular veterinary services for dogs and cats, has a grooming service for long-haired cats.

*Elizabeth Street Veterinary Clinic*, 55 Elizabeth Street, SW1; (020) 7730 9102. An emergency veterinary service 24-hours a day, 365 days a year. The regular day clinic is very good as well. Appointment required.

*K. M. Butt*, 8 Kynance Mews, SW7; (020) 7584 2019.

*Michael Gordon*, 35 Alexander Street, W2; (020) 7229 2040.

*The Village Vet Practice*, 11 Belsize Terrace, Hampstead, NW3; (020) 7794 4948.

# Chapter Twelve: Shopping

London offers an incredible selection of stores to the shopper. There are centuries-old shops selling traditional goods for which Britain is famous. There are chic boutiques offering the latest in international fashion. There is a "high street" in most neighbourhoods offering a wide range options from chains to quaint specialty shops catering to every household need.

The following list of shops is not intended to be inclusive; it simply provides some suggestions. Businesses that are marked by an asterix * have been recently recommended for inclusion by Junior League of London members.

> *"The best piece of advice that someone gave me before I moved to London was to embrace the culture and learn as much about it as possible during your time there. You are no longer living in the US, if you compare everything to America you are unlikely to have a positive experience."* – Junior League member

## SHOPPING AREAS

The main 'high street' shopping areas in the city of London are Oxford Street and Regent Street. On these streets you'll find the flagship stores of most major UK and international chains pretty much shared between them. Other great shopping areas include Neal Street and the Piazza in Covent Garden, King's Road in Chelsea, where you'll find most international designers as well as more quirky, independent shops and then Knightsbridge, which boasts two of London's best department stores, Harrods and Harvey Nichols.

If you're seeking the convenience of the typical American one-stop mall, you'll need to head out of London to Bluewater (08456 021021). Just off junction 2 of the M25 at Greenhithe in Kent, Bluewater is Europe's largest mall, where you find a vast array of upmarket shops, more than 40 restaurants, and a 12-screen cinema. Smaller in size and a bit less posh, Lakeside (01708 869933) is located at junction 30/31 of the M25, at West Thurrock, in Essex.

## SALES

The vast majority of London's shops have only two sales per year, one in January and one in July. Outside of these times, you can find a listing of current sales in and around London in the 'Sale Finder' on www.gooddealdirectory.co.uk. You can also call (01367) 860 016 to order the book the Good Deal Directory, detailing how to buy brand names for less than the usual high street prices, as well as information on over 3,100 outlets and discount businesses.

## LATE OPENINGS

Most stores in central London are open late one night of the week (usually until around 19.00). Those in Chelsea/Knightsbridge and Kensington stay open late on Wednesday, while those in the West End (Oxford Street to Covent Garden) stay open late on Thursdays. Most shops are not open on Sundays, except in the weeks leading up to Christmas.

> *"For the first several months that we were here, we converted everything back into dollars, which made shopping, going to the movies, taking taxis...very unpleasant I know that most people do this for a while, and it's a waste of energy and frustration. Eventually you just settle into the fact that London is an expensive city and the sooner you stop thinking in dollars, the sooner you will start enjoying everything that the city has to offer. I know I do!"* – Junior League member

## ART AND ANTIQUES

Antique hunting in London is a joy. No matter how elegant or humble the establishment, gracious haggling is always permitted. Dealers are often prepared to come down 10 percent, which they say is a trade discount. If they do not come down, do not persist, as the price may genuinely be the best they can give.

### Antique Shops

If you are looking for a specialist dealer, *The British Antique Dealers Association*, 20 Rutland Gate, SW7; (020) 7589 4128, will send a list of members on request.

Choice, and expensive, antiques can be found in Bond Street, the South Kensington end of Fulham Road and Kensington Church Street, which also has shops specialising in china and glass. Pimlico Road is interesting for unusual and decorative pieces. King's Road also has an array of antique shops.

*The Millinery Works*, 87 Southgate Road, N1, (020) 7359 2019. Open 11.00-18.00 Tuesday through Saturday and 12.00-17.00 on Sunday. Closed Mondays. Specialise in arts & crafts furniture.

* *Chevertones of Edenbridge*, (01732) 863 196. Outside London. Monday – Saturday 09.00 – 17.30. Great prices and friendly service.

### Antique Markets

There are antique markets all over London where groups of dealers, specialising in a variety of antiques or collectibles at all different price levels, display their goods. (See the Markets section for outdoor street markets specialising in antiques.) The following indoor markets contain numerous permanent stalls that deal in smaller items such as silver, prints, and ceramics.

*Admiral Vernon*, 141-9 Portobello Road, W11; (020) 7727 5242; (www.portobello-antiques.co.uk). Only open on Saturday. The busiest arcade on Portobello Road, it features 17th to 19th-century porcelain, advertising art, and antique textiles among its stalls.

*Alfie's Antique Market*, 13-25 Church Street, NW8; (020) 7723 6066; (www.ealfies.com). Closed Sunday and Monday. Source of some real bargains. The basement is packed with antique textiles, 19th century furniture, jewellery and accessories, while on the upper levels you might find French country furniture or '60s furniture and lighting.

*Antiquarius*, 131-141 King's Road, SW3; (020) 7351 5353. Closed Sunday. Good for browsing. There are over 120 dealers at this Chelsea arcade featuring glassware, classic luggage, silverware and costume jewellery.

*Bond Street Antiques Centre*, 124 New Bond Street, W1; (020) 7493 1854. Closed Sunday.

*Chelsea Antique Market*, 253 King's Road, SW3; (020) 7352 1424. Closed Sunday.

*Gray's Antique Market & Grays in the Mews*, 58 Davies Street and 1-7 Davies Mews, W1; (020) 7629 7034; (www.graysantiques.com). Closed Saturday and Sunday. The front hall has an enormous collection of antique jewellery and silverware dealers. The Mews is a bit cheaper but offers no less desirable collectibles, particularly tin-plate toys.

*London Silver Vaults*, 53-64 Chancery Lane, WC2; (020) 7242 3844. Closed Sunday. These subterranean vaults are home to over 40 dealers offering every imaginable kind of silver item from antique to modern. Prices range from £10 to £100,000+, so you should find something to suit you. Some stalls also offer clocks, watches and jewellery.

### Antique Fairs

There are way too many Antiques Fairs in and around London to list them all. The BBC has a good website at www.bbc.co.uk (click on categories and then antiques) that will give you a listing of fairs when you input the region, month and even day you are looking to visit a fair.

Some of the Junior League of London members' favourites are:

- ✓ The Chelsea Antiques Fair held in the Chelsea Old Town Hall in both the autumn and spring
- ✓ The Decorative Antiques and Textiles Fair held in Battersea Park generally in January, April and September
- ✓ The Grosvenor House Art & Antiques Fair held in June
- ✓ The Fine Arts & Antiques Fair held in Olympia in February, June and November
- ✓ The West London Antiques Fair held in the Kensington Town Hall in January

Also, BADA, the British Antique Dealers' Association holds Antiques & Fine Art Fairs. They can be contacted at (020) 7589 4128 or visit their website at www.bada.org for a listing of their fairs. The Association of Art and Antiques Dealers (LAPADA) also host several fairs a year. Call (020) 7823 3511, or visit www.lapada.co.uk for more information. The LAPADA website lists their fairs and others as well.

For complete listings of regularly scheduled Sunday fairs in London and throughout the UK, check the weekly newspaper, *The Antiques Trade Gazette* and two monthly magazines, *The Antique Collector* and *The Antique Dealer and Collector's Guide* and *Time Out*. All are available at larger newstands.

## Auction Houses

Auction houses are the best place for antique hunting if you have the time. Items for auction are on view a few days before the sale. At the viewing, you can purchase a catalogue, usually about £15, which includes descriptions and estimates for each lot. Bidding is easy - you register, take a paddle with a number, then raise your hand when the lot you want comes up. The auctioneer will take your bid. If you are successful, he or she will note your number. It's that simple! It can be great fun and can be one of the cheapest places to buy antiques.

The main auction houses are *Christie's* and *Sotheby's*. Most of the firms listed below (and others) advertise their auctions in *The Daily Telegraph*, *The Times* and *The Financial Times* as well as weekly events magazines such as *Time Out*. For a comprehensive listing of auctions by region and by month and date, visit www.bbc.co.uk and click on Antiques and then in the "Local to You" section click on Auctions.

*Bonham's*, Montpelier Street, SW7; (020) 7393 3900. Holds regular sales of fine furniture, paintings, objets d'art, jewellery, silver, clocks, ceramics (Oriental, European and Contemporary), tribal art antiquities, cars, musical instruments, books, guns and fountain pens. Two other locations, contact (020) 7629 6602 for Bonham's on New Bond Street; or (020) 7313 2700 for Bonham's at 10 Salem Road.

*Christie's*, 8 King Street, SW1; (020) 7839 9060. Regular sales of period furniture, Victorian, Georgian and Edwardian furniture, Art Deco, Art Nouveau, Chinese, Japanese, and Persian works of art, ceramics, jewellery, and general ephemera. Old masters, 19th century, impressionists, modern and contemporary art. Contact for special sales and viewing dates.

*Christie's South Kensington*, 85 Old Brompton Road, SW7; (020) 7581 7611. Regular sales of antiques, carpets, embroidery and textiles, Art Deco and Art Nouveau, furniture, pictures, prints, and works of art from the Victorian period, porcelain, ceramics, English and Continental watercolours on Tuesdays, Wednesdays and Thursdays. Contact for viewing dates and sale times.

*Lots Road Auctions*, 71 Lots Road, SW10; (020) 7376 6800. Two sales every Sunday. At 14.00 a selection of contemporary household furnishings ranging from sofas, tables, and rugs to ceramics, prints and engravings. The main auction of period quality furniture and objects d'art begins at 16.30. Viewing Thursday-Sunday, prior to the sale.

*Roseberry's Auction Rooms*, 74-76 Knight's Hill, SE27; (020) 8761 2522. Two sales each month - general (including ceramics and glass, pictures, prints and furniture, silver and jewellery, works of art and rugs) and antiques. Ring for dates.

*\*Sotheby's*, 34-35 New Bond Street, W1; (020) 7293 5000. Regular sales of antique furniture, Edwardian, Victorian, and modern 20th century furniture, rugs, and carpets, porcelain, glass, prints, works of art and general small collectibles. Contact for viewing times.

## Art Galleries

London has many fine art galleries whatever your taste, be it Old Masters or young contemporary artists. The more expensive dealers are concentrated in St. James's and Mayfair, others are scattered throughout the city. A few well-known galleries are listed below, but you may also want to visit The Society of London Art Dealers website at www.slad.org.uk to see it's lists of fairs, and the locations and specialities of all it's member shops.

*Agnew's*, 43 Old Bond Street, W1; (020) 7290 9250; (www.agnewsgallery.com). Excellent source of Old Masters, watercolours, drawings, prints, Modern British and contemporary pictures.

*Colnaghi*, 15 Old Bond Street, W1; (020) 7491 7408; (www.colnaghi.co.uk). Specialises in Old Master paintings and drawings, British 1500 to 1850, 19th Century European.

*\*The Fine Art Society*, 148 New Bond Street, W1; (020) 7629 5116; (www.faslondon.com). 19th and 20th century British and Scottish paintings, sculpture and decorative arts.

*Richard Green*, 147 New Bond Street, W1; (020) 7493 3939; (www.richard-green.com). Also 39 Dover Street, W1 and 33 New Bond Street, W1. Offers British sporting and marine paintings, French Impressionists, modern British, Victorian, European and Old Master pictures.

*Marlborough Fine Arts*, 6 Albemarle Street, W1; (020) 7629 5161. Source of Impressionist, Post-Impressionist and leading contemporary artists.

*Photographers' Gallery*, 5 & 8 Great Newport Street, WC2; (020) 7831 1772. Offers largest collection of original photographs for sale in the country.

*Special Photographers' Company*, 21 Kensington Park Road, W11; (020) 7221 3489. Well known for selling top-quality works.

*Waddington Galleries Ltd.*, 11, 12 and 34 Cork Street, W1; (020) 7850 2200; (www.waddington-galleries.com). Large commercial art gallery specialising in 20th century paintings, sculpture post 1900 and works on paper.

## ART MATERIALS

Most major department stores offer a selection of materials.

*Cowling and Wilcox*, 26-28 Broadwick Street, W1; (020) 7734 5781.

*Daler Rowney*, 12 Percy Street, W1; (020) 7636 8241.

*Green and Stone Ltd.*, 259 King's Road, SW3; (020) 7352 0837. Expensive but conveniently located.

*London Graphic Centre*, 16-18 Shelton Street, WC2; (020) 7240 0095; (www.lgc-unlimited.co.uk). Good prices and selection.

## BAKERIES

*Clarkes*, 122 Kensington Church Street, Kensington, W8; (020) 7229 2190; (www.sallyclarke.com). Offers delicious cakes, patisseries and deli fare, but it's specialty is over 30 types of bread. Try the rosemary and raisin, oatmeal honeypot, fig and fennel, or if you're less adventurous stick with the superb rye, sourdough or French bread.

*Jane Asher Party Cakes*, 24 Cale Street, SW3; (020) 7584 6177. This is the cake shop to end all cake shops. You can specify your design or pick from a vast portfolio of ideas.

*Konditor & Cook*, 10 Stoney Street (near Borough Market), SE1; (020) 7407 5100. Visit on a Friday or Saturday and catch the market as well. This bakery features fancy fondant covered cakes in vibrant hues of fuschia, violet and lime. Modern messages and a bespoke cake service. Also near Waterloo and on Chancery Lane.

*Maison Blanc*, 37 St. John's Wood High Street, NW8; (020) 7586 1982. Also branches in Chelsea, Chiswick, Hampstead, Holland Park and Richmond.

*Patisserie Valerie*, 44 Old Compton Road, Soho, W1; (020) 7437 3466; (www.patisserievalerie.co.uk ). Founded in 1921, this is the most famous of the many French patisseries in Soho. Fabulous wedding cakes and one of the best breakfasts in town. With branches throughout the city. The one down the street from Harrod's makes a great stop for tea or coffee and a treat while shopping in Knightsbridge and Chelsea.

## BATH PRODUCTS - See Toiletries

## BOOKS

Chain bookstores like Waterstone's and W. H. Smith are ubiquitous in London. And there are numerous other bookstores with branches throughout London, including Books Etc., Borders, Foyles and Hatchard's, which offer a good general selection of standard books in print.

But if you're looking for specialty books, maybe something old, out of print, or an art book, you're in luck because London is still peppered with small, independent bookstores. Many sell a mix of new and used books, often devoted to specialist themes to differentiate themselves from the chains, while others are devoted exclusively to dusty and dog-eared second-hand books or rare first editions and leather-bound gems. The heart of London's book trade is to be found in the Bloomsbury area where a number of fine bookshops are clustered around the British Museum, among them Unsworths Booksellers, Ulysses and Gekoski. You also might want to visit Henry Sotheran as well as Cecil Court, where you'll find a number of specialist book, poster and print shops devoted to, among many subjects, travel, ballet and Italiana.

(See Chapter Eight: Children under 'Shopping' for specialty children's bookstore.)

*Bertram Rota*, 31 Long Acre, Covent Garden, WC2; (020) 7836 0723. Antiquarian bookseller offering a huge selection of first editions, with an emphasis on English literature.

*Biblion*, 1-7 Davies Mews (behind Bond Street Station), Mayfair, W1; (020) 7629 1374. A site where a wide variety of antiquarian booksellers are all located under one roof. You can while away hours here sampling the merchandise.

*Books for Cooks*, 4 Blenheim Crescent, W11; (020) 7221 1992; (www.booksforcooks.com). A vast array of cookbooks is stacked floor to ceiling. The knowledgeable staff will help with suggestions or special orders. A small kitchen at the back where they test recipes and offer lunch – but you'll need to book early to get one of the few tables for lunch!

*Cinema Bookshop*, 13-14 Great Russell Street, WC1; (020) 7637 0206. Offers best selection of film books and paraphernalia, including biographies, stills, screenplays and movie guides.

*Comic Showcase*, 76 Neal Street, WC2; (020) 7240 3664. Specialises in adult comics and books by well-known cartoonists.

*Daunt Books for Travellers*, 83 Marylebone High Street, W1; (020) 7224 2295. Aims to provide a complete picture of a country. Stocks cookery books, histories, biographies and novels as well as a range of guides and maps.

*Dillon's Bookstore*, 82 Gower Street, WC1; (020) 7636 1577. Excellent and very wide choice. Also stocks academic books. Has specialty branches including Dillon's Art Bookshop on Long Acre, WC2; (020) 7836 1359. Also other branches throughout London.

*The Economist Bookshop*, Clare Market, Portugal Street, WC2; (020) 7405 5531. Specialises in social sciences. (Not to be confused with The Economist magazine!).

*Edward Stanford*, 12-14 Long Acre, WC2; (020) 7836 1321; (www.stanfords.co.uk). Maps and globes are their specialty, but they also have a great range of travel literature and guides.

*Forbidden Planet*, 71-5 New Oxford Street, WC1; (020) 7836 4179. Specialises in sci-fi, fantasy and horror with a range of comics, magazines, books and collectibles.

*Gay's the Word*, 66 Marchmont Street, WC1; (020) 7278 7654; (www.gaystheword.co.uk). London's only exclusively gay and lesbian bookshop offering fiction, biography, travel literature and sex manuals.

*Gekoski*, Pied Bull Yard, 15A Bloomsbury Square, Bloomsbury, WC1; (020) 7404 6676. Antiquarian books.

*Hatchard's*, 187 Piccadilly, W1; (020) 7439 9921. Excellent selection; the oldest and one of the best bookstores in London. Has various branches throughout London.

*Henry Sotheran*, 2-5 Sackville Street, W1; (020) 7439 6151. Has a handsome ground floor room of wall-lined, glass-fronted cabinets packed with antiquarian books, supplemented by a downstairs print gallery.

*Maggs Brothers*, 50 Berkeley Square, W1; (020) 7493 7160. Arguably the most prestigious antiquarian bookseller in London, selling pre-20th-century manuscripts and first editions, with an outstanding selection in literature and travel.

*Murder One*, 71-73 Charing Cross Road, WC2; (020) 7734 3485. Specialises in crime books.

*\*Pan Bookshop*, 158-162 Fulham Road, SW10; (020) 7373 4997. Good general selection, non-academic.

*Silver Moon Women's Bookshop*, 64-8 Charing Cross Road, WC2; (020) 7836 7906 (www.silvermoonbookshop.co.uk ). Europe's largest women's bookshop.

*Sportspages*, 94-6 Charing Cross Road, WC2; (020) 7240 9604; (www.sportspages.co.uk). Football rules here, but the books, videos, fanzines and magazines cover most sports.

*Talking Books*, 11 Wigmore Street, W1; (020) 8491 4117; (www.talkingbooks.co.uk); Massive selection of spoken-word CDs and tapes.

*Travel Bookshop*, 13-15 Blenheim Crescent, W11; (020) 7229 5260. Exclusively books on travel.

*Zwemmer*, 24 Litchfield Street, WC2; (020) 7379 7886; (www.zwemmer.com ). Has the finest choice of art books in London. The branch at 80 Charing Cross Road specialises in photography and cinema.

## BUTCHERS

*J. Seal Butchers*, 7 High Street, SW13; (020) 8876 5118. Sell grass-fed Aberdeen Angus beef, grass-fed lamb from Dorset, and free-range pork, chicken, game in season, and organic turkeys and geese at Christmas.

*\*John Wells*, (01483) 282 524. Sells and delivers American beef. Good turkeys as well; however, if you want to order for Thanksgiving, order early.

*Kent & Sons*, 59 St. John's Wood High Street, NW8; (020) 7722 2258. Offers a wide range of convenient, ready to cook items like breaded veal escalopes and chicken or lamb kebabs. Excellent service and outstanding selection of the highest quality.

*Mackden Bros.*, 44 Turnham Green Terrace, W4; (020) 8994 2646. High-quality Scotch beef; free-range poultry, pork and lamb; fresh duck; home-made sausages; haggis; quail; wild rabbit; hare and venison.

*Miller of Kensington*, 14 Stratford Road, W8; (020) 7937 1777. This butcher sells organic meat, chicken, quail and veal, as well as offers Middle Eastern specialities like Baklava, cow's milk feta cheese, and marinated olives. A festive offering is Victorian Royal Roast – a goose stuffed with duck, in turn stuffed with pheasant, then chicken, partridge and quail, all boned!

*Organic World*, 23 Friars Stile Road, TW10; (020) 8940 0414. Completely organic, this shop offers a wide range of meat and poultry, game is season, and frozen wild rabbit and venison throughout the year. In the summer, they have a good selection of ready-marinated meats and poultry for barbecuing. And, at Christmas Bronze turkeys are on offer.

*Randall's*, 113 Wandsworth Bridge Road, SW6; (020) 7736 3426. Outstanding selection and excellent service. If you're looking to have your meat cut in a special way or boned for you, no problem. About a quarter of the quality beef, lamb and poultry on offer is organic and the majority of the rest is free range. Wide variety of game in season, as well as MacSween's haggis, home-made sausages, venison and wild boar. Kelly Bronze turkeys are available at Christmas. A cheese counter at the back offers British and continental cheeses.

## CARPETS

*Terry Raven Oriental Carpets*, O.C.C., 105 Eade Road, N4, (020) 8802 2929. By appointment only.

## CHINA AND CRYSTAL

All major department stores offer a large selection, although many have to order required items or large numbers of items.

*Asprey & Garrard*, 167 New Bond Street, W1; (020) 7493 6767.

*Bridgewater China and Glass*, 739 Fulham Road, SW6; (020) 7371 9033. Emma Bridgewater's sponged china.

*China Craft*, 134 Regent Street, W1; (020) 7734 4915. Branches throughout London.

*The Dining Room Shop*, 62-64 White Hart Lane, Barnes, SW13; (020) 8878 1020.

*General Trading Company*, 144 Sloane Street, SW1; (020) 7730 0411.

*Rosenthal*, 158 Regent Street, W1; (020) 7734 3076.

*George Jensen*, 15B New Bond Street, W1; (020) 7499 6541. Stocks Royal Copenhagen.

*Thomas Goode & Co.*, 19 South Audley Street, W1; (020) 7499 2823.

*Waterford Wedgwood*, 158 Regent Street, W1; (020) 7734 7262.

## Discount China

*Aynsley*, Sutherland Road, Longton, Stoke-on-Trent, Staffordshire ST3; (01782) 599 499.

*C. Hartley & Sons Ltd.*, Ley Avenue (and other locations) Letchworth, Hertfordshire; (01462) 679 483. Fifteen per cent off china and crystal, first quality only. They will take phone orders and deliver in London at no extra charge.

*Minton Bone China and Royal Doulton*, London Road, Stoke-on-Trent, Staffordshire ST4; (01782) 292 121. Located 3 miles from Crown Staffordshire.

*Portmeirion*, Sylvan Works, Normacot Road, Longton, Stoke-on-Trent, Staffordshire, ST3; (01782) 326 412.

*Reject China Shop*, 71 Regent Street, London W1R; (020) 7434 2502. Discounts on first and second quality china and crystal.

*Reeves & Son*, 142 High Street, Rochester, Kent ME1; (01634) 843 339. First quality china, 20 percent discount, some discount on crystal as well.

*Royal Crown Derby Factory Shop*, 194 Osmaston Road, Derby, Derbyshire DE23; (01332) 712 833

*Royal Worcester*, Worcester Royal Porcelain Ltd., Severn Street, Worcester WR1; (01905) 23221.

*Spode Ltd.*, Church Street, Stoke-on-Trent, Staffordshire ST4; (01782) 744 011. Outlet.

*Waterford Wedgwood*, Barlaston, Stoke-on-Trent, Staffordshire ST12; (01782) 204 141. Outlet.

## Discount Crystal

*Dartington Crystal Ltd.*, Linden Close, Great Torrington, Devon, EX38; (01805) 626 262.

*Edinburgh Crystal*, Eastfield, Penicuik, Midlothian, EH26; (01968) 675 128.

*Royal Brierley Crystal*, Moor Street, Brierley Hill, West Midlands DY5; (01384) 573 580.

*Stuart Crystal*, Stuart & Sons Ltd., Redhouse Glassworks, Stourbridge, West Midlands DY8; (01384) 828 282.

*Tudor Crystal*, Dennis Hall Crystal, Cookley Wharf Industrial Estate, Leyes Road, Brockmoor, Brierley Hill, West Midlands DY5; (01384) 483 218.

## CLOTHES

### DESIGNER AND BESPOKE

If you're looking for a wide range of labels under one roof, try Harvey Nichols, Harrods, Liberty or Selfridges (see Department Stores). In Chelsea (SW3) on the King's Road, start at Joseph (sale shop) and work your way all the way down to World's End for Vivienne Westwood. In Covent Garden (WC2), you'll find Agnes B, Jones and Paul Smith. In Knightsbridge (SW1 & SW7), explore Alberta Ferretti, Armani, a new Chanel boutique, Christian Dior, Gucci, Hermes, MaxMara and Tommy Hilfiger. Head to South Kensington (SW1 & SW3) where on the Brompton Road you'll find Emporio Armani, Issey Miyake, Betty Jackson, Paul Costelloe, while close by on Draycott Avenue are Betsey Johnson and Galerie Gaultier.

The biggest cluster of designer boutiques is in Mayfair (W1). For a designer whirlwind, head to Avery Row for Paul Smith's sale shop. On Brook Street you'll find Comme des Garcons and Pleats Please. Further along on Conduit are Alexander McQueen, Issey Miyake, Moschino, Krizia, Vivienne Westwood and Yohji Yamamoto. Burberry, Calvin Klein, Donna Karan, Collesioni Armani, Emporio Armani, Fenwick, Louis Vuitton, Miu Miu, Nicole Farhi, Ralph Lauren, Tommy Hilfiger and Yves Saint Laurent are all located on New Bond Street. While on Old Bond Street, you'll find Anna Milinari, Blumarine, Dolce & Gabbana, DKNY, Gianni Versace, Joseph and Prada.

Following are designer shops that are unique to London:

*A la Mode*, 36 Hans Crescent, SW1; (020) 7584 2133. Stocks mostly European and British designers.

*Ally Capellino*, 66 Sloane Avenue, SW3; (020) 7591 8200.

*Amanda Wakeley*, 80 Fulham Road, SW3; (020) 7590 9105.

*Belville Sasson*, 18 Culford Gardens, Blacklands Terrace, SW3; (020) 7581 3500. Cocktail and evening wear.

*Ben de Lisi*, 40 Elizabeth Street, SW1; (020) 7730 2994. Glamorous yet understated.

*Betty Jackson*, 311 Brompton Road, SW3; (020) 7589 7884.

*Bruce Oldfield*, 27 Beauchamp Place, SW3; (020) 7584 1363. Couture to order.

*Browns*, 23-27 South Molton Street, W1; (020) 7491 7833. Also located on Sloane Street. Offers designer collections.

*Caroline Charles*, 56-57 Beauchamp Place, SW3; (020) 7589 5850.

*Elspeth Gibson*, 7 Pont Street, SW1; (020) 7235 0601.

*Ghost*, 14 Hinde Street, W1; (020) 7486 0239. Pretty clothes, separates.

*Jacques Azagury*, 50 Knightsbridge, SW1; (020) 7245 1216. Sleek evening dresses.

*Mane*, 29 Holland Street, W8; (020) 7937 7030. Dresses and special occasion wear. Bespoke dresses as well.

*Matches*, five locations in Wimbledon Village and two locations in Richmond; (020) 8542 9416. Designer ladies' (and men's) wear including European and British labels such as *Prada, Gucci, D&G, Ghavani Strok* and *Missoni*.

*\*Ronit Zilkha*, 34 Brook Street, W1; (020) 7499 3707. Suits and evening wear.

## English Classics

Well cut raincoats and fine woollens are the trademarks of classic English clothing. Your best bet when out looking for these is to head towards Regent Street and Piccadilly (or to Department Stores such as Harrods and Harvey Nichols). Others include:

*Aquascutum*, 9 Brompton Road, SW3; (020) 7581 4444.

*Brora*, 344 King's Road, SW3; (020) 7352-3697. Cashmere sweaters, scarves, etc.

*\*Burberrys*, 18-22 Haymarket, SW1; (020) 7930-3343. Also located on Regent Street and Brompton Road (within *The Scotch House*).

*\*N. Peal*, 37 Burlington Arcade, Piccadilly, W1; (020) 7493 5378. Men's shop located at 71 Burlington Arcade. Classic knitwear including classics from the Shetland Isles and lambswools and cashmeres from Scotland.

*Patricia Roberts*, 60 Kinnerton Street, SW1; (020) 7235 4742. Wonderful range of sweaters in lambswool, cashmere, cotton, angora and chenille.

*\*Portobello Road Cashmere Shop*, 166 Portobello Road, W11, (020) 7792 2571, (www.portobellocashmere.com).

*\*The Scotch House*, 2 Brompton Road, SW1; (020) 7581 2151. Also located on Regent Street; (020) 7734 0283.

## Casual Wear

For everyday wear, as well as the odd favourite, try the "High Street stores". These stores have branches throughout London and all can be found in the phone book: Austin Reed, Benetton, Episode, French Connection, Gap, Hobbs, Jaeger, Jigsaw, Karen Millen, Kookai, Laura Ashley, Miss Selfridge, Monsoon, Morgan, New Look, Next, Oasis, Principles, River Island, Warehouse and Whistles. And there are many online options, one of our favourites is www.boden.co.uk.

## Maternity Wear

See Chapter Eight: Children in the Pregnancy section.

## Fashion for unusual sizes

Petite ranges are now stocked by many of the High Street stores, e.g. *Marks &*

*Spencer*, *Next*, *Richards*, *Talbots* and *Episode*. While German labels at *Fenwicks* in New Bond Street are suitable for taller women.

*Celia Loe*, 68 South Molton Street, W1; (020) 7409 1627. For the style-conscious petite, offers suits, dresses, skirts and trousers that are well designed and beautifully tailored.

*Long Tall Sally*, 21 Chiltern Street, W1; (020) 8649 9009. Long Tall Sally clothes are contemporary and perfectly proportioned for women over 5'-9". Hundreds of items to choose from in an exciting 40-page colour catalogue. Clothes that really fit tall women in sizes 10 to 22. Free catalogue and 22 nation-wide branches.

*French & Teague*, 69 Gloucester Avenue, NW1; (020) 7483 4174; (www.sixteen47.com). This classic and successful designer line, founded by comic Dawn French and designer Helen Teague, offers chic day and eveningwear in sizes 16-32.

*Ken Smith Designs*, 6 Charlotte Place, W1; (020) 7487 3341. Offers a bevy of stylish bargains mixed with some pricier pieces in sizes 18-30. Includes jeans to special-occasion wear with labels like Cora, Givenchy, Oliver James and Wille.

## TEENS/YOUNG ADULTS

*Top Shop*, 214 Oxford Street, W1; (020) 7636 7700. A fashiondrome for the budget conscious, or the forever shopping teen. Several floors contain all the latest looks in accessories, dresses, shirts, trousers, make-up and there's even a café in the basement for Mom.

*Miss Selfridge*, 40 Duke Street, W1; (020) 7629 1234. The shop for young trend-setters, both those into the streetwise combat or the wannabe rock chick looks.

## MENSWEAR

Available at most department stores, *Harvey Nichols*, *Harrods* and *Liberty* in particular. The many shops on Jermyn Street, Sackville Street, and Saville Row offer custom-made (bespoke or made-to-measure) clothing for the discerning gentlemen. There are numerous gentlemen's stores with branches throughout London such as *Cecil Gee*, *Burton*, *Aquascutum*, *Austin Reed*, *Blazer* and *Next for Men*. The following is a sample of men's clothing retailers unique to London:

*Favourbrook*, 18 Piccadilly Arcade, W1; (020) 7491 2331. Also located on Jermyn Street, W1. Very English style that combines traditional designs with contemporary and period fabrics.

*Hackett*, 136-138 Sloane Street, SW1; (020) 7730 3331. Other locations throughout London. Specialise in tailored, traditional everyday clothing, formal wear and country attire.

*Herbie Frogg Ltd.*, 18-19 Jermyn Street, SW1; (020) 7437 6069. Other locations throughout London.

*Hilditch & Key*, 73 Jermyn Street, SW1; (020) 7930 5336. Shirt-makers and tie offerings.

*Lords*, 70 Burlington Arcade, W1; (020) 7493 5808. Knitwear, ties, shirts and blazers.

*Moss Bros.*, 88 Regent Street, W1; (020) 7494 0665. Retail and hire for special occasions, such as "morning suits" for gentlemen.

*Thomas Pink*, 74 Sloane Street, SW1; (020) 7245 0202. Other locations throughout London. Large range of shirts in various patterns including stripes, checks and plain colours. Generously cut with extra long tails.

*Timberland*, 72 New Bond Street, W1; (020) 7495 2133. Casual menswear and shoes.

*Turnbull & Asser*, 71-72 Jermyn Street, SW1; (020) 7808 3000. Shirtmakers.

## Shops for Tall Men

*High and Mighty*, 81-83 Knightsbridge, SW1; (020) 7589 7454; 81-3 Knightsbridge, Knightsbridge, SW1; (http://www.highandmighty.co.uk). Other locations: 145-7 Edgware Road, Paddington, W2 (7723 8754); The Plaza, 120 Oxford Street, Fitzrovia, W1; (7436 4861). Larger (17in-21in collar), broader (44in-60in chest) and taller (over 6ft 2in) men have an extensive range from which to choose, including jeans, casuals and suits.

## CLOTHING SIZE CHARTS

The tables below should be used as an approximate guide, as the actual sizes may vary according to the manufacturer, as well as the country of origin. Small sizes are generally difficult to obtain. It is advisable to try the clothing on to ensure the correct size. (See Chapter Eight: Children under 'Shopping' for children's clothing size chart.)

### Adults

*Women's Dresses, Suits and Coats:*

| American | 6 | 8 | 10 | 12 | 14 | 16 |
|---|---|---|---|---|---|---|
| British | 8 | 10 | 12 | 14 | 16 | 18 |
| Continental | 36/38 | 38/40 | 40/42 | 42/44 | 44/46 | 46/48 |

*Women's Sweaters and Blouses:*

| American | 6 | 8 | 10 | 12 | 14 | 16 |
|---|---|---|---|---|---|---|
| British | 8/30 | 10/32 | 12/34 | 14/36 | 16/38 | 18/40 |
| Continental | 36/38 | 38/40 | 40/42 | 42/44 | 44/46 | 46/48 |

*Women's Shoes:*

| American | 5½ | 6 | 6½ | 7 | 7½ | 8 |
|---|---|---|---|---|---|---|
| British | 3½ | 4 | 4½ | 5 | 5½ | 6 |
| French | 36 | 36½ | 37 | 37½ | 38 | 38½ |
| Italian | 36½ | 37 | 37½ | 38 | 38½ | 39 |

| American | 8½ | 9 | 9½ | 10 |
|---|---|---|---|---|
| British | 6½ | 7 | 7½ | 8 |
| French | 39 | 39½ | 40 | 40½ |
| Italian | 39½ | 40 | 40½ | 41 |

*Men's Suits and Overcoats:*

American and British sizes are the same, although British sizes run narrower in the shoulder.

| American/ British | 36 | 38 | 40 | 42 | 44 |
|---|---|---|---|---|---|
| Continental | 46 | 48 | 50 | 52 | 54 |

*Men's Shirts or Collar Sizes:*

| American/ British | 14 | 14½ | 15 | 15½ | 16 | 16½ | 17 |
|---|---|---|---|---|---|---|---|
| Continental | 36 | 37 | 38 | 39 | 40 | 41 | 42 |

*Men's Shoes:*

| American | 8 | 8½ | 9 | 9½ | 10 | 10½ | 11 | 11½ |
|---|---|---|---|---|---|---|---|---|
| British | 7½ | 8 | 8½ | 9 | 9½ | 10 | 10½ | 11 |
| Continental | 41 | 42 | | 43 | | 44 | | 45 |

## COFFEE & TEA

*Algerian Coffee Stores*, 52 Old Compton Street, W1; (020) 7437 2480. Established in 1887, this shop sells a variety of coffees and an equally impressive array of teas, both from all over the world.

*R Twining & Co*, 216 Strand, WC2; (020) 8353 3511. The world's most famous tea merchant, established on these premises in 1706. Sells a dazzling array of teas and there's a small museum of the firm's history.

*The Tea House*, 15A Neal Street, WC2; (020) 7240 7539. Offers an outstanding range of some 60 teas from around the world.

## COMPUTERS & GAMES

*Virgin Megastore* and *HMV* are both good sources for games.

*Computer Exchange*, 32 Rathbone Place, W1; (020) 7536 2666. New, used and imported games and PC software, plus second-hand hardware.

*Gultronics*, 52 Tottenham Court Road, W1; (020) 7637 1619/ mail order (020) 7436 3131, (www.gultronics.co.uk). Numerous branches throughout London. A decent range of PCs, though prices are not always the cheapest to be found.

*Micro Anvika*, 245 Tottenham Court Road, W1; (020) 8636 2547; (www.microanvika.co.uk). Central London's leading Mac specialist offering reasonably priced computers but rather expensive software.

*\*PC World*, (08705) 464 464, (www.pcworld.co.uk). A chain of computer stores that can satisfy almost every computer need. Some stores also have in-store technicians to answer questions regarding computer problems you may have.

### DEPARTMENT STORES

The list below contains a mixture of large department stores with multiple branches, as well as smaller, specialty department stores.

*Army and Navy Stores*, 101 Victoria Street, SW1; (020) 7834 1234. Not related to the American store. Offers fashions and household basics.

*Barkers of Kensington*, 63 Kensington High Street, W8; (020) 7937 5432.

*BHS*, 252-258 Oxford Street, W1; (020) 7629 2011.

*C&A*, 501-519 Oxford Street, W1; (020) 7629 7272.

*Debenhams*, 334-348 Oxford Street, W1; (020) 7580 3000.

*Dickins & Jones*, 224 Regent Street, W1; (020) 7734 7070; (www.houseoffraser.co.uk). Though it does carry ranges of sensible, high-quality furniture and home goods, D&J is mainly devoted to clothing and beauty. Women's fashion tends towards classic designers such as Jasper Conran and Betsey Johnson, while the underrated menswear department includes Kenzo, Burberry and London's only Crombie concession.

*D. H. Evans*, 318 Oxford Street, W1; (020) 7629 8800. Women's, men's and children's clothing plus linens and electrical appliances.

*Fenwick of Bond Street*, 63 New Bond Street, W1; (020) 7629 9161. Upmarket clothes and accessories.

*Fortnum and Mason*, 181 Piccadilly, W1; (020) 7734 8040; (www.fortnumandmason.co.uk). Offers old-world charm atmosphere. The ground floor houses a formal food hall stocked with specialty teas, fabulous "hamper" gifts, and a genteel setting for an afternoon tea. Classic women's-wear and the quintessential attire of the English gent are to be found on the first and third floors respectively. The fourth floor contains furniture and home-ware, while the basement is the place to go for made-to-order hampers.

*\*Harrods*, 87-135 Brompton Road, SW1; (020) 7730 1234. London's most famous emporium. Unequalled grandeur fills their hallowed food halls. Known for their twice yearly sales and amazing range of goods (exotic animals to medieval instruments). Offers over 60 fashion departments, including an excellent selection of designer shoes. However, beware the out-of-date dress code: anyone arriving wearing shorts, torn jeans or carrying a rucksack may be asked to leave.

*Harvey Nichols*, 109-125 Knightsbridge, SW1; (020) 7235 5000. A shrine to the fine and divine. The "Bergdorf Goodman" of London, offers a fabulous array of designer collections and exquisite home furnishings. Don't miss their drinks bar and cafe on the Fifth Floor which sits alongside their food hall filled with minimalist-packaged products. The window displays are legendary as well.

*John Lewis*, 278-306 Oxford Street, W1; (020) 7629 7711; (www.johnlewis.co.uk). The homely matron of London department stores. Known for their curtain department and household items selection, but boasts a comprehensive and vastly underrated electronics section and a good range of stylish, functional clothing. Its famed 'never knowingly undersold' policy means prices, as a rule, are very reasonable.

*Liberty*, 214 Regent Street, W1; (020) 7734 1234; (www.liberty.co.uk). Offers beautiful fabrics, home furnishings and designer fashions. Not only has a great needlepoint department, but has a reputation for the funkiest women's fashion in London. Most other departments - especially accessories, furniture, fabrics and jewellery - offer an above- average selection of goods, while the small space of the cosmetics department, on the ground floor, is filled with a mix of cult and big names.

*Marks & Spencer*, 458 Oxford Street, W1; (020) 7935 7954; (www.marks-and-spencer.com). Known for their food halls, which specialise in ready meals and their staples like socks and underwear. Also carry women's, men's, and children's fashions focusing on good value at the right price. Branches throughout London.

*Peter Jones*, Sloane Square, SW1; (020) 7730 3434. Affiliated with The John Lewis Partnership.

*Selfridges*, 400 Oxford Street, W1; (020) 7629 1234; (www.selfridges.co.uk). Universal love of most Londoners. Large and varied selection of cutting edge, but not intimidating fashions, including children's. Boasts London's largest cosmetics hall, a spectacular toy department, and an amazing food hall. Has a number of in-store restaurants that range from sprawling family-oriented affairs to hip little coffee bars.

## DO IT YOURSELF (DIY)

There are many local DIY stores. We have only listed the large chains that can be found throughout London. Look in your Yellow Pages for a complete listing.

*B&Q*, Western Avenue, Greenford, UB6; (020) 8575 7175. Also Alexandra Road, Wimbledon SW19; (020) 8879 3322, and other branches throughout London. A wide selection of DIY and garden needs. The only DIY to offer free delivery.

*Homebase*, 195 Warwick Road, W14; (020) 7603 6397. Also other branches throughout London. All your DIY needs, plus Laura Ashley, Vogue Carpets, Schreiber Kitchens, curtains, and gardening supplies, including plants. Open 7 days per week.

## DRESSMAKING FABRICS

*Allans of Duke Street*, 75 Duke Street, W1; (020) 7629 3781. Sells wide range of fabrics at discount prices. Has large array of pure silks.

*Jason's of Bond Street*, 71 New Bond Street, W1; (020) 7629 2606.

*Viyella*, Head Office, 136 Regent Street, W1; (020) 7200 2900. Sells full range of men's and women's Viyella clothing. Also stocks the fabric! Also available at *Fenwicks*, *Debenhams* and *House of Fraser*.

## ELECTRICAL AND GAS APPLIANCES

Most major department stores, including *Peter Jones, John Lewis* and *Selfridges*, offer a range of appliances from toasters to microwave ovens. Other places include:

*London Electricity Board* (LEB) listed under 'Electricity' in the telephone directory.

*British Gas* listed under 'Gas' in the telephone directory.

*American Appliance Centre*, (020) 8443 9999; (www.americanappliances.com). Larger appliances, refrigerators, washer/dryers, etc.

*Comet*, discount warehouses throughout London selling electrical and domestic appliances. Or visit www.comet.co.uk where their regular online offers beat their in-store prices.

*Currys*, discount warehouses throughout London selling electrical and domestic appliances.

*P.M. Linpower*, 8 Micklethwaite Road, SW6; (020) 7385 2349. Installation of American appliances and general household plumbing. Has partner who converts electrical goods from 110 watts to 240 watts.

*Power Plus Direct* (0700) 234 0700. If you're looking for a washing machine, fridge, freezer, tumble dryer, television set, hi-fi or camcorder, shop around. Once you find the product you want, make a note of the product code. Then phone *Power Plus Direct* on and they will usually beat the best price you have found. They deliver anywhere in the UK, but there is a charge, except for some items over £300.

### Online sources:

www.24-7electrical.co.uk, Sells everything from vacuum cleaners to TVs, and DVDs to microwaves. Brands include Bosch, Panasonic, Hoover and Electrolux.

www.rdo.co.uk, Sells discount kitchen appliances including dishwashers, ovens and freezers. Brands include Zanussi, Smeg, Belling and Creda. Delivery in the UK is free.

## FISHMONGER'S

*Chalmers and Gray Fishmongers*, 67 Notting Hill Gate, W11; (020) 7221 6177.

*Cope's Seafood Company*, 700 Fulham Road, SW6; (020) 7371 7300.

## FLOWERS

Some major department stores have flower departments, including Harrods and Harvey Nichols and offer Interflora services. See also Markets, for those specialising in flowers. And see Chapter Eleven: Services for florists who will arrange flowers in private homes or for parties.

*Flower Van,* Michelin Building, 81 Fulham Road, SW3; (020) 7589 1852.

*\*Jane Packer Flowers,* 56 James Street, W1; (020) 7935 2673. Unique and creative floral arrangements. Once famous for 'doing Princess Di's wedding'.

*Kensington Flowers,* 3 Launceston Place, W8 5RL; (020) 7937 0268.

*Mary Jane Vaughan Design in Flowers,* 609 Fulham Road, SW6; (020) 7385 8400; (www.maryjanevaughan.co.uk). From Simple arrangements to extravagant affairs.

*Molly Blooms,* 787 Fulham Road, SW6; (020) 7731 1212.

*Moyses Stevens,* 157-158 Sloane Street, SW1; (020) 7493 8171.

*New Covent Garden Market,* Nine Elms Lane, SW8; (020) 7720 2211. Bulk sales of fruit, vegetables and flowers to the trade. Individuals may enter by paying a parking fee (£2) and may buy flowers and produce at the vendors' discretion. Market hours: Monday to Friday 03.00 to 11.00, Saturdays 04.00 to 09.00.

*Paula Pryke,* 20 Penton Street, N1; (020) 7837 7336. Absolutely beautiful and unique arrangements.

*Pot Pourri,* 255 Chiswick High Road, W4; (020) 8994 2404.

*Pulbrook & Gould,* 127 Sloane Street, SW1; (020) 7730 0030. Offers Inter-flora service.

*Silk Landscape Contracts,* 164 Old Brompton Road, SW5; (020) 7835 1500.

*Wild at Heart,* 49a Ledbury Road W11; (020) 7727 3095.

## FURNITURE

Most major department stores offer furniture ranging from traditional to modern styles; some have antiques. There are also specialist furniture stores that deal in reproductions. Also see Art and Antiques section in this Chapter.

*\*Albrizzi,* 1 Sloane Square, SW1; (020) 7730 6119. Italian and continental contemporary furniture designs.

*And So To Bed,* 638-640 King's Road, SW6; (020) 7731 3593. Specialises in brass beds. Also furniture and linens.

*\*Conran Shop,* 81 Fulham Road, SW3; (020) 7589 7401. Modern and contemporary furniture and accessories.

*Furniture Village,* 145 Tottenham Court Road, W1; (020) 7387 7000. Reproductions of traditional pieces.

*General Trading Company*, 144 Sloane Street, SW1; (020) 7730 0411. Antiques, ethnic artefacts, china, etc.

*George Smith Furniture & Fabrics*, 587 King's Road, SW6; (020) 7384 1004. Fine custom-made classic sofas and armchairs.

*\*Habitat*, 208 King's Road, SW3; (020) 7351 1211; Tottenham Court Road, W1; (020) 7631 3880. Other branches, owned by the Conran Group. Reasonably priced.

*\*Heal's*, 234 King's Road, SW3; (020) 7349 8411. Modern international selection. Inspiring room sets. Good selection of English contemporary furniture. Also on Tottenham Court Road.

*IKEA*, Brent Park, 255 North Circular Road, NW10; (020) 8208 5600. Swedish budget furniture. Contemporary, inexpensive and hard wearing.

*Kingcome*, 302-304 Fulham Road, SW10; (020) 7351 3998. Sofa and chair specialists.

*\*Liberty*, Regent Street, W1; (020) 7734 1234. Interesting selection of modern furniture from some of the best designers in Europe.

*Purves & Purves*, 80-81 and 83 Tottenham Court Road, W1; (020) 7580 8223. Good selection of fine contemporary European furniture, furnishings and accessories.

*Tulley's*, 153-155 Wandsworth High Street, SW18; (020) 7352 1078.

*Zarach*, 225 Ebury Street, SW1; (020) 7730 3339. Modern furniture.

## GARDEN CENTRES AND NURSERIES

From the most elaborate garden to the simplest flower box, London is in bloom most of the year. The following are a few suggestions to put some colour into your life. Christmas trees can be bought at nurseries, flower shops, flower stalls on street corners and at Columbia Road Market or New Covent Garden. (See Chapter Eleven: Services for where to "chop your own" Christmas tree).

*Barralets of Ealing Ltd.*, Houseplant Centre, 34 Central Chambers, Broadway W5; (020) 8566 0754. Garden and horticultural centre. Also supplies indoor plants and organises window box displays.

*B&Q*, Western Avenue, Greenford, UB6; (020) 8575 7175. Also Alexandra Road, Wimbledon SW19; (020) 8879 3322, and other branches throughout London. A wide selection of DIY and garden needs. The only DIY to offer free delivery.

*\*The Chelsea Gardener*, 125 Sydney Street, SW3; (020) 7352 5656. Comprehensive garden centre selling everything from shrubs and plants to gardening furniture and books. Also has excellent selection of houseplants and a florist department.

*Clifton Nurseries*, 5A Clifton Villas, W9; (020) 7289 6851. An excellent all-purpose garden centre. Services also include garden designing and delivery.

*Columbia Road Market*, E2. Sundays 08.00-12.30. Outside street market selling plants, shrubs, flowers and garden accessories.

*Fulham Palace Garden Centre*, Bishop's Avenue, SW6; (020) 7736 2640. Good selection of plants, pots and shrubs. Garden landscaping and delivery available.

*\*Homebase*, 195 Warwick Road, W14; (020) 7603 6397. Also other branches throughout London. All your DIY needs, plus Laura Ashley, Vogue Carpets, Schreiber Kitchens, curtains, and gardening supplies, including plants. Open 7 days per week.

*Rassell's Nursery*, 80 Earl's Court Road, W8; (020) 7937 0481. Garden plants and shrubs, window boxes and hanging baskets made to order.

*Royal Horticultural Society*, 80 Vincent Square, SW1; (020) 7834 4333. Have a comprehensive reference library available to non-members.

Online resource: Crocus Online at www.crocus.co.uk

## GIFTS

All major department stores have special departments for distinctive and unusual gifts. In addition, most of London's large museums have excellent gift shops, in particular London's Transport Museum, the British Museum, the V&A and the Tate Modern offer good selections. Here are a few shops and stores that carry many different and fun items.

*Alfred Dunhill*, 48 Jermyn Street, SW1; (020) 7290 8622. Also in Knightsbridge. Men's accessories.

*\*Asprey & Garrard*, 167 New Bond Street, W1; (020) 7493 6767. Fine gifts, silver and china.

*BBC World Service Shop*, Bush House, The Strand, WC2; (020) 7557 2576; (www.bbc.co.uk/worldservice). A wide range of BBC merchandise, plus books on a variety of arts and media subjects.

*\*Boleslawiec Polish Pottery*, (01273) 483 449, (www.baltictrader.co.uk).

*Cargo Home Shop*, 245-249 Brompton Road, SW3; (020) 7584 7611. Other branches throughout London. General household items at reasonable prices.

*\*The Chocolate Society*, 36 Elizabeth Street, SW1, (020) 7259 9222, (www.chocolate.co.uk).

*\*Conran Shop*, Michelin House, 81 Fulham Road, SW3; (020) 7589 7401. Designer household items from furniture to kitchenware.

*\*General Trading Company*, 144 Sloane Street, SW1; (020) 7730 0411. Upmarket items for the entire house, including furniture, china, kitchenware and eclectic accessories.

*Graham & Green*, 4, 7 and 10 Elgin Crescent, W11; (020) 7727 4594. Unusual collection of household accessories.

*Halcyon Days*, 14 Brook Street, W1; (020) 7629 8811. Also 4 Royal Exchange, EC3; (020) 7626 1120. Enamel boxes, clocks and many other decorative items.

*Neal Street East*, 5 Neal Street, WC2; (020) 7240 0135. London's leading ethnic emporium has a huge range of Oriental and South American goods, including clothing, jewellery, books, home-wares and gifts.

*\*Nina Campbell*, 9 Walton Street, SW3; (020) 7225 1011. Eclectic assortment of decorative items for the home.

*\*Oggetti*, 133 Fulham Road, SW3; (020) 7581 8088. Everything for the kitchen.

*Oliver Bonas*, 137 Northcote Road, SW11; (020) 7223 5223. Many branches throughout London. Stocked with well-chosen merchandise, much of it in natural materials.

*Osborne & Little*, 304-308 King's Road, SW3; (020) 7352 1456. Interior designer, household gifts.

*The Pen Shop*, 199 Regent Street, W1; (020) 7734 4088; (www.penshop.co.uk). Pens by Lamt, Waterman, Cross, Shaeffer and Parker, plus Yard O Led's distinctive silver pens and Mont Blanc's chic black models.

*The Tintin Shop*, 34 Floral Street, WC2; (020) 7836 1131. A tiny shop devoted to Hergé's much loved reporter. The stock includes key-rings, stationery, collectibles, plus, of course, the full range of books.

*The Wedding List Company*, 91 Walton Street, SW3; (020) 7584 1222.

*Thomas Goode*, 19 South Audley Street, W1; (020) 7499 2823. China, crystal and antiques.

### GROCERIES

The major supermarkets are Sainsbury's, Tesco, Waitrose, ASDA, Morrisons and Safeway (although not the same Safeway as in the US). You can also buy groceries from smaller, independent stores peppered throughout London, as well as in the food halls of most major department stores. The best food halls are in Fortnum & Mason, Harrods, Harvey Nichols and Selfridges. While variety is limited in these venues, the quality is quite good.

Note, in most supermarkets you will be required to bag your own groceries. If bagging your own groceries and even going out to shop for them is not your thing, simply order online. Both Sainsbury's (www.sainsburys.com) and Tesco (www.tesco.com) have excellent online grocery services.

## HATS

Fenwicks, Harrods, Harvey Nichols and Peter Jones have good selections. Liberty has what many consider the most exquisite selection in town.

*James Lock*, 6 St. James's Street, SW1; (020) 7930 8874. Hats for gentlemen and ladies.

*John Boyd*, 16 Beauchamp Place, SW3; (020) 7589 7601. You can have your hat specially designed for you or you can select from stock.

*Herbert Johnson*, 54 St. James's Street, SW1; (020) 7408 1174. Large selection of hats for men and women. Great source for Ascot.

*David Shilling*, 5 Homer Street, W1; (020) 7262 2363. A hat designer with a theatrical flair! Expensive but the quality and service are great. Call first for an appointment.

*Philip Treacy*, 69 Elizabeth Street, SW1; (020) 7259 9605. Amazingly imaginative yet glamorous hats.

*Fred Bare*, 14 Lamb Street, E1; (020) 7247 9004. Offers a mix of cosy pull-ons to extravagant special-occasion hats

*Stephen Jones*, 36 Great Queen Street, WC2; (020) 7242 0770. Cutting-edge, crafted fashion statements.

## HI-FI AND VIDEO EQUIPMENT

Most major department stores, such as *Harrods, Peter Jones, John Lewis* and *Selfridges*, have an excellent selection of equipment.

*Hi-Fi Experience*, 227 Tottenham Court Road, W1; (020) 7580 3535; (www.hifilondon.co.uk). Offers hi-fi and home cinema equipment in eight demo rooms. Expert staff.

*Richer Sounds*, 2 London Bridge Walk, SE1; (020) 7403 1201; (www.richersounds.com). Good hi-fi separates at rock-bottom prices.

*Thomas Heinitz*, 35 Moscow Road, W2; (020) 7229 2077. Carries video and hi-fi equipment.

## HOBBIES

*Beatties*, 202 High Holdborn, WC1; (020) 7405 6285; (www.beatties.net). Numerous branches offering toys, model railways, model kits and all the accessories.

*London's Dolls' House Company*, Unit 29, The Market, Covent Garden, WC2; (020) 7240 8681. Amazingly detailed Victorian-style dolls' house with a variety of handmade furniture.

*Spink & Son*, 69 Southampton Row, WC1; (020) 8563 4000; (www.spink-online.com). Britain's foremost authority on coins & medals.

*The Bead Shop*, 21A Tower Street, Covent Garden, WC2; (020) 7420 0931. Offering a vast array of glass, wooden and ceramic beads with all the necessary accoutrements.

## INTERIOR DESIGN

Most major department stores carrying decorating materials will advise and do drapery, upholstery and other work. Fabric and wallpaper are sold by the metre. Liberty fabrics are world famous and of a consistently high quality. John Lewis and Peter Jones are also known for their excellent haberdashery and own label quality fabric departments.

Equivalents:

| | | |
|---|---|---|
| 1 inch | = | 2.5 centimetres |
| 1 foot | = | 30 centimetres |
| 1 yard | = | 0.9 metres |
| 1 centimetre | = | 0.333 inch |
| 1 metre | = | 39.37 inches |

For other measurement conversions see Chapter One: Moving and Chapter Nine: Cooking, Food and Drink. Also Conversion Charts at the back of the book.

*Cole & Son*, Chelsea Harbour Design Centre; (020) 7376 4628. Specialise in hand-printed wallpapers and own range paints.

*Colefax & Fowler*, 39 Brook Street, W1; (020) 7518 8500. Also branch on Fulham Road. Famous for chintz.

*Conran Shop*, Michelin House, 81 Fulham Road, SW3; (020) 7589 7401.

*Curtain Mill*, 256b Wimbledon Park Road, SW19; (020) 8785 3366. Sell discount designer fabrics.

*Designer's Guild*, 277 King's Road, SW36; (020) 7351 5775. Wide range of contemporary, colourful wallpaper, fabric and paint, sheets and towels.

*Farrow & Ball*, 249 Fulham Road, SW3; (020) 7351 0273. Traditional wallpaper and paint.

*Fiona Campbell*, 259 New King's Road, SW6; (020) 7731 3681. Fabric, wallpaper and paint.

*\*Habitat*, 208 King's Road, SW3; (020) 7351 1211. Also branches on Tottenham Court Road and Finchley Road.

*Jane Churchill*, 151 Sloane Street, SW1; (020) 7730 9847. Fabric, wallpaper and paint.

*John S. Oliver Ltd.*, 33 Pembridge Road, W11; (020) 7221 6466. Produce a unique range of paints that match their hand-made wallpapers.

*Laura Ashley*, 7-9 Harriet Street, SW1; (020) 7235 9797. Other branches throughout London.

*\*Liberty*, 214 Regent Street, W1; (020) 7734 1234.

*Mary Fox Linton Ltd.*, Chelsea Harbour Design Centre, SW10; (020) 7351 9908. Fabric.

*Nina Campbell*, 9 Walton Street, SW3; (020) 7225 1011. Sells her own fabric and wallpaper.

*Osborne & Little Ltd.*, 304-308 King's Road, SW3; (020) 7352 1456.

*The Paint Library*, 5 Elystan Street, SW3; (020) 7823 7755. Wallpaper and paint.

## JEWELLERY

*Angela Hale*, 5 The Royal Arcade, 28 Old Bond Street, W1; (020) 7495 1920; (www.angelahale.co.uk). Has deco and '50s-style costume jewellery, from beaded bracelets to chunky cufflinks and tiaras

*Argenta*, 82 Fulham Road, SW3; (020) 7584 4480; (www.argenta.co.uk). Offers a wide range of contemporary jewellery and watches, including over 1,000 wedding rings.

*Electrum Gallery*, 21 South Molton Street, W1; (020) 7629 6325. More like an art gallery than a shop, Electrum sells sparkling contemporary jewellery.

*Frontiers*, 37 & 39 Pembridge Road, W11; (020) 7727 6132. Specialises in old and new jewellery from North Africa and Asia, packed with exotic items.

*\*Tiffany's*, 25 Old Bond Street, W1; (020) 7409 2790; (www.tiffany.com).

*\*Total Jewels*, (020) 7828 2801 or (020) 7233 9399, by appointment. Unique hand-crafted jewellery from India. Plain silver or gold plated silver and semi-precious stones.

*Wright & Teague*, 1A Grafton Street, W1; (020) 7629 2777; (www. wrightandteague.com). Contemporary jewellery with an emphasis on crosses and hearts. Inscriptions are also popular, especially on the chunky silver pieces.

## KITCHEN EQUIPMENT

Most major department stores offer a large selection of kitchen equipment, particularly good are: Conran's, Habitat, Peter Jones/John Lewis, Harrods and Selfridges. Some of the better known shops are listed below.

*Anything Left-Handed*, 57 Brewer Street, W1; (020) 7437 3910. Stocks left-handed kitchen equipment. Catalogue available.

*David Mellor*, 4 Sloane Square, SW1; (020) 7730 4259.

*Divertimenti*, 139-141 Fulham Road, SW3; (020) 7581 8065. Also 45-47 Wigmore Street, W1; (020) 7935 0689.

*Elizabeth David*, Unit 3A North Row, The Market, Covent Garden, WC2; (020) 7836 9167.

*Fairfax Kitchen Shop*, 1 Regency Parade, NW3; (020) 7722 7648.

*General Trading Company*, 144 Sloane Street, SW1; (020) 7730 0411.

*Hansen's Ltd.*, 306 Fulham Road, SW10; (020) 7351 6933.

*Jerry's Home Store*, 80-81 Tottenham Court Road, W11, (0870) 840 6060, (www.jerryshomestore.com). A store with an American flair. Great for kitchen and trendy home items.

*Kitchen Works of Hampstead*, 92 Heath Street, NW3; (020) 7431 0469. Fitted kitchen retailer with many appliances.

*Leon Jaeggi & Sons Ltd.*, 77 Shaftesbury Avenue, W1; (020) 7580 1974. Caters to commercial trade, good for appliances.

*Oggetti*, 133 Fulham Road, SW3; (020) 7581 8088. Offers British and continental accessories.

## LEATHER ACCESSORIES, HANDBAGS AND LUGGAGE

Again, the large department stores all carry excellent selections. Harrods has probably the best selection. Selfridges has a range of inexpensive, value-for-money luggage with many of the best-known makes, as does Peter Jones. Marks & Spencer carries a range of own-brand luggage that is durable and well-priced. And of course, luxury leather accessories can be found at designer boutiques such as Gucci, Hermes and Prada.

*Accessorize*, Branches throughout London. Specialises in accessories including jewellery, watches, belts, gloves, tights and scarves.

*Anya Hindmarch*, 15-17 Pont Street, SW1; (020) 7838 9177. Creative and customised bags and gifts

*Bill Amberg*, 10 Chepstow Road, W2; (020) 7727 3560. Timeless designs with universal appeal. Bags are the mainstay of Amberg's business, but he also makes home accessories and furniture (by commission).

*Loewe*, 130 New Bond Street, W1; (020) 7493 3914.

*Lulu Guinness*, 3 Ellis Street, SW1; (020) 7823 4828.

*Mulberry*, 41-42 New Bond Street, W1; (020) 7491 3900. Other locations and also available in boutiques in *Liberty*, *Harrods* and *Harvey Nichols*. Medium-priced range of quintessentially English clothing, luggage, handbags, belts and other accessories.

*Osprey*, 11 St. Christopher's Place, W1; (020) 7935 2824. Reasonably priced, handmade leather bags and accessories.

*Pickett Fine Leather*, 149 Sloane Street, SW1; (020) 7823 5638. Also in Burlington Arcade.

## LINENS

Most department stores carry a wide selection of linens. Other stores are listed below.

*Albary Linens*, 6 Baker Street, W1; (020) 7487 4105. Large selection of American size sheets and towels.

*Givans*, 207 King's Road, SW3; (020) 7352 6352.

*The Irish Linen Shop*, 35-36 Burlington Arcade, W1; (020) 7493 8949.

*Linen Cupboard*, 21 Great Castle Street, W1; (020) 7629 4062.

*The Monogrammed Linen Shop*, 168 Walton Street, SW3; (020) 7589 4033. Personalised items; will also embroider your own items.

*The White House*, 102 Waterford Road, SW6; (020) 7629 3521.

## LINGERIE

Marks and Spencers is well known for reasonably priced underwear, and you will find lingerie available in most major department stores. Selfridges is highly recommended by several of our League members, as they will actually take the time to fit you. Following are a few more favourites.

*Agent Provocateur*, 6 Broadwick Street, W1; (020) 7439 0229 (www.agentprovocateur.com). Lingerie with 1950's pin-up appeal, silk nightwear, hosiery, and even their own perfume.

*La Perla*, Sloane Street, King's Road, and numerous locations throughout London. Beautiful, luxurious lingerie.

*Rigby & Peller*, 2 Hans Road, SW3; (020) 7589 9293 (www.rigbyandpeller.com). Lingerie in ALL sizes and they will fit you to ensure you're in the correct size. Second branch in Mayfair.

## MARKETS

London's street markets are great fun to visit and offer some of the most competitive prices.

### Antiques Markets

Everything from fine silver to genuine fakes can be found at the many different markets in London - be very careful!

*Bermondsey Market* (*New Caledonian Market*), Long Lane and Bermondsey Street, SE1. Open 05.00-14.00 Fridays. Specialises in paintings, silver and jewellery. Best before 9.00.

*\*Camden Passage*, Camden Passage, N1. Open 10.00-14.00 Wednesdays and 10.00-17.00 Saturdays. Specialises in prints, silver, 19th century magazines, jewellery and toys.

*\*Portobello Road Market*, Portobello Road, W10. 07.00-17.30 Saturdays (for antiques and junk). Has over 2,000 stalls displaying jewellery, old medals, paintings, silver and *objets d'art*. Famous for its achingly hip new and vintage clothes stalls. Also has some good food and flower stalls on Saturdays.

## General Markets

*Berwick Street Market*, Berwick Street, W1. Open 09.00-18.00 Monday-Saturday. All kinds of fruit and vegetables as well as fabrics, household goods and leather handbags.

*Brick Lane Market*, Brick Lane, E1. Open daybreak-13.00 Sunday. Furniture, old books, jewellery, watches, food, bicycles, handbags - offers something for everyone!

*Brixton Market*, Electric Avenue, SW9. Open 08.30-17.50 Monday, Tuesday, Thursday-Saturday; 08.30-13.00 Wednesday. All kinds of wonderful Afro-Caribbean food from goat's meat to plantains.

*Camden Lock Market*, Buck Street, NW1. Open 09.00-17.00 Thursday and Friday; 10.00-18.00 Saturday and Sunday. Handmade crafts, new and second-hand street fashions, books, records, etc.

*East Street Market*, East Street, SE17. Open 08.00-17.00 Tuesday, Wednesday, Friday and Saturday; 08.00-14.00 Thursday and Sunday. On Sundays has over 250 stalls selling fruit, vegetables, flowers, clothes, electrical and household goods.

*\*Greenwich Market*, Antiques Market Greenwich High Road, SE10. Open 9am-5pm Sat, Sun; closed Mon-Fri. Central Market off Stockwell Street, SE10. Open *Outdoor* 7.00 – 18.00 Sat; 7.00 – 17.00 Sun; closed Mon-Fri. Indoor (Village Market) 10.00 – 17.00 Fri, Sat; 10.00 – 18.00 Sun; closed Mon-Thur. Crafts Market *College Approach*, SE10. Open *Antiques* 7.30 – 17.00 Thur; closed Mon-Wed, Fri-Sun. *General* 9.30 – 17.30 Fri-Sun; closed Mon-Thur. Food Market off Stockwell Street, SE10. Open 10.00 – 16.00 Sat; closed Mon-Fri, Sun.

*Leadenhall Market*, Whittington Avenue, EC3. Open 07.00-16.00 Monday through Friday. It's not a traditional London market, but Leadenhall Market, whose retailers include clothes shops Jigsaw and Hobbs and foodie paradises Butcher & Edmonds and RS Ashby, is worth visiting alone for the beautiful Victorian arcade in which it's situated.

*Petticoat Lane Market*, Middlesex Street, E1. Open 09.00-14.00 Sunday. Leather goods, clothes, watches, jewellery and toys.

*Shepherd's Bush Market*, Goldhawk Road, W12. Open 09.30-17.00 Monday-Wednesday, Friday and Saturday; 09.30-14.30 Thursday. West Indian food, Asian spices and cheap electrical and household goods.

*Walthamstow Market*, Walthamstow High Street, E17. Open 08.00-18.00 Monday through Saturday. Walthamstow's answer to the East End's Petticoat Lane claims to be Europe's longest daily street market, with 450 stalls selling cheap clothing, fruit and veg, as well as household items.

### Fruit, Veg and Flower Markets

*Berwick Street Market*, Berwick Street & Rupert Street, W1. Open 08.00-18.00 Monday through Saturday. Offers best and cheapest selection of fruit and veg in central London, although the area is genuinely seedy. There are also good cheese, fish, bread, and herb and spice stalls.

*Borough Market*, between Borough High Street, Bedale Street, Winchester Walk & Stoney Street, SE10; (www.londonslarder.org.uk). Open noon to 18.00 Friday; 0900 to 16.00 Saturday. This superb farmers' market, nicknamed London's Larder, recently started opening to the public every weekend. There are some good cut flowers, as well as quality coffees, fruit, vegetables and meat. A number of traders offer organic produce.

*Columbia Road Flower Market*, Columbia Road (between Gosset Street & the Royal Oak pub), E2. Open 08.00 to 13.00 Sundays only. Without question this is the prettiest street market in town. Flowers, shrubs, bedding plants and other horticultural delights are spread in all directions, while the shops stock flowers, garden accessories, and even gifts and furniture. Visit in December to pick up a Christmas tree, poinsettias and wreaths.

*Spitalfields Market*, 65 Brushfield Street, Spitalfields, E1; (020) 7377 1496. Open 10.00 to 16.00 Monday through Friday. Crafts and antiques stalls are set up through the week, but on Friday and, particularly, Sunday, the market comes alive with a dozen or so organic producers selling relishes, pickles, herbs and spices, breads and cakes, and fruit and vegetables.

### MUSIC

The HMV in Oxford Circus is the largest record store in the world and caters to all tastes in music. There are branches of HMV, Virgin and Tower Records throughout London. And most major department stores, such as Harrods, Peter Jones, John Lewis and Selfridges, have music departments.

If you like browsing through more atmospheric shops, head to Soho's Berwick Street. On Berwick, you'll find Jamaican music at Daddy Kool at number 12, Indi at Selectadisc at number 34, and general cut-price CD's at Mr CD at number 80.

And, for second-hand CD's head to Hanway Street, located at the intersection of Oxford Street and Tottenham Court Road, where you'll find On the Beat at number 22 and Division One at number 36.

Following are several favourite specialist music shops:

*Black Market*, 25 D'Arblay Street, W1; (020) 7437 0478; (www.blackmarket.co.uk). A tiny corridor with nodding DJs behind the counter offering a good selection of imported house and drum 'n' bass.

*Harold Moores Records*, 2 Great Marlborough Street, W1; (020) 7437 1576; (www.hmrecords.co.uk). Offers an enormous selection of classical music and opera on CDs upstairs and LPs downstairs.

*Honest Jon's Records*, 276-278 Portobello Road, W10; (020) 8969 9822; (www.honestjons.co.uk). Eclectic and self-consciously cool, specialises in jazz, R&B, reggae and dance records and compact discs.

*Intoxica!*, 231 Portobello Road, W11; (020) 7229 8010 (www.intoxica.co.uk). Considered to be one of the best second-hand record shops in London, where you'll find '60's and '70's rock, funk and soul, ska, punk and new wave.

*MDC Classic Music*, 437 The Strand, WC2; (020) 7240 2157 (www.mdcmusic.co.uk). Other branches throughout London. Offers classical tapes and CDs at discount prices.

*Mole Jazz*, 311 Gray's Inn Road, WC1; (020) 7278 0703; (www.molejazz.co.uk). Bebop, nostalgia, male and female vocal, free jazz, traditional as well as avant garde are offered in all formats: CDs, records, books and videos.

*Ray's Jazz*, 180 Shaftesbury Avenue, WC2; (020) 7240 3969. Upstairs they offer jazz and downstairs it's blues, folk, world music, soul, and reggae.

*Rough Trade*, 130 Talbot Road, W11; (020) 8229 8541; (www.roughtrade.com). Branch in Covent Garden. Offers obscure American post-rock, Japanese noisecore, the freeest of free jazz and anarchic fanzines. Go just to find out what this is!

## OUTLET SHOPPING

*\*Bicester Villa*, Bicester; (01869) 323 200 (www.bicester-village.co.uk). Junction 9 off M40. Outlet centre offering great stores, including Tods and Petit Bateau.

*\*Burberry Outlet*, 29-52 Chetham Place, (Bethal Green Tube stop), (020) 8985 3344.

*Clarks Village Factory Shopping*, Farm Road, Street, Somerset BA16 OBB; (01458) 840 064. Nearly 60 shops.

*Merchants Quay*, Brighton Marina, Brighton, East Sussex BN2 5UF; (01273) 693 636. 10 shops.

*Great Western Designer Outlet Village*, Churchward Village, Swindon, Wiltshire, Junction 15 off M4.

*\*Costco*, (01923) 213 113. Membership warehouse.

## PERFUMES AND TOILETRIES

*The Body Shop*, 54 King's Road, SW3; (020) 7584 0163; (www.the-body-shop.com). Other branches throughout London. Chain of shops in London and most towns in Britain offering natural hair, bath, body and skin care products made with natural ingredients. None of the products or ingredients are tested on animals. Customers may refill or recycle their product containers at the shops.

*Crabtree & Evelyn*, 6 Kensington Church Street, W8; (020) 7937 9335. Other branches throughout London. Sells a wide range of popular men's and women's skin and hair care products. Also carries a selection of high quality products for children and home. Will assemble gift baskets.

*Culpeper Ltd.*, 8 The Market, Covent Garden, WC2; (020) 7379 6698. Employs herbal and floral remedies as bases for their natural, therapeutic toiletries. Make cosmetics, hair preparations, potpourri, pomanders as well as oils for aromatherapy.

*Czech & Speake*, 39c Jermyn Street, SW1; (020) 7439 0216. Flower-based scents and toiletries for men and women.

*G. F. Trumper*, 9 Curzon Street, W1; (020) 7499 1850. Scents and toiletries for men. Also on Jermyn Street.

*J. Floris*, 89 Jermyn Street, SW1; (020) 7930 2885. Uses recipes that are hundreds of years old - still manufacture flower-based scents sold in the 19th century.

*\*Jo Malone*, 150 Sloane Street, SW1; (020) 7581 1101. Trendy perfumery which sells perfumes, soaps, bath oils, candles, and room sprays.

*L'Occitane*, 70 Kensington High Street, W8; (020) 7938 4135. Fragrances, soaps, hair and skincare from Provence.

*Lush.* Two locations: 123 Kings Road, Chelsea, SW3; (020) 7376 8348. The Piazza, Covent Garden, WC2. Fresh handmade cosmetics. Specialise in freshly made facial masks, cosmetics, soaps and bath products derived from fresh fruit, vegetables, essential oils and safe synthetics.

*Molton Brown*, 58 South Molton Street, W1; (020) 7499 6474. Sells a range of natural cosmetics, body and haircare products.

*\*Neal's Yard Remedies*, 15 Neal's Yard, Covent Garden, WC2; (020) 7379 7222. Also outlet in Chelsea Farmer's Market. Uses traditional herbal and floral remedies as base for natural and therapeutic remedies.

*Penhaligon's*, 16 Burlington Arcade, W1; (020) 7629 1416. British perfumery which sells traditional toilet water and other exotic scents.

## PHARMACIES (DRUGSTORES) AND CHEMISTS

Your local Police Station holds a list of chemists in your area that are available at all hours in case of an emergency. (See Chapter Seven: Healthcare for a partial list of Late Night Chemists).

*John Bell & Croyden*, 50-54 Wigmore Street, W1; (020) 7935 5555. Open Monday-Friday, 09.00-18.30, Saturday 09.30-18.00.

*Bliss Chemist*, 33 Sloane Square, SW1; (020) 7730 1023. Open Monday-Saturday 8.30-19.00, Sunday 10.00-17.00.

*\*Boots*, 44-46 Regent Street, W1; (020) 7734 6126. Open Monday-Friday, 08.30-20.00, Saturday 09.00-20.00. Branches all over London; some open Sundays. A chain of drugstores selling toothpaste to toddlers' clothing.

*Dajani Pharmacy*, 92 Old Brompton Road, SW7; (020) 7589 8263. Open Monday-Friday, 09.00-22.00, Saturday 09.00-21.00, Sunday 10.00-20.00, Bank Holidays 10.00-20.00.

*Dennis and Co.*, 12 Pembridge Road, W11; (020) 7229 0958. Open Monday - Friday, 09.00-19.00, Saturday 09.00-18.00.

*Trident Pharmacy*, 187 Worple Road, SW20; (020) 8946 6282. Open Monday - Friday, 09.00-19.00, Saturday 09.00-18.00.

*Warmen-Freed*, 45 Golders Green Road, NW11; (020) 8455 4351. Open 08.30 - 24.00 every day (including Bank Holidays).

## SHOES

### Women's Shoes

Shoes can, of course, be found in the designer shops and most department stores (*Selfridge's* has a particularly large selection). Harrod's carries a wide range of designer shoes under one roof. There are also many "High Street" shoe shops with multiple locations throughout London, such as:

| | |
|---|---|
| *Bally* | *Office* |
| *Bertie* | *Pied a Terre* |
| *Church's* | *Ravel* |
| *Hobbs* | *Russell & Bromley* |
| *Jones Bootmaker* | *Shellys* |

Of particular note are these favourites for shoes:

*Bruno Magli*, 207 Sloane Street, SW1; (020) 7235 7939.

*Charles Jourdan*, 39 Brompton Road, SW3; (020) 7581 3333. Excellent shoes and boots, handbags and evening shoes.

*Christian Louboutin*, 23 Motcomb Street, SW1; (020) 7823 2234. Elegant French shoes.

*Emma Hope*, 53 Sloane Square, SW1; (020) 7833 2367. Special shoes for all occasions.

*Gina*, 189 Sloane Street, SW1; (020) 7235 2932. Beautiful shoes from a London designer.

*Jimmy Choo*, 20 Motcomb Street, SW1; (020) 7235 6008. Perfect strappy sandals and more.

*Joseph Azagury*, 73 Knightsbridge, SW1; (020) 7259 6887. Fashionable, refined shoes.

*Kurt Geiger*, 49 New Bond Street, W1; (020) 7491 8562.

*L. K. Bennett*, 31 Brook Street, W1; (020) 7491 3005. Wide range of styles. Branches throughout London.

*Manolo Blahnik*, 49-51 Old Church Street, SW3; (020) 7352 8622. For the ultimate pair of shoes.

*Patrick Cox*, 30 Sloane Street, SW1; (020) 7235 5599.

*Robert Clergerie*, 67 Wigmore Street, W1; (020) 7935 3601.

*Stephane Kelian*, 48 Sloane Street, SW1; (020) 7235 9459.

## Narrow Fittings for Women

*N. Potulski's "Bible"* on shoe shops lists shops with extra small or large sizes/widths.

*Babers*, 299 Oxford Street, W1; (020) 7639 3371. This shop is great for narrow fittings at reasonable prices.

*Crispins*, 28-30 Chiltern Street, W1; (020) 7486 8924. Narrow fitting designer fashion shoes (average price £60). Sizes range from 4 to 11 in AA and 8½ to 11 in B and C fittings as well. Occasionally AAA available.

*K Shoes*, 324 Oxford Street, W1; (020) 7629 3656. AA fittings in sizes 2-9 (including half sizes). Other locations throughout London.

*Tall and Small Shoe Shop*, 71 York Street, W1; (020) 7723 5321. AA fittings. Large sizes start at 9, small at 2½.

## Men's Shoes

Both traditional and trendier designers and manufacturers shoes can be found in the department stores - the best being Fortnum & Mason, Harrods and Harvey Nichols. Most of the "High Street" shoe stores stock both men's and women's shoes. Other stores include:

*John Lobb*, 9 St. James's Street, SW1; (020) 7930 3664. Specialises in hand-made classic footwear. Ready to wear shoes available at 88 Jermyn Street, SW1; (020) 7930 8089.

*Next for Men*, 327-329 Oxford Street, W1; (020) 7409 2746. Other branches throughout London. Good for casual shoes.

*Wildsmith & Co.*, 13 Princes Arcade, Jermyn Street, SW1; (020) 7437 4289. High quality hand-made shoes.

## SPORTSWEAR AND SPORTING EQUIPMENT

*Captain O. M. Watts*, 7 Dover Street, Piccadilly W1; (020) 7493 4633. Boating equipment and leisure wear.

*Debenham's Basement*, 1 Welbeck Street, W1; (020) 7580 3000. Good selection of sporting goods.

*Farlow's of Pall Mall*, 5 Pall Mall, SW1; (020) 7839 2423. London's oldest fishing tackle shop. Has large selection of fishing tackle, shooting accessories and country clothing including Barbour waxed clothing.

*\*Harrods*, Knightsbridge, SW1; (020) 7730 1234. Large selection of goods.

*Holland & Holland*, 31 Bruton Street, W1; (020) 7499 4411. Also at 171 Sloane Street, SW1; (020) 7235-3475. Sporting guns, shooting accessories and country clothing.

*\*Lillywhites*, 24-36 Regent Street, SW1; (020) 7915 4000. Large department store devoted solely to sporting goods.

*Oddball Juggling*, 200B Chalk Farm Road, NW1; (020) 7284 4488. Juggling equipment and unicycles.

*On Your Bike Ltd.*, 52-54 Tooley Street, London Bridge, SE1; (020) 7407 1309. Bicycles for adults.

*Purdey*, 57-58 South Audley Street, W1; (020) 7499 1801. Hunting and shooting shop with classic English country clothing.

*Ray Ward*, 24 Lowndes Street, SW1; (020) 7235 2550. Sporting guns, shooting accessories and English country clothing.

*Run & Become*, 42 Palmer Street, SW1; (020) 7222 1314. Running gear.

*Snow & Rock Sports Ltd.*, 188 Kensington High Street, W8; (020) 7937 0872. Skiing and mountaineering equipment for the entire family. Also rollerblade and swim gear.

*Sports Division*, 301 Oxford Street, W1; (020) 7409 2619. Branches throughout London. All types of sporting goods for children and adults.

*Swaine Adeney*, 54 St. James's Street, SW1; (020) 7409 7277. Very upmarket horse riding gear and English country accessories.

*William Evans*, 67A St. James's Street, SW1; (020) 7493 0415. Sporting guns and shooting accessories.

*W & H Gidden Ltd.*, 15d Clifford Street, W1; (020) 7734 2788. Wide range of traditional riding equipment including saddles, boots, whips, etc. Small range of children's gear.

*Y.H.A. Adventure Shop*, 14 Southampton Street, Covent Garden, WC2; (020) 7836 8541. Wide range of travel and adventure clothing and equipment. Also on Kensington High Street.

## STATIONERY

Most major department stores and some larger chemists offer a selection of stationery. Also try the High Street "quick print" shops for a selection of inexpensive personalised paper.

*Able Direct*, Northampton NN6; (01604) 810 781. Very reasonably priced personalised stationery and return address stickers by mail order.

*\*Alastair Lockhart*, 97 Walton Street, SW3; (020) 7581 8289. Fine personalised stationery, invitations and announcements.

*CLD Stationery*, 7 Imperial Studios, Imperial Road, SW6; (020) 7610 9292.

*Paperchase*, 213 Tottenham Court Road, W1; (020) 7580 8496. Has wide range of cards, pens, wrapping paper, ribbons, plus paper gifts and all kinds of party things. Branches throughout London.

*\*Papyrus*, 48 Fulham Road, SW3; (020) 7584 8022. Fine personalised stationery, invitations and announcements as well as gift items.

*Pencraft*, 119 Regent Street, W1; (020) 7734 4928. Has full range of pens by Mont Blanc, Watermans, Parker and Sheaffer.

*\*Phoenix Trading*, (020) 8875 9944, (www.phoenix-trading.co.uk). A wide selection of invites, thank you notes, and note cards.

*Ryman*, branches throughout London. Excellent for office supplies and stationery.

*\*Smythson of Bond Street*, 40 New Bond Street, W1; (020) 7629 8558. The Queen's Stationer stocks the finest personal stationery as well as leather bound address books, diaries, blotters and pencil holders. Also on Walton Street.

*Tessa Fantoni*, 73 & 77 Abbeville Road, SW4; (020) 8673 1253. Has wonderful paper-covered boxes, photo frames and albums which are sold in specialist stationery shops, Conran's and her own shop in Clapham.

*\*The Wren Press*, 26 Chelsea Wharf, 15 Lots Road, SW10; (020) 7351 5887. Fine engraving and printing at affordable prices - everything from letterheads to party invitations.

*W. H. Smith*, branches throughout London.

## WINES, SPIRITS, BEERS

The best known chains are Oddbins (www.oddbins.co.uk), Nicolas, Thresher and Victoria Wines. Many chain food stores (e.g. Sainsbury's, Waitrose) and department stores (e.g. Harrods, Harvey Nichols, Marks & Spencer) have a good selection of wine and/or beer and some sell spirits as well.

*Gerry's*, 74 Old Compton Street, W1; (020) 7734 4215. Spirits and liqueurs from all corners of the globe, sold by friendly staff who will happily explain away some of the more unique bottles on their shelves. A favourite of London's cocktail barmen and -women.

*\*Handford*, 12 Portland Road, W11, (020) 7221 9614. Master of wine, great shop and they also offer classes in wine and tasting.

*Milroy's of Soho*, 3 Greek Street, W1; (020) 7437 9311; (www.milroys.co.uk). The only whisky shop in London, Milroy's has a huge selection (over 400) of whiskies from Scotland, Ireland and America.

*Majestic Wine Warehouse*, Albion Wharf, Hester Road, Battersea SW11; (020) 7223 2983, sells beer and wine by the case, at a discount. Cases can be mixed and they carry a large selection of French, Californian and Australian wine. Also for sale are soft drinks, mixers and bar necessities at a discount. There are 12 other Greater London locations. Call the main number (020) 7736 1113 for the location nearest you.

*The Beer Shop*, 14 Pitfield Street, N1; (020) 7739 3701; (www.pitfieldbeershop.co.uk). A massive selection of bottled (and some draught) beer from Britain, Belgium and Germany is offered at this friendly store.

## VALUE ADDED TAX (VAT)

You are only eligible to reclaim the VAT on items you buy in Great Britain if you have not been in the United Kingdom for more than 365 days in the two years before the date you purchase the item. You must also intend to leave the United Kingdom with the purchased items within three months of the purchase date.

If you have lived in the UK for more than 365 days, in the two years before the date you purchase the items, you are considered a departing UK resident, and different VAT regulations apply.

To reclaim the VAT on items you buy in Great Britain, you must have the retailer fill out the export documentation, Form VAT 435.

Instead of taking your items through customs at the port or airport when you leave the UK, the retailer ships your goods directly to the ship or the freight forwarder for export. For more details, contact the Customs and Excise Department, or your international carrier.

# Chapter Thirteen:
# Continuing Education

The opportunities for continuing education in London are immense. Since we could not possibly list the thousands of programmes offered in London every year, this chapter focuses on those that are well known and repeatedly attended by members of the Junior League of London.

The cost of the courses varies and some mentioned here are quite costly. Do not hesitate to ask about the cost of the course at the same time that you enquire about dates and availability.

## COURSE LISTINGS

Don't let this list of courses limit you. There are a plethora of courses offered throughout Greater London. Floodlight and Hotcourses are the standard references for courses offered in London (www.floodlight.co.uk, www.hourcourses.co.uk). Floodlight guides are published three times a year: the March edition list summer courses, the July edition lists part-time and short courses offered throughout the academic year, and the October edition lists full-time courses. Hotcourses (formerly On Course) publishes Hotcourses Magazine, Hotcourses University and Career Guide, and Hotcourses World Study Guide.

These publications can be found at most bookshops and newsagents, but should you have difficulty they can also be ordered through Central Books on (020) 8986 4854.

## ADULT EDUCATION COURSES

Contact your local borough town hall for information on hundreds of adult education classes, ranging from pottery, car mechanics and Italian to degrees in social work. The fees are usually very reasonable because they are government subsidised and classes are held at various locations within your neighbourhood.

## ART HISTORY COURSES

Prices vary depending on the duration of the course and the institution. Many courses follow a semester or school year schedule; therefore it is advisable to call well in advance to secure a place. Additionally, many course offerings change based on current interest. For the most current curriculum content and schedule, call the school and ask for a brochure.

## Intensive Courses

Christie's Education, 5 King Street, St. James's, SW1Y, (020) 7747 6800, (www.christies.com). Christie's aim is to give students a firm and practical foundation of knowledge in the arts of the western world.

One year diploma courses or certificate courses (3 terms of 10 weeks each) are offered for the following:

The Early European Art Diploma Course – antiquity to Renaissance; Fine and Decorative Arts – Renaissance to present day; and Modern Art – late 19th century through contemporary

Evening Courses are also offered. They meet one evening a week for eight weeks and cover a variety of specialised subjects.

*The History of Art Studies*, 13 South Terrace, SW7, (020) 7584 6086, fax (020) 7584 0705, (www.historyofarts.com). Courses are held at the Linnean Society, Burlington House, Piccadilly, W1. Nearest tube: Piccadilly. Certificate and general interest lecture courses are available. Additionally, there are short courses on special topics, trips abroad, private views to exhibitions, and lectures held at various London museums.

*The New Study Centre*, 21 Palace Gardens Terrace, W8, (020) 7229 3393. Courses are held at The Royal Entomological Society, 41 Queen's Gate, SW7. The Decorative Arts Course is divided into four self-contained parts (which can be taken separately): 16th and 17th century, 18th century I, 18th century II, and 19th and 20th century. Other short courses and day visits to country houses are also available.

*Sotheby's Institute in London*, 30 Oxford Street, W1, (020) 7462 3232, (www.sothebys.com). The Institute runs over 30 courses in all aspects of fine and decorative art at both undergraduate and postgraduate levels. Internationally recognised courses offer unique first-hand examination of works of art with privileged access to auction rooms.

Full-time Courses are available in a large range of topics including: Styles in Art – An Introduction to Art history; Foundation Course in Asian Art; 17th and 18th Century Decorative Art; 19th and 20th Century Decorative Art; 19th and 20th Century Fine Art;; The Works of Art Course – MA in Fine and Decorative Art; MA in Contemporary Art; MA in Art Business; MA in East Asian Art; PhD in Applied and Decorative Arts. Acceptance by application and interview.

Evening Classes meet on weekday evenings from 6.00 to 8.00 p.m. starting in January, April and September each year. Classes include: English Furniture; Glass; Drawings and Prints; Silver; Decorative Interiors; British Art; Oriental Ceramics; European Pottery and Porcelain; London: The Contemporary Art Scene; Wine; Jewellery.

## One Day and Short Courses

*The Art Study Circle*, Sara Hebblethwaite, (020) 8788 6910. Art history lectures given weekly in an informal setting by experts in their fields. Some tie in with current exhibitions and include visits.

## COOKERY COURSES

### Books for Cooks

*Le Cordon Bleu Cookery School*, 114 Marylebone Lane, W1, (020) 7935 3503, (www.lecordonbleuparis.com). Nearest tube: Bond Street. Offers career training, short and part-time courses, practical and demonstration classes. Because this school is world famous, there is often a waiting list for its diploma and certificate courses. Cookery demonstrations are open to the public but require advance booking.

*Leith's School of Food and Wine*, 21 St. Alban's Grove, W8, (020) 7229 0177, (www.leiths.com). Nearest tube: High Street Kensington. Associated with Leith's restaurant, the school offers diploma and certificate courses in food and wine for all levels, and a variety of short cookery courses.

*Tante Marie School of Cookery*, Woodham House, Carlton Road, Woking, Surrey GU21, (01483) 726 957, (www.tantemarie.co.uk). Offers both certificate and diploma courses as well as occasional short course demonstrations. A wide range of cuisine is covered.

*Constance Spry Ltd.*, Moor Park House, Moor Park Lane, Farnham, Surrey GU9 8EN, (01252) 734 477, (www.constancespry.com). Offers a wide variety of one day cooking demonstrations held in conjunction with flower arranging courses (see Flower Arranging). Several week-long summer courses in entertaining also available.

## FLOWER ARRANGING COURSES

*Jane Packer Flower School*, 32-34 New Cavendish Street, W1, (020) 7486 1300, (www.janepacker.com). Nearest tube: Bond Street. Offers a four-week career course, a three day introductory course in Flower Arranging as well as courses in Dried Flowers, Christmas Decoration, Wedding Flowers and more. Evening and Saturday classes also available.

*Kenneth Turner*, 58 South Moulton Street, W1, (020) 7409 2560, (www.kenturnerflowerschool.com). One, two and three day courses available on a variety of arranging subjects.

*Paula Pryke Flowers*, 20 Penton Street, N1, (020) 7837 7373, (www.paula-pryke-flowers.com). One day courses on a variety of themes. Four day intensive courses and a four week career course available.

*Constance Spry Ltd.*, Moor Park House, Moor Park Lane, Farnham, Surrey GU9 8EN; (01252) 734 477, (www.constancespry.com). One day flower workshops and two day short courses covering a variety of arranging subjects.

## GARDENING COURSES

The British take great pride in their gardens, and the following courses are very comprehensive.

*The English Gardening School*, The Chelsea Physics Garden, 66 Royal Hospital Road, SW3, (020) 7352 4347, (www.englishgardeningschool.co.uk). Nearest tube: Sloane Square. Certificate courses in design and horticulture, held 1-2 days per week over a year. One to four day classes, on a wide range of topics such as Christmas wreaths and flower arranging, are offered. Additionally, there is a correspondence course in design available.

*The Inchbald School of Design: Garden Design*, 32 Eccleston Square, SW1, (020) 7630 9011, (www.inchbald.co.uk). Nearest tube: Victoria. A one year diploma course, a 10-week certificate course and a MA course. Subject matter includes: basic principles of design, plant knowledge, the role of fine art in design, garden architecture and business skills.

## INTERIOR DESIGN/DECORATION COURSES

*The Inchbald School of Design*, 7 Eaton Gate, SW1, (020) 7730 5508, (www.inchbald.co.uk). Nearest tube: Sloane Square. A one year diploma course, a 10-week certificate course and a MA course in interior design and decoration. Admission by interview and application.

*KLC School of Design*, 503 The Chambers, Chelsea Harbour, SW10, (020) 7376 3377, (www.klc.co.uk). Nearest tube: Fulham Broadway. Variety of courses in interior design and decoration.

## LANGUAGE COURSES

Institut Francais, 14 Cromwell Place, SW7, (020) 7581 2701, (www.institut.ambafrance.org.uk). The official French government centre of language and culture in London offers courses for all levels part-time or full-time, weekdays or weekends. Enrolment in a course provides access to the Institute's cultural centre, multimedia library, and children's library.

*University of Westminster*, 309 Regent Street, W1, (020) 7911 5000, (www.wmin.ac.uk). Offer courses in most European languages one evening a week from late September through May.

## MUSEUM AND GALLERY LECTURES

Most museums and galleries offer regular free lectures and tours. See Chapter Fourteen for museum addresses and telephone numbers. Call for a schedule of events, and to be placed on mailing lists. Information on talks and lectures, as well as new exhibits, can be found in the weekly magazine Time Out.

## UNIVERSITY AND COLLEGE COURSES

There are numerous courses available: undergraduate, graduate, part-time and full-time. Check to see whether the course might be credited to any degree you are planning to complete. Tuition fees vary and, if you have resided in the UK long enough, you might be eligible for 'home student tuition', which is generally half the overseas student fee. Check with the school.

*The Open University*, Walton Hall, Milton Keynes, MK7 6AA, (01908) 653 231, (www.open.ac.uk). Offers university courses to any resident of the European Union and Switzerland over 18 years of age. Methods of instruction include television courses, tutorials and correspondence work.

*The University of London*, Birkbeck College, Malet Street, London WC1, (020) 7631 6633, (www.bbk.ac.uk). Nearest tube: Russell Square. Offers certificate and diploma courses, as well as one and two term courses to anyone over 18 years of age. Classes usually meet 2 hours a week for 24 weeks.

## WINE COURSES

*Christie's Education*, 5 King Street, St. James's, SW1, 020 7747 6800, (www.christies.com). Offers an Introduction to Wine Tasting course (primarily focusing on French wines) that meets 1 evening a week for 5 weeks, available 6 times per year. Also runs one off Master Classes on fine and rare wines and occasional classes on wines of the New World. Wine Seminars abroad are also available.

*Sotheby's Wine Department*, 34-35 New Bond Street, W1, (020) 7293 6423, (www.sothebys.com). Nearest tube: Bond Street. Separate courses covering varietal and regional wines, running 1 evening a week for 5 weeks, offered twice per year. Occasional "one off" wine seminars are also available.

# Chapter Fourteen: Sports and Leisure

Sports and games are a huge part of British life. Many sports were invented, developed or codified by the British - golf, skiing, tennis and football to name but a few. Just about every sport is played somewhere, from the most popular "sport" of angling, with over 2.2 million participants, to the more arcane sports of lawnmower racing and curling. However, team games traditionally have a higher profile, with association football, rugby football and cricket the most popular, although golf, racing and motor sports have huge followings too.

## Brief British sporting vocabulary guide

| | |
|---|---|
| Test match | An international rugby or cricket match |
| Touts | Scalpers. Expensive and illegal sources of hard-to-find tickets. |
| Racing | Racing horses. Never horse-racing. |
| Athletics | Track and field |
| Football | Theoretically can be either association football (soccer) or rugby football, but usually refers to the former. NFL football is known as "American football". |
| Rugby | In London, usually taken to mean Rugby Union (15 a side), but in the North, Rugby League (13 a side) is more common. |
| Hockey | Always field hockey, and played by men and women. Ice hockey is ice hockey. |
| Rounders | A version of softball, usually played at school. |
| FA Cup | The main football knock-out competition, open to all clubs, amateur and professional, in England and Wales. |
| Premiership | An elite league of the best 20 football clubs in England and Wales |
| Six Nations | Premier northern hemisphere rugby competition between England, Wales, Scotland, Ireland, France and Italy, held in Jan/Feb. |
| The Open | The (British) Open Championship in golf. |
| Royal Ascot | A race meeting at Ascot in Berkshire in the third week in June, attended by the Queen. |

| The Derby | (Pronounced "dar-bee") Classic flat race for three year old horses in June, run on Epsom Downs in Surrey since 1780. |
|---|---|
| Grand National | World's best known race over fences, run at Aintree in early April. |
| Henley | Rowing regatta in the first week of July at Henley in Oxfordshire. |

## Spectator sports

Tickets to see the biggest sporting events are incredibly difficult to obtain, with the most sought after being Wimbledon tennis, the FA Cup Final, home Six Nations fixtures, Test cricket matches and the Formula One British Grand Prix. In addition, many Premiership football matches are season ticket only, with long waiting lists. Unless you have very good connections, or are prepared to pay vastly inflated prices on the black market, your best bet if you wish to experience one of these events may be to encourage your employer to purchase a corporate hospitality package, or best of all, to get yourself invited to someone else's corporate box or tent. Try *The Sporting Traveller* The Old Forge, 36b West Street, Reigate, Surrey RH2 9BX (01737) 244 398 and www.thesportingtraveller.com, or *Matchpoint* on (020) 8332 7384 or at www.matchpoint.co.uk which both offer deals for all these events. Your best advice: regardless of where you buy or find your tickets, get them early.

## Football

Association football, also known as soccer, is the national game, and every visitor should experience at least one game. The season runs from August until April, ending with the drama and passion of the *FA Cup Final* in May. FA Cup Finals are being temporarily held for the next few years at the Millennium Stadium in Cardiff, Wales until a new English national stadium is built. Nearly all tickets are allocated to season ticket holders of the two clubs contesting the Final, but there are always hospitality packages available for a price - expect to pay at least £500 per ticket (see agencies listed above).

## Premier League/Nationwide League

There are 12 professional football teams in London, of which six are currently in the Premier League. Of those six, *Arsenal*, *Chelsea*, and *Charlton* are season ticket only, with lengthy waiting lists. If you wish to see Premiership level soccer in London, it is possible to obtain match tickets relatively easily to see *Fulham*, *West Ham United* or *Tottenham Hotspur*. You will need to book several weeks in advance for "derby" matches against local London rivals, or matches against well-known teams such as Manchester United, but for other games it should be possible to purchase tickets a few days ahead. Most football clubs allow you to book via telephone or online. For fixtures and tickets try Ticketmaster on (020) 7316 4709 (www.ticketmaster.co.uk) or the individual club websites www.fulhamfc.co.uk, www.whufc.co.uk and www.spurs.co.uk. Alternatively, for easier access to tickets and a more representative taste of the national game, you could try one of the London clubs in Nationwide Division One (just below the Premier League). *Crystal Palace FC* (www.cpfc.co.uk) in south London has a reputation for being especially family-friendly.

## Going to the Game – some handy hints

- Professional football matches take place at weekends and on weekday evenings. The traditional kick-off times are 3pm Saturday, and 7.45pm during the week, but always be sure to check the day before because the time on your ticket can change at short notice due to TV schedules and police requests.

- Most football clubs welcome children, but book seats in the designated family areas, which will be non-smoking and specially stewarded.

- Expect opposing supporters to be strictly segregated. If you are ever offered a match ticket, check where it is. Avoid sitting with the away supporters unless you and your family are die-hard fans of the away team. Equally, you may be asked to leave by the stewards if you are seen to be supporting the away team in a home area.

- Take public transport to the game if at all possible. Roads around the ground may be blocked and parking will be virtually impossible.

- Do not try to take food or drink with you, as it will probably be confiscated. Not only do clubs prefer you to buy food from their own concessions, but cans and bottles are regarded as a safety hazard. Beer is available inside the stadium before the match, but cannot be taken to your seat and the bar will close as soon as the match is underway. This applies to corporate boxes as well.

- And finally: wrap up warm. Unless you are in a box, there will be no heating and your seats may not even be under cover. Matches are usually played rain or shine.

## Rugby football

There are two types of rugby played in England – rugby union (15 a side) and rugby league (13 a side). In London and the south, rugby union is far more popular. The English national team plays at Twickenham in West London, where Test matches, including the three "Six Nations" home matches, are played. In general, rugby matches have a more relaxed and friendly atmosphere than football matches and opposing supporters are not separated. Tailgate parties in the car park before and after matches are a longstanding Twickenham tradition.

Tickets for Twickenham are notoriously hard to obtain. Unless you are a playing or coaching member of a rugby club, your best bet is to book a hospitality package, which will include a ticket, lunch, tea and drinks. These are not cheap, and most are bought for corporate entertainment. Try Compass 0845 30 50 900 or *Peter Parfitt Sport* (01423) 874 874. Do not risk buying tickets from a tout – not only will it be very expensive but it's illegal and they may be forgeries. For more details and fixtures, visit www.rfu.com.

If you would like to see a domestic rugby match, there are several professional clubs based in London. The *Harlequins* (0871) 871 8877 (www.harlequins.co.uk) play just down the road from Twickenham, and tickets are usually easy to obtain.

## Golf

The biggest annual golfing event is the Open Championship, which is rotated around links (seaside) courses around England and Scotland. Admission tickets and hospitality may be booked online at www.britishopengolf.co.uk or by phone on (01253) 780 000. You will need to book in early spring for general admission tickets.

## Tennis

Tennis is a minority sport in the UK with a very low profile - except for during the All-England Championships (otherwise known as "Wimbledon") fortnight in June when the whole nation seems to go tennis-mad, particularly if a British player manages to survive the first week. There are four main ways to see the tournament:

Firstly, put an application into the public ballot for a pair of show court tickets. You will need to send a stamped self-addressed envelope to: The All England Lawn Tennis & Croquet Club, PO Box 98, Wimbledon, London SW19, between August 1 and December 31 the year before you wish to attend.

Secondly, if your family is a member of the Lawn Tennis Association, you may enter the LTA Advantage ballot for tickets. For more details contact (020) 7381 7037 or www.lta.org.uk/advantage.

Thirdly, some tickets go on sale on the day of play. Be warned that queues are very long. Expect to have to queue overnight for show court tickets, or to start queuing at 7am for Ground Admission Tickets, of which 6000 are available each day. These entitle use of the No.2 Court standing enclosure and unreserved seating and standing round Courts 3-19. Alternatively, many Londoners choose to visit Wimbledon in the late afternoon/early evening, when show court tickets are resold for charity once their original holders (often corporate hospitality guests) have left for the day.

Catering at Wimbledon is excellent, if expensive. Strawberries, champagne, lobster and Pimms are all available within the grounds, but you can also take your own picnic. There is a large, atmospheric grassy picnic area known as "The Hill" with a large screen relaying live action from the show courts.

Lastly, if all else fails, there is always corporate hospitality. Try:

*Keith Prowse*, 4th Floor, Elvin House, Stadium Way, Wembley, Middlesex HA9 0DW (020) 8795 2222 (www.keithprowse.co.uk)

*Sportsworld*, New Abbey Court, Stert Street ,Abingdon, Oxon OX14 3JZ, (01235) 555 844 . Expect to pay at least £500 per person for the day.

# RACING

## Cheltenham National Hunt Festival

The most important jump racing meeting in the calendar, featuring the Gold Cup, takes place in March. Apply for tickets and book accommodation from 30 September. Discount scheme for early purchases. Cheltenham Racecourse, Prestbury Park, Cheltenham, Gloucestershire. (0124) 251 3014 (www.cheltenham.co.uk).

## Grand National

The Grand National, held at Aintree in Liverpool, is perhaps the most famous steeplechase in the world: a 4.5 mile race over very challenging fences. Tickets are relatively inexpensive and plentiful - contact (0151) 522 2929 (www.aintree.co.uk) for details.

## Ascot

Race meetings are held at Ascot year round – jump racing in the winter and flat racing in the summer. Royal Ascot, in June, is perhaps the most famous meeting: the Queen, who is herself an avid owner, always attends it. Foreign nationals may obtain tickets for the Royal Enclosure at Royal Ascot by application to their embassy or high commission. Morning dress, military dress or national dress for men, and hats and skirts for ladies must be worn. Alternatively, you can buy tickets for other enclosures from Ascot Racecourse, Ascot, Berkshire, (01344) 622 211.

# CRICKET

Cricket is the English summer national game, and is famously said to be incomprehensible to foreigners. In fact, it shares many of the same principles as baseball and is easy to follow once the basic terms are understood. Many argue that there is nothing more peaceful than spending an afternoon beside a village cricket green lounging on a picnic rug, reading the weekend papers and sipping a cup of tea or glass of wine. Alternatively you can experience the excitement and atmosphere of a one-day international or a five-day Test match at either the Oval or Lord's cricket grounds in London. Contact the *English Cricket Board* on 0870 533 8833 or at www.ecb.co.uk for fixtures and tickets.

# US SPORTS

## Basketball

London has its own basketball team, the *London Towers* whose season runs from September until March. Although most of the players are North American, the standard is unsurprisingly not as high as in the NBA. The Towers play home fixtures at the Crystal Palace National Sports Centre, off Anerley Hill, Upper Norwood, SE19 - ring (020) 8776 7755 for fixtures and tickets.

## Ice Hockey

London has a professional ice hockey team, the *Knights*. Based at the London Arena in the Docklands, the Knights play teams from across Europe, from September until March. For fixtures and tickets: ring (020) 7538 1212, (www.knightice.co.uk) or Ticketmaster.

## Baseball/ Softball

Baseball is more or less non-existent in the UK as a spectator sport. Several of the big US law firms, management consultancies and banks have softball teams that play in London parks.

See Chapter 8 - Children for children's sports, including basketball and softball leagues.

## FITNESS AND SPORTS FACILITIES

Most boroughs have a variety of public recreational facilities, such as pools, tennis courts, aerobics classes and parks. Call your local council for location, costs, and availability. Some councils run a residents discount scheme, such as Westminster's ResCard, which entitles members to substantial reductions on public gym memberships.

Below are listed some of the more 'well known' facilities that are frequented regularly by League members and their families. For a more complete list, refer to *London Man*, a reference guide to London clubs and facilities, published annually. Also, check your local residents' magazine (e.g., *The Hill* magazine for Kensington residents) for the most up-to-date information on new club openings.

### Private Health Clubs and Gyms

There are many health clubs and gyms located throughout London. Membership rates and services provided vary according to the quality and location of the club. Many clubs have off peak memberships that cost less than a full membership and, in general, allow you to use the club on weekdays from 09.00-17.00. Additionally, many have flexible payment schedules to accommodate instalments on a monthly basis. Telephone for membership rate information.

---

*Did you know...*London health clubs and gyms are generally expensive to join and often demand a guarantee of at least one year's commitment. When thinking about joining one, always ask for at least a fortnight's trial, and if necessary shop around to find the right one for you.

---

*Alan Herdman Studios*, 17 Homer Row, W1, (020) 7723 9953. Nearest tube: Edgware Road. Practices the Pilates Technique, including body conditioning and corrective exercise.

*The Armoury*, 25 Pond Street, Hampstead, NW3; (020) 7431 2263. Nearest tube:

Belsize Park. Aerobic classes, Treadmills, Stairmaster, Lifecycle, free weights, Cybex equipment, personal training, children's classes and sunbed facilities.

*The Berkeley Club and Spa*, The Berkeley, Wilton Place, SW1, (020) 7201 1699. Nearest tube: Knightsbridge. Expensive, but one of the only pools in London with a sliding roof for summer, and a good place to spot filmstars staying at the hotel. Full spa service, aqua aerobics, personal training, Powersport runners, Lifestride treadmill, Lifecycles, Concept II rower and Cybex weight machines.

*Cannons Sports Clubs*, Many locations across the City, making it handy for after work visits. Some have pools, some do not. Good value. (020) 7283 0101.

*Champneys, The London Club*, 21A Piccadilly, W1, (020) 7255 8000. Nearest tube: Piccadilly. Expensive. Pool, squash, gym, Cybex machines, sauna, steam room, solarium, beauty facilities, two dance studios and restaurant.

*Cottons Health and Fitness*, London Bridge City, Tooley Street, SE1, (020) 7403 1171. Nearest tube: London Bridge. Pool, squash, aerobics, fitness training, jacuzzi, sauna, steam room, beauty facilities, physiotherapy and restaurant.

*The Dorchester Spa*, The Dorchester, 53 Park Lane, W1, (020) 7629 8888. Nearest tube: Hyde Park Corner. Precor treadmills, Technogym weight equipment, Stairmasters, rowers, Lifecycle bike, Concept II rower, personal training and spa treatments.

*Esporta*, Fitness centre chain with more spacious facilities than most: some, such as the Riverside Club in Chiswick, are more like country clubs with tennis courts, outdoor swimming pools and lots of children's facilities. London branches include: Wandsworth, Chiswick, Kingston, Islington, Swiss Cottage and Wimbledon. (0118) 912 3500, (www.esporta.com).

*The Harbour Club*, Watermeadow Lane, SW6, (020) 7371 7700. Nearest tube: Fulham Broadway. Pool with separate baby area, tennis (indoor/outdoor), aerobics, fitness training, restaurant, beauty facilities, crèche and a variety of children's activities, including gymnastics, karate, ballet, tennis and swimming.

*Holmes Place*, An upper end chain with 28 branches in Greater London. Be warned that facilities can vary enormously between branches while prices tend not to. Most have pools; a few have indoor running tracks, separate men's and women's gyms, crèches and restaurants. Varied studio programme includes aerobics, spinning, Pilates and yoga. (0800) 106 050, (www.holmesplace.co.uk).

*Living Well*, Another national chain – mid-priced. (0870) 600 7001 for your nearest location or see www.livingwell.co.uk. All the basics, not too many frills.

*The Peak*, Hyatt Carlton Hotel, Cadogan Place, Knightsbridge, SW1; (020) 7858 7008. Beautifully located in an atrium of the hotel, offers a pool, yoga and pilates classes, full fitness studio, restaurant and bar. A variety of treatments are available.

> **Did you know...**If you still have questions regarding the right health club for you, Health and Fitness magazine has a good web-site with a comprehensive summary of what London has to offer (www.hfonline.co.uk/features/feature16/peak.html).

## Cycling

Cycling on the streets of London is legal but can be dangerous. Cycle routes and lanes are marked throughout the city for safer riding. A map of cycle routes is available at your local council office and libraries. Please note that lights are compulsory after dark if you are cycling on the street, and that cycling on pavements (sidewalks) is illegal.

*Hyde Park* – on marked bicycle paths. On Sundays, South Carriage Drive and Constitution Hill and the Mall near Buckingham Palace are closed to cars.

*Off Road Cycling* – parts of Wimbledon Common and Richmond Park.

*Road Safety Unit*, Royal Borough of Kensington and Chelsea, The Town Hall, Hornton Street, W8, (020) 7361 3170. Children's cycling safety classes.

*London Cycling Campaign*, Tree House, 3 Stamford Street, SE1, (020) 7928 7220. Can provide very good cycling maps of London.

*Kensington and Chelsea Cyclists*, 24 Bartok House, 30 Lansdowne Walk, W11, (020) 7727 8872. Contact: Paul Krebbs.

## Dance and Fitness Classes

*British Military Fitness*, (020) 7751 9742, (www.britmilfit.com). For something different, try army-style training in London's parks! Classes are held by army or marine instructors most days in Hyde Park, Battersea Park, Clapham Common and Blackheath for varied ability ranges.

*Danceworks*, 16 Balderton Street, W1, (020) 7629 6183. Nearest tube: Bond Street. A variety of dance, aerobic and Pilates classes.

*English National Ballet*, 39 Jay Mews, SW7, (020) 7581 1245. Adult ballet class one evening a week. All levels.

*The Grove*, 182-184 Kensington Church Street, W8, (020) 7221 2266. Nearest tube: Kensington High Street or Notting Hill. Personalised exercise classes based on Pilates; also one-on-one training.

*The Life Centre*, 15 Edge Street, W8, (020) 7221 4602. Nearest tube: Kensington High Street or Notting Hill. Classes include yoga, Pilates and tai chi.

*Pilates Institute*, Wimborne House, 151 - 155 New North Road, N1, (020) 7253 3177, (www.pilates-institute.co.uk). This organisation will provide you with a list of qualified Pilates teachers in and around London.

*The Pineapple Dance Studio*, 7 Langley Street, WC2, (020) 7836 4004. Nearest tube: Covent Garden. A variety of dance classes for beginners to professionals.

*Triyoga*, 6 Erskine Road, Primrose Hill, London NW3, (020) 7483 3344 (www.triyoga.co.uk). Vast array of yoga and Pilates classes for all standards and ages. Also offers post-natal yoga and baby massage classes.

*The Health Yoga Studio*, Ofra Graham, 171 West, Heath Road, Hampstead, NW3

## Golf

There are, unsurprisingly, very few golf courses in central London, although there are some hidden- away driving ranges. The courses and ranges below are all open to the public (and you do not need a handicap to play but offer preferential rates and booking times if you become a member. Do not expect golf carts – these are rare in the UK.

Note that at smarter and more traditional golf clubs, shirts with collars are obligatory for both sexes, and ladies shorts should be knee length. Some clubs also require men to wear knee length socks with shorts. Ask your host beforehand if in any doubt.

### Driving ranges/ Golf lessons

*Alex Saary*, (07799) 676 307, (alexsaary@zoom.co.uk). Excellent young, professional golf instructor based in Northwest London. Specialises in short game, golf psychology and fitness, but highly recommended all round.

*Ealing Golf Range*, Rowdell Road, Northolt, (020) 8845 4967. Big range very convenient for the A40. Tuition (lessons), pro shop, bar and new short game area.

*Knightsbridge Golf School*, 47 Lowndes Square, London SW1, (020) 7235 2468, (www.knightsbridgegolfschool.com). An underground driving range in a converted squash court! Good reputation for tuition. KGS members receive a discount on green fees at Stoke Park Golf Club in Buckinghamshire.

*Regent's Park Golf School*, Outer Circle, Regent's Park, NW1, (020) 7724 0643. Short driving range, small pitching area, tuition and shop.

*TopGolf*, Bushey Mill Lane, Watford, Hertfordshire, (01923) 222 045, (www.topgolf.co.uk). A bit further out of London, but worth it for the heated bays, food delivery service and the microchips inside each ball, which tell you exactly how far and where each ball is hit. Tuition, putting course, shop, café, children's parties.

### Golf courses

All the below welcome non-members on a casual basis.

*Central London Golf Centre*, Burntwood Lane Wandsworth SW17, (020) 8871 2468, (www.clgc.co.uk). Young, informal club with a 9 hole course and driving range.

Club hire available and tuition (lessons) offered, including a good value group beginners course.

*Chiswick Dukes Meadow Golf Course*, Chiswick, W4, (020) 8995 0537. Driving range and an all par-3 9-hole golf course. Instruction available, but no club hire.

*Richmond Golf Course*, (020) 8876 3205. Two 18-hole golf courses.

*Stockley Park Golf Course*, (near Heathrow) (020) 8561 6339. 'Pay as you play' European PGA 18-hole golf course.

**Hiking** – see Walking

**Ice Skating**

*Queen's Ice Bowl*, Queensway, W2, (020) 7229 0172. Skate hire on premises.

*Broadgate Ice Rink*, Broadgate Circle, EC2, (020) 7505 4068. Nearest tube: Liverpool Street. Small circular outdoor rink is open October to early April. Skate hire and lessons available.

*Somerset House*, The Strand. Nearest tube: Charing Cross. (020) 7845 4670, (www.somerset-house.org.uk). December to January only.

**Martial Arts**

*The Budokwai*, GK House, 4 Gilston Road, SW10, (020) 7370 1000. Nearest tube: South Kensington or Gloucester Road. Offers a range of instruction in judo, karate and aikido for beginners through advanced level. Judo classes for children.

*Kamon Wing Chun at the Pineapple Dance Studios*. Address as above, and www.kamonwingchun.com. Kevin Chan teaches this very direct and practical version of kung-fu, called Wing Chun.

**Personal Trainers**

Personal fitness trainers are an increasingly popular alternative/addition to the use of health club facilities. They can provide a programme to meet your individual fitness needs within your time schedule.

*Brian Brown*, (07973) 896 102. Over 15 years experience in the fitness industry. Specialising in pre and post natal and weight-loss programmes in the Kensington and Chelsea area.

*British Military Fitness* (see Fitness classes above)

*Citifit*, (020) 7299 9595 (www.citifit.com). Offers one to one fitness training in the gym or at home; also sport specific training and nutritional advice. Prices start from £35 for an individual session.

*Julia Swift*, RSA; (020) 7289 0494. Individualised programmes for cardiovascular fitness, body sculpting, pre and post natal exercise and diet and nutrition. Works with individuals or very small groups.

# Rowing

There are many boat clubs along the Thames which train and compete in crews for regattas and "head" races, the most famous of which are the Henley Royal Regatta in July, and the Head of the River Race on the Thames in March. Most also have active social programmes and are an excellent way to meet new people.

*Thames Rowing Club*, Embankment, Putney, SW15. Nearest tube: Putney Bridge. (www.thamesrc.co.uk). A big, successful club with men's, women's and junior sections. Beginners welcome.

*Kingston Rowing Club*, The Boathouse, Canbury Gardens, Lower Ham Road, Kingston-on-Thames (020) 8546 8592, (www.kingstonrc.co.uk). Men/women – beginners welcome.

# Running

*British Military Fitness*, (see Fitness classes above) Running club in Hyde Park on Thursday evenings.

# Riding

Equipment can usually be hired from the stables for a small fee. Hard hats are compulsory in the UK.

*Hyde Park Riding Stables*, 63 Bathurst Mews, W2, (020) 7723 2813. Nearest tube: Lancaster Gate. Also has (more expensive) stables and livery at 11 Elvaston Mews, SW7, (020) 7823 7300. Nearest tube: Gloucester Road. Horses available for hire to ride in Hyde Park. Lessons available.

*Kingston Riding Centre*, 38 Crescent Road, Kingston Upon Thames, KT2, (020) 8546 6361. Lessons available. Famous for their "Pimm's Hacks" through Richmond Park on summer evenings.

*Wimbledon Village Stables*, 24A/B High Street, SW19; (020) 8946 8579. Lessons available.

# Sailing

*Little Ship Club*, Bell Wharf Lane, Upper Thames Street, London, EC4, (020) 7236 7729, (www.little-ship-club.co.uk). Unique sailing club based in the City of London with restaurant, bar and guest rooms. Holds sailing trips and rallies at clubs across Southern England, plus RYA training and lots of social events. New members welcome to visit on Tuesday nights – and no boat of your own is required!

*Ranelagh Sailing Club*, Embankment, Putney SW15, (020) 8788 4986, (www.ranelagh-sc.co.uk). Friendly club offering year round sailing on the Thames. Contact the Commodore, Christopher Edwards on (020) 8788 3094.

*Sail UK*, Lake Yard, Poole; Ocean Village, Southampton; & East Cowes (01202) 668 410 www.sailuk.net. Offers sailing lessons in the Solent.

### Shooting

*West London Shooting School*, Northolt; (020) 8845 1377. Sporting clays.

*Holland & Holland*, West Ruislip (01923) 825 349. Sporting clays. All the instructors are good, but Ken Davies is especially recommended.

### Swimming

Your borough council can provide a list of local public pools. A list of all swimming pools and their facilities in Greater London may be obtained from Sport England, P.O. Box 480, Jubilee Stand, Crystal Palace National Sports Centre, Ledrington Road, SE19, (020) 8778 8600. Also see Private Health Clubs and Gyms.

### Tennis

There is a range of options for the tennis enthusiast in London. You can either enjoy the luxurious facilities of a private club, or take advantage of the public courts in the parks, which can be extremely good value.

### Public/open courts

*Battersea Park*, (020) 8871 7542. 19 courts. No racquet hire available.

*Hyde Park*, South Carriage Drive, Hyde Park, (020) 7262 3474. Six courts. Racquet hire available.

*Regents Park Tennis Centre*, York Bridge, Inner Circle, Regent's Park NW1, (020) 7486 4216, (www.rptc.co.uk). Nearest tube: Baker Street or Regents Park. 12 hard courts in a lovely setting. Tuition (lessons), café, changing rooms. Membership is not essential.

### Private Tennis Clubs

*The Campden Hill Lawn Tennis Club*, 9 Aubrey Walk, W8; (020) 7727 4050.

*Carlton Tennis Club*, 1 Alfred Road, Westbourne Green, W2; (020) 7286 1985.

*David Lloyd Tennis Centre*, 1 Southall Lane, Hounslow, Middlesex PW5, (020) 8573 9378. Located near Heathrow Airport. Tennis (10 indoor/9 outdoor courts), squash, badminton, pool, aerobics, fitness training, crèche, restaurant and beauty facilities.

*The Harbour Club* (see Private Health Clubs and Gyms).

*Magdalen Park Tennis Club*, SW18, (020) 8874 8313. Very friendly and social, with nice clubhouse. 8 hard courts, 6 floodlit. Juniors welcome. New members are advised to visit at weekends between 12 and 4pm and ask for a committee member.

### Walking

### Inside London

See the list of parks further on in this chapter. In addition, there are a number of established routes and guided tours to try:

The *Thames Path* is a 180 mile-long National Trail that follows the course of the Thames, from Thames Head near Kemble in the Cotswolds, to the Thames Barrier in east London. As well as passing through central London, it also takes in historic places such as Oxford, Henley, Windsor and Greenwich. This would be a good route to tackle in sections over a number of weekends. For more information, try the book *Thames Path – by David Sharp* or write for the free guide *Accessible Thames: Ten easily accessible walks by the Thames in West London* with a 44p SAE from Thames Landscape Strategy, Holly Lodge, Richmond Park, Richmond TW10 5HS.

*Saturday Strolls*, The Inner London Ramblers Association (ILRA) runs regular free guided walks in the London area. They are 5 - 7 miles long and start and finish at public transport points within Travelcard zones. You do not need to book - just turn up at the designated station entrance. Call the ILRA hotline on (020) 7370 6180, contact the organiser, Les Douglas at 8 Faircroft, 37 St Andrew's Grove, London N16, or visit www.zoom.connectfree.co.uk/inlonarea for a list of upcoming walks

*Canal and riverside walks* The ILRA also runs free Wednesday evening walks featuring a canal or river. The pace is gentle and there are frequent stops along the route and places of interest pointed out. All walks start at 18.45 and last for approximately two hours, with both the start and finish accessible by public transport. The walks always end with a visit to a nearby pub! Details on the website above or contact the walk leader Mike Biggs on (020) 7274 1853.

Also, the following three guides may be useful to you:

✓ *Time Out Book of London Walks (Vols 1 & 2) – ed Andrew White* A compendium of London walks contributed by famous London residents

✓ *WALK THIS WAY – architecture and history at your feet* – two guides to walks in London which can be obtained for free by ringing (020) 7928 2442

✓ *Travelcard Walks in West London – Margaret Sharp.*

## Outside London

In addition, within as little as one hour from central London by train or car, you can walk in beautiful countryside on many public footpaths and trails. Two easily accessible trails by train are the North Downs Way (see the *Official Guide to the North Downs Way* by Neil Curtis and Jim Walker) and the 1066 Country Walk (see *The 1066 Country Walk* by Brian Smailes or visit www.1066country.com).

Try the following for more ideas and information on hiking and walking in the UK:

✓ *Trail* magazine is a useful resource for ideas on where to walk in the UK and Europe.

✓ *Ramblers Association* (020) 7339 8500 (www.ramblers.org.uk). The "Ramblers" are a leading British hiking organisation and pressure group. Their website contains a list of and links to all the National Parks, Forests and Areas of

Outstanding Natural Beauty in the UK, plus general information and advice on walking, routes and accommodation, as does their book, *The Rambler's Yearbook and Accommodation Guide*. The Ramblers have a central London branch which runs regular day long walks in the South of England for its members. Contact the Membership Secretary for Westminster, Kensington and Chelsea: Sue King, 161 Shirland Road, London W9, (020) 7286 6447.

✓ *The Long Distance Walkers Association*, 63 Yockley Close, Camberley GU15, (www.ldwa.org.uk). A members' organisation would be worth joining if you are planning to do some serious walking while in the UK. The website has information on all the UK's Long Distance Paths.

## PARKS

There are over 80 parks within a seven-mile radius of Hyde Park Corner. Most parks are open from dawn until dusk.

*Alexandra Park and Palace*, Wood Green, N22; Skating rink, boating pool, children's concerts, pitch and putt, animal enclosures, adventure playground and play park.

*Battersea Park*, Albert Bridge Road, SW11; Boating lake, zoo, deer park, tennis, children's play park (adventure playground), London Peace Pagoda and herb garden.

*Chelsea Physic Garden*, 66 Royal Hospital Road, SW3

*Classed Park*, Green Lane, N4; Fishing lake, bowling green, adventure playground, croquet lawn, football, tennis and putting green.

*Crystal Palace Park*, Penge, Thicket Road, SE19; Boating and bands during the summer; adventure playground.

*Golders Hill Park*, North End Road, Golders Green, NW11. Playground, nice sandpit, lots of animals to feed (deer, goats, ducks and flamingoes), good cafe and beautiful gardens.

*Greenwich Park*, SE10, Deer park, bird sanctuary and Royal Observatory.

*Hampstead Heath*, Parliament Hill, NW3. Ponds, concerts in summer, grass skiing, adventure playground and tennis. (See Cultural Events for more details)

*Hampton Court Palace*, Surrey, KT8. Famous maze, open March to October, "great vine", ponds and natural farmland.

*Highgate Woods*, Several entrances; Muswell Hill Road, Fortis Green, N6-N10 and Archway Road. Wonderful new adventure playground (for under 5's and over 5's), picnic area and lovely vegetarian cafe.

*Holland Park*, (W8) Nearest tubes: Holland Park and Kensington High Street. Tulip and rose gardens, peacocks, tennis, adventure playground, sandpits, and a playground for children under 5. There is opera in summer against a backdrop of Holland House.

*Hyde Park*, (W2) Nearest tubes: Hyde Park Corner, Marble Arch, Lancaster Gate. Lake for fishing, boating, swimming, riding, tennis, concerts and fairs.

*Kensington Gardens*, (W2) Nearest tubes: Bayswater, South Kensington. Peter Pan's statue, children's playgrounds and round pond for model boats, the Princess Diana Memorial playground.

*Primrose Hill*, (NW1) Nearest tubes: Camden Town, Chalk Farm. Excellent views of London, and a famous bonfire and firework display on Guy Fawkes Day.

*Regent's Park*, (NW8) Nearest tubes: Baker Street, Regent's Park. Home of London Zoo and the Open-Air Theatre. Tennis, golf, boating lake and rose garden.

*Richmond Park*, Surrey, (TW10) Fish ponds, deer park, golf, riding and cycling paths.

*Royal Botanic Garden*, Kew, (TW9); Lake, aquatic garden, pagoda, Kew Palace and Palm House.

*St. James's Park* and *Green Park*, (SW1) Nearest tubes: Green Park, Charing Cross. Oldest Royal Park with lake, bridges and bird sanctuary.

*Thorpe Park*, Staines Road, Chertsey, Surrey; (01932) 562633. Amusement park for children offering attractions, shows, rides and exhibits. Open June to August, seven days a week. Other times vary.

---

**Did you know...**For an excellent resource on all that England has to offer, join the National Trust. This is a guide to stately properties throughout the UK and entitles you discounts on many admissions. (08704) 584 000.

---

# Chapter Fifteen:
# Travel and Culture

The opportunity to travel throughout the United Kingdom and Europe is one of the great advantages of living in London.

Guidebooks, bucket shops for discount tickets and travel agents are good resources for planning your trip. Package tours can be arranged for inexpensive or luxurious holidays and include airfare for either a scheduled or charter flight and hotel accommodation. Package tours may include airport transportation, sightseeing trips, private accommodation in a villa, ski chalet, or apartment and car hire. It is easy to book package tours through any travel agency or tour operator.

If you are interested in staying in smaller inns or Bed and Breakfasts, it is advisable to call them directly to make arrangements, as most travel agencies do not book smaller lodgings.

It is normally advisable to arrange your holidays well in advance, especially for peak holiday times. School and traditional holidays, such as Christmas and Easter, bank holiday weekends and the month of August are popular holiday times. Most English, Europeans and Americans take their holidays in August; it may be wise to avoid this busy month for trips to resort areas, although major European business cities are quieter and will often offer special rates.

If you have the flexibility, it is possible to make a late booking just a few weeks or even days in advance. Prices for package holidays drop considerably when airline seats, reserved hotels or ski chalets are not filled to capacity.

## Before you travel

### Paying for your holiday

Be aware that some ticket brokers and travel agents will charge you extra to pay by credit card for holidays and flights. It may be worth doing so, however, because most credit card companies provide refunds if you have paid with their card and your travel agent or ticket broker then goes out of business.

### Health & safety

The British *Foreign Office* can provide you with up-to-date country specific advice, which can be vital if you are travelling outside Europe and North America. Call (020) 7008 0232 (www.fco.gov.uk/knowbeforeyougo).

For health information and tips on travelling in tropical countries, visit the website of *University College London Hospital* at www.uclh.org/services/htd/advice.shtml. If you think you may require immunisations before travelling, contact the not-for-profit organisation *MASTA (Medical Advisory Services for Travellers Abroad)* at www.masta.org or on (09068) 224 100 at least 6 weeks before you travel. MASTA will provide you with a Health Brief specifying which jabs (immunisation shots) you need, which you can then take to one of their network of travel clinics (call 01276 685 040 to find the nearest one), to another clinic such as the walk-in *British Airways Travel Clinic*, 156 Regent Street W1, (020) 7439 9584, *Trailfinders* (020) 7938 3999 www.trailfinders.com or to your own doctor. Some immunisations, such as Polio and tetanus, and sometimes hepatitis and meningitis, are free on the NHS, while others may be charged for or may not be easily available at your doctor. If you need several immunisations, it may be worth shopping around as prices vary considerably.

Lastly, the Department of Health's travel site offers advice on getting treatment when you are abroad, via the reciprocal health care agreements the UK has with other countries. (www.doh.gov.uk/traveladvice).

## Insurance

Package tour operators will always try to sell you their own holiday insurance. It is rarely worth buying it – for one thing if the operator goes out of business you have nowhere to turn. Better value, if you travel abroad more than twice a year, is annual multi-trip cover bought independently. Try www.fco.gov.uk/travel for a list of reputable travel insurers and tips on what to look for in your policy, American Express is reliable and helpful and offers multi-trip insurance from £56 on www.americanexpress.co.uk or call (0800) 028 7573.

## Five unique ideas for short holiday breaks from London...

1) Spend a relaxing week steering a narrow boat along one of Britain's many canals. Try *Hoseasons* (0870) 902 3113 or www.hoseasons.co.uk

2) Fly to Dublin for a weekend of Guinness-drinking, music and local "craic". Stay at the ultra cool *Morrison Hotel* tel +353 1 887 2400.

3) Catch the Eurostar to Brussels for a sumptuous gourmet lunch or maybe just a plate of "moules frites". Contact (0990) 186 186 (www.eurostar.co.uk).

4) Go walking in the Lake District. Rent a cottage from *Heart of the Lakes*, (01539) 432 321 or www.heartofthelakes.co.uk.

5) Sip lingonberry vodka cocktails in the IceBar and sleep on reindeer skins at the *IceHotel* in northern Sweden, +46 980 66 800 or go to www.icehotel.com

## Buying air tickets

Most British and European airlines will not offer you the best available rates if you call the airline directly – discounts are only obtained from ticket brokers, bucket shops or travel agents.

The exceptions to this rule are the low-cost, low-frills airlines, such as *Go, Buzz, Ryanair* and *EasyJet*. These airlines offer low prices to many European cities direct to the customer. Be warned however, that many of the low cost airlines' routes do not fly to the closest airport to the city advertised and that you may face a long journey to reach the city centre – for example Ryanair's London-Venice route is in reality Stansted - Treviso.

## Ticket Brokers and Bucket Shops

Ticket brokers offer charter flights at a discount. Most charter flights are linked to package tours, but ticket brokers will sell tickets on a seat-only basis. Some brokers also offer discounted seats on "scheduled" (non-charter) airlines.

Bucket shops sell unofficially discounted air tickets on charter and scheduled routes to the Continent, Asia and elsewhere at large reductions. A good bucket shop only requires a nominal deposit. If booking a flight through a bucket shop, check with the airline directly to make sure that you are listed on the passenger list.

You will find ticket broker and bucket shop advertisements in the travel sections of the Sunday and daily newspapers and in the back of *Time Out Magazine*.

Always confirm the terms and conditions of any discount fares, which may include a required length of stay and cancellation charges. You may want to purchase travel insurance for coverage in the event of cancellation. It is recommended to only use IATA (International Airline Transport Association), ABTA (Association of British Travel Agents) or ATOL (Air Tours Operators Licence) approved travel agents and ticket brokers, as many travellers have been stranded when some of the less reliable companies suddenly folded.

## Travel Agents

Call *The Air Travel Advisory Bureau* (020) 7636 5000 to find out which travel agencies offer the best fares to your destinations.

The following travel agents are IATA, ABTA and ATOL approved:

| | | |
|---|---|---|
| Abercrombie & Kent | (020) 7730 9600 | |
| Flightbookers | (020) 7757 2000 | |
| Goodacre & Townsend | (020) 7702 1166 | |
| Thomas Cook | (020) 7499 4000 | |
| Trailfinders | (020) 7938 3939 | (long haul) |
| | (020) 7937 5400 | (European and Trans-Atlantic) |

## AIRPORTS

There are five airports conveniently located close to London. The British Airports Authority (BAA) operates the largest three. Its very useful website www.baa.co.uk

has real-time arrivals boards for each airport which you can check before setting out to meet a flight.

## London Heathrow Airport

Hounslow, Middlesex TW6 1JH
(020) 8759 4321 (flight enquiries)
(0345) 405 000 (car park information)

Heathrow, 15 miles to the west of London, is the busiest international airport in the world, with over 90 airlines carrying over 60 million passengers a year. It is also very large, with four terminals and a fifth planned. Terminal 4, the newest, is a considerable distance by road from the others, and extra time should be allowed to reach it, or to transfer between terminals. Check your departure terminal before you begin your journey to Heathrow.

*In general*, departures are scheduled as follows:

Terminal 1: British and Irish airlines; British Airways' domestic and (most) European flights.

Terminal 2: European airlines

Terminal 3: International airlines

Terminal 4: British Airways: all its intercontinental flights, and its flights to Paris, Amsterdam, Moscow, and Athens.

You can travel to Heathrow by train, tube, bus, taxi or car. Most services run between 05:00 and 23:30.

*Train,* The Heathrow Express is the fastest way to reach the airport from Central London. The journey takes 15 minutes between Paddington station and Terminals 1, 2 or 3, and 20 minutes to Terminal 4. Trains run every 15 minutes. A one-way ticket costs £14 if bought on the train, or £11 if purchased online or by phone. If you have heavy luggage, be warned that there is a fairly long walk at the other end to reach the terminals. (0845) 600 1515, (www.heathrowexpress.co.uk).

> **Did you know...** You can check your baggage for some airlines at Paddington Station.

*Tube,* The Piccadilly Line connects central London and Heathrow's two tube stations (one for Terminals 1,2 and 3, and one for Terminal 4). Trains run every 5 minutes at peak times and every 9 minutes off peak and at weekends. Journey time is roughly one hour from Central London.

*Bus,* The A2 Airbus runs every 30 minutes from King's Cross to Heathrow, via Knightsbridge and Kensington. Passengers are dropped off close to check-in at each terminal. The journey takes approximately 55 minutes from the stop outside

**TRAVEL AND CULTURE**

Holland Park tube and 90 minutes from Kings Cross. Pay the £7 one way fare on board. (020) 8400 6690, (www.gobycoach.com).

**Licensed black cabs** in central London will always take passengers to Heathrow. The fare will vary on traffic and time of day but is generally £40-50 from central London. Some black cab drivers will accept pre-booked trips for a set fare.

**Fly Away Valet** is a service for travellers who wish to drive themselves to Heathrow. They will collect your vehicle from you at the terminal, and have it waiting for you upon your return. For an additional fee they will wash, wax and service your car while you are away. Call (020) 8759 1567 or (020) 8759 2020 with your terminal, travel dates and time.

## London Gatwick Airport

Gatwick, West Sussex RH6 0NP
(01293) 535 353

Gatwick, 28 miles to the south of London, is the busiest single runway airport in the world, handling over 30 million passengers a year. Although it is further from central London than Heathrow, many consider travelling from Gatwick to be a more pleasant experience.

There are two terminals at Gatwick – North Terminal, mainly dedicated to British Airways scheduled flights, and South Terminal, from which most other scheduled services and all holiday charter flights depart. The main train station is in the South terminal, but there is a free, shuttle train service that will take you to the North terminal in a couple of minutes.

**Train** The fastest and best value way to reach Gatwick is via the Gatwick Express, a non-stop service which departs from Victoria Station. Trains leave every 15 minutes between 06.00 and 20:00 and every 30 minutes between 04:00-06:00 and 20:00-23:30. Journey time is approximately 30 minutes and it costs £11 one way. Booking is not necessary. Go to www.gatwickexpress.co.uk or call 08705 30 15 30 for schedules, and for train schedules from Charing Cross and London Bridge to Gatwick.

**Bus** The A5 Airbus service connects Victoria Coach station and Gatwick. Contact details as Heathrow Airbus above.

**Taxi** The black cab fare is roughly £80 from central London, and takes about 90 minutes: you will usually be better off taking the train. A chauffered car will be slightly less expensive, and more luxurious- try Checker Cars (South terminal 01293 502808; North terminal 01293 501377) which charges £75 one-way.

**Car** Gatwick Airport parking is available through the PAS Gatwick Parking Services. For bookings and enquiries call (01293) 502 390.

## Stansted Airport

Essex CM24 1QW
(01279) 680 500
Car park information: (01279) 651 192

Several low-cost airlines, including Go and Ryanair, fly from Stansted, a very modern airport 37 miles north-east of London.

**Train** The Stansted Express service operates from Liverpool St station, and takes 41 minutes. The one-way fare is £13. (www.stansted-express.co.uk or 08705 301 530).

**Bus** The A6 Airbus departs from Victoria, via St Johns Wood, Baker Street, Marble Arch and Hyde Park Corner. It operates up to every 20 minutes (and half hourly throughout the night). Contact details as Heathrow Airbus above.

## Luton Airport

Luton, Bedfordshire LU2 9LY
(01582) 405100
Car park information: (01582) 395 270

City of London Airport
Royal Docks E16 2PX
(020) 7646 0000

## AIRLINES

For a complete listing of airlines, consult the London Yellow Pages under "Airlines".

## CHANNEL TUNNEL

The Channel Tunnel, which links England and France, has greatly reduced travel time to the Continent: Paris is now only three hours from London. The tunnel is rail-only - you cannot drive through it, although there is a "drive-on" service.

*Eurostar* (passengers only), Leaves from Waterloo station, with destinations to: Paris (Gare du Nord and Disneyland, Paris), Brussels (Gare du Midi), Lille (Europa), Bourg St. Maurice, Moutiers and Calais. Contact (0990) 186 186 (www.eurostar.co.uk) for information and reservations. Be warned that tickets are priced in a similar way to flights, and to obtain the best deals you will probably need to buy a non-flexible ticket with a Saturday night stay.

*Le Shuttle* (passengers and cars). A drive on service from Folkestone, in Kent, to Calais. For information and reservations contact (0990) 353 535 or go to www.eurotunnel.co.uk .

## Accommodation

Whether you are seeking to rent a cottage in Wales or a suite in a European city hotel, your first stop should be the travel supplements of the weekend papers. The

Observer (Sunday), the Telegraph (Saturday and Sunday) and the Times (Sunday) are particularly good, and frequently feature special offers and discounts available exclusively to their readers. Late spring is a particularly good time to look for reduced room rates and upgrade packages as the tour operators and cruise lines seek to get rid of unsold capacity. In major business cities, such as London itself, August is the best month to find excellent room rates.

## London hotels

Central London hotels are notoriously expensive. To get the most for your money, explore the online hotel room brokers, which are probably the cheapest source of accommodation in London. Next, try calling the hotel and asking for the best rate they can offer for the nights you are thinking of. If all else fails, see if you can obtain a special rate via your corporate travel agency or American Express, if you have an Amex card.

Some tried and tested online resources for London hotel rooms:

✓ www.ebookers.co.uk

✓ www.lastminute.com

✓ www.expedia.co.uk

✓ www.travelocity.co.uk

Some London families open up their homes to welcome travellers on a bed-and-breakfast basis. Try the *London Bed and Breakfast Agency* on (020) 7586 2768 (www.londonbb.com) which offers both rooms in family homes, and self-catering flats, for stays of two or more nights. Also, be sure to look under the 'Hotels' section in Chapter Eleven: Services.

Did you know...The Orient Express operates day and weekend trips around the UK. For a special occasion, this is a wonderful way to see the countryside. (www.orient-express.com)

## Elsewhere in Britain

Room rates sharply fall once you are outside London, and there is a much bigger variety of hotel, bed and breakfast, and self-catering accommodation to sample. The British Tourist Board website www.visitbritain.com has a full list, but here are some other resources:

✓ *The Good Bed and Breakfast Guide* 2002 by Elsie Dillard

✓ *Ramblers Association Accommodation Finder* (www.ramblers.org.uk). Sorted by proximity to Long Distance Paths.

✓ *Lakeland Cottage Company,* Cumbria/Lake District (01539) 530 024 or www.lakelandcottageco.com

✓ *English Country Cottages,* (0870) 444 1155, (www.english-country-cottages.co.uk)

✓    *Country Cottages* in Scotland, (0870) 585 1133, (www.cc-scot.co.uk)

✓    *Country Holidays*, (08700) 781 200, (www.country-holidays.co.uk)

✓    *Farm Stay UK*, Rooms and cottages on working farms. (02476) 696 909 (www.farmstayuk.co.uk)

✓    *Bed and Breakfast Nationwide*, www.bedandbreakfastnationwide.com, (01255) 831 235

✓    *Macdonald Hotels*, Traditional inns and hotels. (0870) 400 9191, (www.heritage-hotels.co.uk )

✓    *Stapleford Park*, Stapleford Park, near Melton Mowbray, Leicestershire, LE14 2EF, (01572) 787 522, (www.stapleford.co.uk). Hotel, spa and sporting estate. Luxury getaway outside of London.

## CULTURE IN BRITAIN

### MUSEUMS, GALLERIES AND NATIONAL TRUST HOUSES

Many major museums have `Friends' programmes which make it easier to view major exhibitions as well as giving discounts on museum entrance and functions. Information can be obtained from each museum. A leader among the many worthwhile charities is the National Art-Collections Fund, 20 John Islip Street, SW1; (020) 7225 4800. This charity is dedicated to keeping Great Britain's art treasures in Great Britain by helping museums and galleries purchase works of art they could not otherwise afford. Membership provides one with reduced or free admission to most galleries and exhibitions as well as information regarding many cultural events in and around London.

© Indicates that the museum or gallery is particularly good for children.

*Bankside Gallery*, 48 Hopton Street, SE1; (020) 7928 7521. Home of the Royal Society of Painters in Water-Colours, founded in 1804 and the Royal Society of Painter-Etchers and Engravers, founded in 1880. Contemporary and historical exhibitions from Great Britain and abroad. Charge for admission.

*Banqueting House*, Whitehall Palace, SW1; (020) 7839 7569. The Banqueting House was built between 1619 and 1622 during the reign of James I. Designed by Inigo Jones it is the only surviving building of the vast Whitehall Palace, destroyed by fire nearly 300 years ago. Charge for admission.

*Barbican Art Gallery*, Barbican Centre for Arts and Conferences, Barbican EC2; (020) 7638 4141. Selected pieces from the important collection belonging to the *Corporation of London* are sometimes on show. Major exhibitions as well. Charge for admission.

©*Bethnal Green Museum of Childhood*, Cambridge Heath Road, E2; (020) 8983 5200. Children's dolls, doll houses, toys, etc., and an important collection of 19th century decorative arts, including continental art nouveau and Tiffany glass. Free admission, donations encouraged.

©*British Museum*, Great Russell Street, WC1; (020) 7636 1555. World renowned collection of antiquities, art, prints, drawings and manuscripts. Among the decorative arts on display are the Rosetta Stone, the Magna Carta, the Elgin Marbles and many other treasures. Donations encouraged.

*Buckingham Palace*, The Mall, SW1; (020) 7930 4832. Built in 1702 by the Duke of Buckingham, it has served as the British Monarch's London residence since the reign of Queen Victoria. Open Tuesday-Sunday, August-September only. Charge for admission.

*Cabinet War Rooms*, Clive Steps, King Charles Street, SW1; (020) 7930 6961. The hidden underground rooms where Churchill and his government lived and worked during dangerous moments of World War II. Charge for admission includes sound guide.

*Carlyle's House (National Trust)*, 24 Cheyne Row, SW3; (020) 7352 7087. Paintings, decorative arts, personal effects, manuscripts and the library of Mr. and Mrs. Carlyle. Charge for admission.

*Chiswick House*, Burlington Lane, W4; (020) 8995 0508. 18th century villa set in extensive grounds built by Lord Burlington, influenced by Palladio and Indigo Jones. Gardens by William Kent. Charge for admission.

©*Commonwealth Institute*, 230 Kensington High Street, W8; (020) 7603 4535. Permanent and extensive exhibitions pertaining to historical, cultural, social and commercial traditions of the Commonwealth countries. Also an art gallery with changing exhibitions and a library. Free admission.

*Courtauld Institute Galleries*, Somerset House, The Strand, WC2; (020) 7873 2526. The important Courtauld collection of Impressionist and Post-Impressionist paintings as well as other notable painting and drawing collections. Charge for admission.

©*The Dickens House Museum*, 48 Doughty Street, WC1; (020) 7405 2127. Period house and museum restored to the time of Dickens' occupation. Site where he wrote some of his best known works with original manuscripts on exhibit. Charge for admission.

*Dulwich Picture Gallery*, College Road, SE21; (020) 8693 8000. Important collection of Old Master paintings, including works by Van Dyck, Rembrandt, Gainsborough and Poussin. Charge for admission. Free on Fridays.

*The Fan Museum*, 12 Croome Hill, SE10; (020) 8858 7879. Delightful private collection of 2,000 fans from different countries displayed in an 18th century townhouse within walking distance of other Greenwich attractions. Charge for admission.

*Fenton House (National Trust)*, Windmill Hill, NW3, (Hampstead Grove); (020) 7435 3471. A late 17th century house with walled gardens and an outstanding collection of porcelain and early keyboard instruments. Charge for admission.

*©Geffrye Museum*, Kingsland Road, E2; (020) 7739 9893. British period rooms especially arranged for children's enjoyment and participation. No charge for admission.

*Goldsmith's Hall*, Foster Lane, EC2; (020) 7606 7010. Antique silver and gold plate collection of importance. Largest collection of modern silver and jewellery in Britain. By appointment unless a special exhibition is being held. Charge for admission.

*Guildhall*, Gresham Street, EC2; (020) 7606 3030. Centre of City of London's government. The gallery exhibits the permanent collection belonging to the Corporation of London and contains the Guildhall library and clock museum. Free admission.

*Gunnersbury Park Museum*, Gunnersbury Park, W3; (020) 8992 1612. Transportation collection containing coaches belonging to the Rothschild family from their former country residence. Free admission.

*Ham House (National Trust)*, Ham Street, Ham, Richmond, Surrey; (020) 8940 1950. Superb 17th century house along the Thames with important collection of Stuart and early Georgian furnishings. Charge for admission.

*©Hampton Court Palace*, Hampton Court, Surrey KT8 9AU; (020) 8781 9500. With its 500 years of royal history Hampton Court Palace has something to offer everyone. Set in sixty acres of world famous gardens the Palace is a living tapestry of history from Henry VIII to George II. Charge for admission.

*Hayward Gallery*, South Bank Centre, Belvedere Road, Waterloo, SE1; (020) 7928 3144. Temporary exhibitions of historical and contemporary fine and decorative arts of major importance. Charge for admission.

*Hogarth's House*, Great West Road, Hogarth Lane, W4; (020) 8994 6757. The artist's Queen Anne house and studio for the last 15 years of his life. Contains a number of his works. Free admission.

*©Horniman Museum*, 100 London Road, Forest Hill, SE23; (020) 8699 1872. Impressive collection of musical instruments, decorative arts and natural history, and gardens. Free admission.

*©H.M.S. Belfast*, Morgans Lane, Tooley Street, SE1; (020) 7940 6300. Reached by ferry from Tower Pier. Floating naval museum. Charge for admission.

*©Imperial War Museum*, Lambeth Road, SE1; (020) 7416 5000. Permanent exhibitions of all aspects of wars in which Britain has been involved since 1914. Includes weaponry, vehicles, photographs, war paintings and posters. Archival films shown on weekends and holidays. Charge for admission. Free after 16.30.

*Institute of Contemporary Arts (ICA)*, 12 Carlton House Terrace, The Mall, SW1; (020) 7930 3647. Changing exhibitions of avant garde art. Charge for admission.

*Jewish Museum,* Woburn House, Woburn Place, WC1; (020) 7284 1997. Extensive collection of Jewish religious antiquities. Charge for admission.

*Dr. Samuel Johnson's House,* 17 Gough Square, EC4; (020) 7353 3745. Small library with relics located in furnished period house where Dr. Johnson lived and worked on England's first definitive dictionary from 1748 to 1759. Charge for admission.

*Keats' House,* Wentworth Place, Keats Grove, NW3; (020) 7435 2062. Regency home of John Keats containing relics and manuscripts. Charge for admission.

*Kensington Palace State Apartments,* Kensington Gardens, W8; (020) 7937 9561. Acquired by William and Mary in 1689 when it was called Nottingham House, Kensington. Highlights of a visit include the recently restored Kings Apartments with a magnificent collection of old masters; Tintoretto and Van Dyke amongst others. Charge for admission.

*The Iveagh Bequest,* Kenwood House, Hampstead Lane, NW3; (020) 8348 1286. Robert Adam designed country house with extensive collection of furniture, Old Master paintings, also superb gardens and views over Hampstead Heath. Donations encouraged.

©*Kew Bridge Steam Museum,* Green Dragon Lane, Brentford, Middlesex TW8; (020) 8568 4757. Giant steam engines from 1820 operating under steam at weekends. Largest of their kind in the world; working forge. Charge for admission.

*Leighton House,* 12 Holland Park Road, W14; (020) 7602 3316. Late 19th century home of the artist Lord Leighton, who designed its notable Arab Hall. Contains works by major Victorian artists. Free admission.

*Linley Sambourne House (Victorian Society),* 18 Stafford Terrace, W8; (020) 8994 1019. Home of the artist Linley Sambourne, cartoonist for `Punch' magazine. The impressive contents of the house remain undisturbed from his day and reflect the taste of the 'aesthetic movement' of the late Victorian period. Charge for admission.

©*London Dungeon,* 28 Tooley Street, SE1; Recorded information: (020) 7403 0606 and General questions: (020) 7403 7221. Definitely not for the squeamish or those under 10; interesting otherwise. Charge for admission.

©*The London Planetarium,* Marylebone Road, NW1; (020) 7935 6861. Exciting astrological displays projected, to scale, on a huge dome. No children under five. Located adjacent to Madame Tussauds. Charge for admission.

©*London Toy and Model Museum,* 21-23 Craven Hill, Bayswater, W2; (020) 7405 5222. Tintypes, toys and Europe's most complete display of model trains. Charge for admission.

©*London Transport Museum,* 39 Wellington Street, Covent Garden, WC2; (020) 7379 6344. Housed in the restored Old Flower Market building, this unique collection includes historic vehicles, buses, trams, trolley buses and railway cars. Charge for admission.

©*Museum of London*, 150 London Wall, EC2; (020) 7600 3699. Leads the visitor through the chronological development of London's history from pre-historic times. Lord Mayor's coach exhibition here. Charge for admission.

*Museum of Garden History*, St. Mary at Lambeth Church, Lambeth Palace Road, SE1; (020) 7261 1891. The church is used for exhibitions of botanical drawings, antique garden implements, etc., and the churchyard contains an interesting collection of plants and flowers. Charge for admission.

©*Museum of Mankind*, 6 Burlington Gardens, W1X; (020) 7437 2224. Ethnographical branch of the British Museum. Donations encouraged.

©*Museum of the Moving Image*, British Film Institute, South Bank, SE1 (under Waterloo Bridge, next to Royal Festival Hall); (020) 7928 3232. History of film and television from the very first images made up to latest technology. Charge for admission.

©*Musical Museum, Kew Bridge*, 368 High Street, Brentford, Middlesex TW8 OBD; (020) 8560 8108. Unique collection of working autopianos, organs and music boxes. Charming lecturette featuring autoroll pianos and organs. Charge for admission.

©*National Army Museum*, Royal Hospital Road, SW3; (020) 7730 0717. Extensive display of army mementoes, equipment and colours from the various British and colonial regiments from 1485. Free admission.

©*National Gallery*, Trafalgar Square, WC2; (020) 7839 3321. World renowned collection of masterpieces from all schools and movements in art. Wonderful holiday quizzes for children. Donations encouraged.

©*National Maritime Museum*, Romney Road, Greenwich, SE10; (020) 8858 4422. Exhibitions relating to all aspects of Britain as a maritime power. The Queen's House by Indigo Jones and the Old Observatory in Greenwich Park, by Wren, are also part of the complex. Greenwich Park stretches up the hill behind the museum. Charge for admission.

©*National Portrait Gallery*, 2 St. Martin's Place, WC2; (020) 7306 0055. Beautifully organised galleries, arranged by period, with portraits of notable personalities from each era in British history from the Tudors to the present. Donations encouraged.

*National Postal Museum*, King Edward Street, EC1; (020) 7239 5420. Extremely interesting collection of postage stamps from all over the world. Free admission.

©*Natural History Museum*, Cromwell Road, SW7; (020) 7938 9123. Innovative exhibitions of zoology, entomology, palaeontology, mineralogy and botany. Charge for admission.

*Osterley Park House (National Trust)*, Isleworth, Middlesex; (020) 8560 3918. Elizabethan mansion transformed by Robert Adam in 1760 to 1780 with Adam decorations and furniture and 140 acres of parkland. Charge for admission.

*Percival David Foundation of Chinese Art*, 53 Gordon Square, WC1; (020) 7387 3909. Contains one of the most impressive collections of Chinese ceramics in the West, covering more than a thousand years of production. Donations encouraged.

©*Pollock's Toy Museum*, 1 Scala Street, W1; (020) 7636 3452. A collection of unusual children's games, dolls, doll houses and mechanical toys. Charge for admission.

*Public Records Office Museum*, Chancery Lane, WC2; (020) 8876 3444. Exhibitions of British national records since the Norman Conquest, including the Domesday Book of 1066. Free admission.

*Queen's Gallery*, Buckingham Palace, Buckingham Palace Road, SW1; (020) 7839 1377, ext. 3351. Changing exhibitions of objects from the Royal Collection. Charge for admission.

*Ranger's House*, Chesterfield Walk, Blackheath, SE10; (020) 8853 0035. Period house with English portraits from the Elizabethan to the Georgian period and a collection of musical instruments. Donations encouraged.

*Royal Academy of Arts*, Burlington House, Piccadilly, W1; (020) 7439 7438. Major changing exhibitions and the Annual Summer Exhibition of work submitted by contemporary artists, held each year without a miss since the 1700's. Charge for admission.

©*Royal Air Force Museum*, Grahame Park Way, Hendon, NW9; (020) 8205 2266. National museum devoted to aviation and the comprehensive history of the RAF. The Battle of Britain wing houses a unique collection of memorabilia and machinery dedicated to the people involved in the 1940 battle. Charge for admission.

©*Royal Hospital Chelsea*, Royal Hospital Road, SW3; (020) 7730 5282. Impressive Wren designed home of the famous scarlet-coated Chelsea pensioners. Paintings and maps. Visitors may also see the famous Chapel (open for services and concerts), the pensioners' dining room and walk in the park. Charge for admission.

©*Royal Mews*, Buckingham Palace Road, SW1; (020) 7839 1377. (Limited opening hours). Splendid collection of state coaches, carriages and the royal horses. Charge for admission.

*Royal Naval College*, King William Walk, Greenwich, SE10; (020) 8858 2154. Housed in a late 17th century hospital on the Thames, partially designed by Christopher Wren. The chapel and Painted Hall in the main building are open to the public every afternoon except Thursday. Charge for admission.

©*Science Museum*, Exhibition Road, SW7; (020) 7938 8008. Comprehensive displays of the history of mathematics, chemistry, physics, engineering, transportation and industry. The `Launchpad' is a popular hands on exhibit for children. Charge for admission.

*Sir John Soane's Museum*, 13 Lincoln's Inn Fields, WC2; (020) 7430 0175. Built in the early 19th century, by the famous architect as his private residence. Contains his collection of art, furniture and antiquities. Excellent tour for limited numbers on Saturday afternoons. Donations encouraged.

*Syon Park*, Brentford, Middlesex TW8; (020) 8560 0881. Impressive Adam interior with furnishings and important picture collection. The extensive gardens were partially designed by Capability Brown; includes a famous conservatory. Charge for admission.

*Tate Gallery*, Millbank, SW1; (020) 7887 8000. The national collection of British art (from the 16th century to the present day) and a collection of modern British and foreign art. Donations encouraged.

©*Theatre Museum*, 7 Russell Street, WC2; (020) 7836 7891. Permanent displays trace the history of the stage since the 16th century. Programmes of special activities and exhibitions, many aimed at children. Charge for admission.

©*Tower of London*, Tower Hill, EC3; (020) 7709 0765. Impressive Norman fortification including chapels, crown jewels and extensive armoury collection. Charge for admission.

©*Madame Tussaud's*, Marylebone Road, NW1; (020) 7935 6861. The famous collection of wax figures of historic and contemporary celebrities. Charge for admission.

©*Victoria and Albert Museum*, Cromwell Road, SW7; (020) 7938 8500. One of the truly great collections of the world. Fine and decorative arts covering most periods and countries. Charge for admission.

*Wallace Collection*, Hertford House, Manchester Square, W1; (020) 7935 0687. Private collection assembled during the 19th century with emphasis on the 18th century French fine and decorative arts. Fine collection of arms and armour as well. Donations encouraged.

©*Wellington Museum*, Apsley House, 149 Piccadilly, Hyde Park Corner, W1; (020) 7499 5676. London home of the Duke of Wellington, containing his art collection and military memorabilia. Charge for admission.

*Wesley's House and Chapel*, 49 City Road, EC1; (020) 7253 2262. Home of the Methodist founder which contains a large collection of his personal possessions. Charge for admission.

William Morris Gallery, Water House, Lloyd Park, Forest Road, Walthamstow, E17; (020) 8527 3782. Childhood home of William Morris. Collections include furniture, pictures, designs, stained glass, wallpapers and textiles designed by Morris and his contemporaries. Donations encouraged.

Wimbledon Lawn Tennis Museum, Church Road, SW19; (020) 8946 6131. Items of interest from games pre-dating lawn tennis and displays relating to the game's development since 1870. Charge for admission.

## THE PERFORMING ARTS

London benefits from a wide range of venues for the performing arts. An essential guide to what is on offer is the listings magazine Time Out, published every Tuesday and available from your local newsagent. It lists dates, times, venues and ticket prices, and includes performance reviews and previews.

### Comedy

*Comedy Café,* 66 Rivington Street, EC2; (020) 7739 5706.

*Comedy Store,* 1a Oxendon Street, W1; (020) 7344 0234.

*Jongleurs (Battersea,* The Cornet, 49 Lavender Gardens, SW11; Bow Wharf, 221 Grove Road, E3; Camden Lock, Dingwalls Building, Middle Yard, Chalk Farm Road, Camden Lock, NW1) (020) 7564 2500.

### Dance

*English National Ballet,* 39 Jay Mews, SW7; (020) 7581 1245. Box office and troupe's home is the Royal Festival Hall.

*Rambert Dance Company,* 94 Chiswick High Road, W4; (020) 8995 4246. The company performs contemporary ballet in various locations.

*Royal Ballet Company,* The Royal Opera House, Covent Garden, WC2, (020) 7240 1200.

*Sadlers Wells,* Roseberry Avenue, EC1; (020) 7713 6000.

### MUSIC

### Classical

*Barbican Hall,* Barbican Centre, EC2; (020) 7638 8891 for information. Home of The London Symphony Orchestra. There are also a number of guest orchestras that perform here.

*Holland Park Theatre,* Holland Park, Kensington High Street, W8; (020) 7602 7856 (box office). Opera, theatre and dance are presented during the summer in the only remaining wing of the 17th century Holland House.

*Kenwood Lakeside,* Hampstead Heath, NW3; (020) 7413 1443 for bookings. Concerts are performed here on summer weekends only.

*Royal Albert Hall,* Kensington Gore, SW7; (020) 7589 3203. A great variety of musical events are staged here, including Christmas Carol Concerts and `The Proms'.

*Royal College of Music,* Prince Consort Road, SW7 2BS; (020) 7589 3643.

*South Bank Centre* (including the Queen Elizabeth's Hall, Royal Festival Hall and the Purcell Room), Belvedere Road, Waterloo, South Bank, SE1; (020) 7928 8800. Home of the London Philharmonic Orchestra, and the Opera Factory among others. A great variety of musical events are held here. For a small subscription fee one can receive a monthly newsletter with concert information and priority booking.

*St. John's Smith Square*, SW1; (020) 7222 1061. Non-profit organisation supported by `The Friends of St. John's Smith Square' that holds all types of recitals and concerts in its restored Queen Anne church-cum-concert hall.

*Wigmore Hall*, 36 Wigmore Street, W1; (020) 7935 2141. A smaller concert hall offering an excellent variety of performances which are often particularly attractive to music connoisseurs.

### Contemporary

*Brixton Academy*, 211 Stockwell Road, SW9; (020) 7771 3000.

*The Forum*, 9-17 Highgate Road, NW5; (020) 7284 1001.

*London Arena*, Lime Harbour, Isle of Dogs, E14; (020) 7538 1212.

*London Astoria*, 157 Charing Cross Road, W1; (020) 7434 9592.

*Royal Albert Hall* (see above).

*Shepherds Bush Empire*, Shepherds Bush Green, W12; (020) 7771 2000.

*Wembley Arena*, Empire Way, Wembley; (020) 8902 1234.

### Jazz

*606 Club*, 90 Lots Road, SW10; (020) 7352 5953.

*Barbican Centre* (see above).

*Jazz Café*, 5 Parkway, NW1; (020) 7916 6060.

*Ronnie Scotts*, 47 Frith Street, W1; (020) 7439 0747.

*South Bank Centre* (see above).

*100 Club*, 100 Oxford Street, W1; (020) 7636 0933.

### Opera

*English National Opera*, London Coliseum, St. Martin's Lane, WC2; (020) 7632 8300. Home of the English National Opera who, notably, sing all their performances in English.

*Glyndebourne Festival Opera*, Glyndebourne, near Lewes, East Sussex (01273) 813 813. Opera in the summer months held in the grounds of an Elizabethan House. Famous for Black-tie picnics on the lawn.

*Royal Opera*, The Royal Opera House, Covent Garden, WC2; (020) 7304 4000.

*The Welsh National Opera* and *The Scottish National Opera* perform in London at various times throughout the year.

**TRAVEL AND CULTURE**

# Theatre

Most people think of the West End when they think of theatre in London. Tickets to most West End shows are available from theatre box offices, ticket agencies, major department stores and hotels. Half-price tickets for same-day performances are available from the Society of West End Theatres' booth located on the south side of Leicester Square (cash only; 4 ticket limit per person). Theatre box offices also offer same-day price reductions on stand-by and returned tickets. Never buy tickets from touts. They charge a premium and there is no guarantee the tickets they sell are genuine. Not to be overlooked are smaller productions at off-West End and fringe theatres. The weekly listings magazine Time Out provides comprehensive coverage of all London theatre productions.

The following are just a sampling of some of the many venues across London.

*The Barbican Theatre/The Pit,* Barbican Centre, EC2; (020) 7638 8891. The venue for various performances, including productions by the Royal Shakespeare Company.

*Lyric Theatre,* King Street, Hammersmith, SW6; (020) 8741 2311. Excellent fringe theatre and a wide variety of children's productions.

*National Theatre* (Cottesloe, Lyttleton and Olivier Theatres), Belvedere Road, Waterloo, South Bank, SE1; (020) 7452 3000, information (020) 7633 0880. For a small annual subscription fee you can join the mailing list and receive advance programme information, priority booking and occasional special offers. Call (020) 7261 9256. Excellent inexpensive seats available at all three theatres from 10.00 on the day of the performance (two tickets per person limit). Back stage tours available.

*Open Air Theatre,* Regent's Park, NW1; (020) 7486 7905. May to August.

*Riverside Studios,* Crisp Road, Hammersmith, W6; (020) 8741 2255. Excellent fringe theatre.

*Tricycle Theatre,* 269 Kilburn High Road, NW6; (020) 7328 1000.

# Chapter Sixteen: Annual Events

To assist you in planning an exciting year, we have provided a month-by-month schedule of events, along with advice on when and where to obtain tickets. For those events requiring advance planning and/or ticket purchase we have added reminders at the time of year when you must send away for tickets.

**Did you know...** if you qualify for a ResCard? Do you live in Westminster? Not many residents of the City of Westminster realise they are eligible for a whole range of special offers and discounted tickets to sights and cultural venues and activities in the area, including discounts to Apsley House (the home of the Great Duke of Wellington), the London Dungeon, London Aquarium, National Maritime Museum, Madame Tussaud's and London Planetarium. You can even obtain reduced price entry to the latest exhibitions at the Hayward and Serpentine Galleries, Tate Britain and some West End shows and cinemas. For information contact (020) 7460 6972 or www.westminster.gov.uk/rescard. Along with the card, you will receive a regular brochure with details of the discounts available at that time.

*Please Note: The following information is accurate at the time of publication, however we suggest that you always verify the details before making your plans. For assistance, contact The London Tourist Board; (020) 7932 2000 (recorded message, updated daily), or The British Tourist Authority; (020) 8846 9000.*

Here are a few other helpful hints:

1. Dress codes are often quite stringent. Ask your host or hostess or someone who has attended the event before for advice.

2. When booking an event, always enclose a self-addressed envelope (s.a.e.) and enquire if it is possible or necessary to book the car park.

3. For more popular events, such as Wimbledon, tickets must be obtained through a lottery or ballot. Entry forms, referred to as ballots, must be submitted by a certain deadline.

4. Individual castles, stately homes and numerous other venues offer their own calendar of events. Telephone, write or email to request one.

## Reminders:

1 JANUARY - 28 FEBRUARY: Applications for Ballots to Trooping the Colour may be submitted. See May and June.

1 JANUARY: Bookings open for Chelsea Flower Show in May, The Derby in June and the Goodwood Festival in July.

31 JANUARY: Tickets for Beating the Retreat available (June).

### NEW YEAR'S DAY
*1 JANUARY* - Bank holiday

The official birthday for all race horses. Lord Mayor of Westminster's parade begins in early afternoon at Piccadilly and ends at Hyde Park. Entertainment continues in Hyde Park throughout the day and concludes with a fireworks display. Marching bands, colourful floats. Free of charge.

### LONDON INTERNATIONAL BOAT SHOW
*EARLY JANUARY*

At Earl's Court, Warwick Road, SW5. The largest boat show in Europe, and among the most prestigious boat shows in the world, displaying the latest designs in pleasure crafts, yachts and equipment. Contact: National Boat Shows Ltd., Meadlake Place, Thorpe Lea Road, Egham, Surrey TW20 8HE, or telephone (0178) 447 3377.

### JANUARY STORE SALES

Most stores have major sales beginning in late December and ending in late January.

### SERVICE COMMEMORATING CHARLES I
*LAST SUNDAY IN JANUARY*

Parade at 11.30 at St. James's Palace to mark the beheading of Charles I on 30 January 1649, followed by a service at Banqueting Hall. Write to: Charles I Service, 70 Hailgate, Howden, North Humberside DN14 7ST. Free of charge.

### CHINESE NEW YEAR CELEBRATIONS
*LATE JANUARY OR EARLY FEBRUARY*

Gerrard Street, W1. Celebrated with a festive march through London's Chinatown complete with papier-maché dragons and extravagant costumes. Usually on the Sunday nearest the date of the New Year. Contact: The Hong Kong Government Office at (020) 7499 9821.

# FEBRUARY

### Reminders:

Early February: Application forms available for submitting work (amateur or professional) to the Royal Academy Summer Exhibition. See May.

## ACCESSION OF H.M. THE QUEEN

*6 FEBRUARY*

Anniversary salute of 41 guns in Hyde Park by the King's Troop of the Royal Horse Artillery, and at the Tower of London a 62 gun salute by the Honourable Artillery Company. No tickets required.

## CLOWN'S SERVICE

*FIRST SUNDAY IN FEBRUARY*

At Holy Trinity Church, Beechwood Road, E8. In memory of the famous clown Joseph Grimaldi. The service is attended by many clowns in full costume. Contact: John Willard (020) 7254 5062. No tickets required.

## GREAT SPITALFIELDS PANCAKE DAY RACE

*LATE FEBRUARY OR EARLY MARCH (SHROVE TUESDAY)*

At The Old Spitalfields Market, Spitalfields, E1. Pancakes are traditionally eaten before Lent. Teams run with frying pans tossing pancakes. (020) 7375 0441.

# MARCH

### Reminders:

30 MARCH: Deadline for obtaining application and sponsorship to the Royal Enclosure at Royal Ascot in June.

## MOTHERING SUNDAY - BRITISH MOTHER'S DAY

*DATE VARIES*

## BRITISH SUMMER TIME BEGINS

*DATE VARIES*

Clocks go forward one hour. UK spring day light savings takes place several weeks before the United States.

## HEAD OF THE RIVER RACE

*END OF MARCH - (USUALLY SATURDAY BEFORE UNIVERSITY BOAT RACE)*

From Mortlake to Putney. Contact: The Amateur Rowing Association on (020) 8748 3632.

## THE UNIVERSITY BOAT RACE (OXFORD V CAMBRIDGE)

*SATURDAY IN MARCH OR APRIL*

Starting time varies according to the tides. From Putney to Mortlake on the Thames. Held annually since 1829. The race can be viewed from many vantage points: bridges, banks, riverside pubs. Timings and maps available on (01992) 505 306; (www.theboatrace.org).

## CHELTENHAM NATIONAL HUNT MEETING

The most important jump racing meeting in the calendar. See Chapter 14: Sports and Leisure.

## CHELSEA ANTIQUES FAIR

At Chelsea Town Hall, King's Road, SW3. Bi-annual antiques fair. (020) 7361 4140 (4150).

## DAILY MAIL IDEAL HOME EXHIBITION

At Earl's Court Exhibition Centre, Warwick Road, SW5. Large annual consumer show for new products for the home. Contact: DMG Angex Ltd., Times House, Station Approach, Ruislip, Middlesex HA4 8NB or (020) 8515 2000; (www.idealhomeshow.co.uk).

## THE CRUFT'S DOG SHOW

Possible the world's most famous dog show, held at the National Exhibition Centre in Birmingham. Contact the Kennel Club on (0870) 606 6750 or at www.crufts.org.uk.

## BASKETBALL

Coca Cola National Cup Finals. At London Docklands Arena, Limeharbour, E14. (020) 7538 1212.

## YONEX ALL ENGLAND BADMINTON CHAMPIONSHIPS

Normally held in the National Indoor Arena in Birmingham. Book direct with the NIA on (0870) 789 8845 or at www.necgroup.co.uk/boxoffice or write to: Badminton Association of England, National Badminton Centre, Bradwell Road, Loughton Lodge, Milton Keynes MK8 9LA, (www.baofe.co.uk).

## APRIL

### Reminders:

First week of April: Deadline for submitting paintings to the Royal Academy Summer Exhibition. See May.

## JOHN STOWE MEMORIAL SERVICE

*5 APRIL*

At St. Andrew Undershaft Church, Great St. Helens, EC3A. Stowe published his survey of London in 1598 age 73. The service marks the anniversary of his death on

5 April and this event is held near this date. The Lord Mayor attends and places a new quill pen in the hand of the Stowe statue.

## FA CUP FINAL

*APRIL OR MAY*

Climax of the English football season. See Chapter 14: Sports and Leisure for more details.

## THE GRAND NATIONAL STEEPLECHASE

Perhaps the most famous steeplechase in the world, run at Aintree Racecourse in Liverpool. See Chapter 14: Sports and Leisure.

## MAUNDY THURSDAY

*THURSDAY BEFORE GOOD FRIDAY*

Held at Westminster Abbey every tenth year and at different cathedrals around the country during the other nine. The Queen distributes purses of specially minted coins to as many poor men and women as the years of her age. Telephone: The Buckingham Palace Information Section; (020) 7930 4832.

## GOOD FRIDAY - Bank holiday.

## BUTTERWORTH CHARITY DISTRIBUTIONS OF BUNS

*GOOD FRIDAY*

At 11.30, Priory Church of St. Bartholomew the Great, West Smithfield, EC1. Tickets not required. (020) 7606 5171.

## HOT CROSS BUN CEREMONY

*GOOD FRIDAY*

At 13.00, Widow's Son Inn, 75 Devon Road, E3; (020) 7515 9072.

## EASTER SUNDAY SERVICE

Seating at 10.00, St. George's Chapel, Windsor Castle, SL4. The Queen and the Royal Family worship together in St. George's Chapel. Visitors can attend. If you are seated toward the front of the Nave and seats are available you may be sitting with the Royal Family in the choir stalls. The queue is long, so arrive early. Many people do not enter the chapel, so do not be discouraged by the size of the queue. Contact: The Chapel Clerk, Windsor Castle, Windsor, Berkshire SL4 1NJ or telephone (01753) 865 538.

## EASTER SUNDAY PARADE

At Battersea Park, SW11. Carnival parade with colourful floats and bands. Tickets not required.

### EASTER SUNDAY PARADE

At the Tower of London. Yeomen Warders in state dress parade at the Tower. (020) 7709 0765.

**EASTER MONDAY** - Bank holiday.

### LONDON HARNESS HORSE PARADE

*EASTER MONDAY*

At Battersea Park. Judging begins at 10.30 with fine breeds from Shires and Suffolks to lighter-weight horses, ponies, carts, brewer's vans and drays parade around the inner circle sometime later. Tickets not required. Contact: The London Harness Horse Parade Society; (0173) 323 4451.

### THE FLORA LONDON MARATHON

*LATE APRIL*

From Blackheath/Greenwich to The Mall. World's largest road race with competitors representing a mixture of international marathon runners, serious runners, celebrities, disabled runners and just-for-fun runners. Large crowds. Telephone: (020) 7620 4117.

### H.M. THE QUEEN'S BIRTHDAY

*21 APRIL*

Gun salutes at the Tower of London (see February).

### SHAKESPEARE'S BIRTHDAY

*23 APRIL*

Shakespeare's birthday is celebrated in his home town of Stratford-upon-Avon every year on the weekend closest to the 23rd April. The highlight is the floral procession of dignitaries from all over the world between his birthplace and Holy Trinity Church. Details from the Stratford Tourist Information Office on (01789) 293 127.

### CRICKET SEASON BEGINS

## MAY

### Reminders:

AFTER 1 MAY: Apply for Steward's Enclosure at Henley Regatta. See June.

### MAY DAY BANK HOLIDAY

*FIRST MONDAY IN MAY*

## THE BADMINTON HORSE TRIALS

*MAY*

At Badminton, Avon, Gloucestershire. International equestrian competition. Contact: The Horse Trials Office; (0145) 421 8375, (www.badminton-horse.co.uk).

## POLO SEASON BEGINS

EARLY MAY TO SEPTEMBER

At Windsor Great Park, matches are held most Saturdays and Sundays. Contact: The Guards Polo Club, Smiths Lawn, Windsor Great Park, Englefield Green, Egham, Surrey TW20 0HP; (0178) 443 4212, (www.guardspoloclub.com).

## GLYNDEBOURNE OPERA SEASON

*MAY TO AUGUST*

International festival of opera. Special train services from Victoria Station to Glyndebourne and return from Lewes. Formal attire. Take a picnic or dine in one of three on-site restaurants. Book early. Contact: Glyndebourne Festival Opera Box Office, Glyndebourne, East Sussex BN8 5UU; (01273) 812 321; (www.glyndebourne.com).

## BEATING THE BOUNDS

At the Tower of London. Harkens back to the days when the majority of parishioners were illiterate, and beating on the boundary marks of the parishes taught them where the boundaries lay. The Tower holds this event tri-annually (last held 1996). Held on Ascension Day. Contact: The Deputy Governor at (020) 7709 0765.

## ROYAL WINDSOR HORSE SHOW

At Windsor, Berkshire. International show with jumping and driving, various displays and numerous trade exhibits. Contact: The Secretary, Royal Windsor Horse Show Club, Royal Mews, Windsor Castle, Windsor, Berkshire SL4 1NG; (0175) 386 0633; (www.royal-windsor-horse-show.co.uk). It is possible to become a member for a fee that allows one access to the Members' Enclosure for the week of the show. For non-member tickets telephone (020) 7341 9341.

## BATH FESTIVAL

Festival of music and arts with concerts, exhibitions, tours and lectures. Contact: The Bath Festival Box Office, 2 Church Street, Abbey Green, Bath, Avon BA1 1NL; (01225) 463 362; (www.bathmusicfest.org.uk).

## TROOPING THE COLOUR

*LAST SATURDAY IN MAY, FIRST REHEARSAL*

From Buckingham Palace along the Mall to Horse Guards Parade, Whitehall and back again, SW1. The first of two rehearsals (the second held in June) to prepare for the actual Trooping the Colour, the second Saturday in June, in the presence of H.M. The Queen. A magnificent parade of colourful military units celebrates the Queen's official birthday. Tickets required. See June for ticket information.

### REGENT'S PARK OPEN AIR THEATRE SEASON

*MAY OR JUNE THROUGH SEPTEMBER*

A full programme of plays, both Shakespeare and more modern works. Open Air Theatre, Inner Circle, Regent's Park, NW1; (020) 7935 5756. Box Office: (020) 7486 2431; (www.open-air-theatre.org.uk).

### CHELSEA FLOWER SHOW

At the Chelsea Royal Hospital Grounds, SW3. Nearest tube: Sloane Square. A four-day event displaying England's best horticultural endeavours, and often visited by the Royal Family. Tuesday, Wednesday and Thursday are reserved for RHS members with admittance to the general public on Thursday and Friday. Limited number of tickets available. Apply to RHS after 1 January. No children under 5 admitted. Contact: The Royal Horticultural Society, 80 Vincent Square, SW1; (020) 7821 3000 for RHS members, (020) 7344 4343 for non-members or book online at www.rhs.org.uk/chelsea. Also watch for RHS Westminster shows approximately every 3 weeks from February to November at Vincent Square.

### ROYAL ACADEMY SUMMER EXHIBITION

*MAY OR JUNE TO AUGUST*

At the Royal Academy of Arts, Piccadilly, W1. A juried exhibition of works by contemporary artists. Telephone: (020) 7300 8000. You may purchase tickets on the day or pre-book tickets by telephoning (020) 7413 1717; (www.royalacademy.org.uk). If you are an amateur or professional artist and would like to submit work to the Summer Exhibition, (e-mail: membershipoffice@royalacademy.org.uk).

### SAMUEL PEPYS MEMORIAL SERVICE

*MAY OR JUNE*

Held during the last week in May or first week in June at the Church of St. Olave, Hart Street, EC3R 7NB. (020) 7488 4318. Attended by the Lord Mayor.

### MALVERN FESTIVAL

Malvern Theatre, Worcestershire. Performances of the works of Sir Edward Elgar and George Bernard Shaw. For more information, contact: Malvern Theatre Box Office, Grange Road, Malvern, Worcestershire WR14 3HB; (0168) 489 2277.

### CHICHESTER FESTIVAL THEATRE SEASON

*MAY TO OCTOBER*

For information, write to: Chichester Festival Theatre, Oaklands Park, Chichester, West Sussex PO19 4AP or telephone (0124) 378 1312. Bookings open late March.

## FESTIVAL OF ENGLISH WINES

*MAY FOR 2 DAYS*

Leeds Castle, Maidstone, Kent. Telephone: (0162) 276 5400. Purchase tickets at the gate.

## OPEN AIR ART EXHIBITIONS

1. MAY THROUGH OCTOBER
   Saturdays - Royal Avenue, King's Road, SW3.

2. WEEKENDS
   Piccadilly on the Green Park Side, W1.

3. MAY TO SEPTEMBER
   Weekends - Heath Street, Hampstead Heath, NW3.

4. SUNDAYS
   Bayswater Road, North Side of Hyde Park, W2.

## OPEN AIR CONCERTS

*MAY TO SEPTEMBER*

At Hyde Park, St. James's Park, Regent's Park, Greenwich Park and Kensington Gardens. Contact: The London Tourist Board, 26 Grosvenor Square, SW1; (020) 7932 2000.

## SPRING BANK HOLIDAY

*LAST MONDAY IN MAY*

## JUNE

## MEDIEVAL JOUSTING TOURNAMENTS

*JUNE TO AUGUST*

For information, write to: Belvoir Castle, Belvoir, Leicestershire NG32 1PD, or telephone (0147) 687 0262. Visit the castle, picnic on the grounds and enjoy the jousting from 15.00 to 16.30. Castle open Easter week until last Sunday in October from 11.00 to 18.00.

## H.R.H. THE DUKE OF EDINBURGH'S BIRTHDAY

Gun salutes. Anniversary salute of 41 guns in Hyde Park by the King's Troop of the Royal Horse Artillery, and at the Tower of London a 62 gun salute by the Honourable Artillery Company. No tickets required.

## TROOPING THE COLOUR (THE QUEEN'S BIRTHDAY PARADE)

First rehearsal is held on the last Saturday in May. Second rehearsal is held on the first Saturday in June. Actual event is held on the second Saturday in June. Tickets are allocated by lottery. Only two tickets per successful entry. Send a self addresses envelope (s.a.e.) between 1 January and 28 February to: Brigade Major, Headquarters Household Division, Horse Guards, Whitehall, SW1 or telephone (020) 7414 2479 for general information. For tickets telephone (0891) 505 453.

## STELLA ARTOIS TENNIS TOURNAMENT

*MID JUNE*

Men's Tournament held two weeks before Wimbledon. Contact: The Queen's Club, Baron's Court, W14 for general information or telephone (020) 7385 3421. Tickets may be purchased 2 months prior to the event by credit card. Telephone: (020) 7413 1414.

## BEATING THE RETREAT

*EARLY JUNE*

Held at Horse Guards Parade. Nearest tube: Charing Cross. A military pageant by floodlight held on 2 consecutive nights with bands to acknowledge retreat of setting sun symbolising the end of fighting in battle for the day. Tickets available after 30 January. Telephone: (020) 7414 2271.

## THE DERBY *(pronounced Dar-by)*

*EARLY JUNE*

On Epsom Downs. The most famous and prestigious horse race in the world. It covers one and a half miles. Created at a noble dinner party in 1779 and named after one of the diners - Lord Derby. Bookings open 1 January at United Racecourses, Esher, Surrey KT10 8AJ. Telephone (01372) 470 047

## THE GARTER CEREMONY

*MONDAY AFTERNOON OF ASCOT WEEK*

At St. George's Chapel, Windsor Castle, SL4. A special service marks the oldest order of chivalry in England. It is attended by the Queen and is preceded by a colourful procession with the Household Cavalry and Yeomen of the Guard. 1,500 people will be admitted at the gate on a first-come first-served basis. Telephone: The Buckingham Palace Information Section; (020) 7930 4832 or for admittance information telephone (01753) 868 286.

## BIGGIN HILL INTERNATIONAL AIR FAIR

At Biggin Hill Airport, Biggin Hill, Kent. Jet formation aerobatics, historic aircraft rally and extensive ground exhibition. Tickets are available 4 weeks in advance or at the gate. Write to: Biggin Hill Airport, Kent TN16 3BN or telephone (0195) 957 2277.

## PRINCE WILLIAM'S BIRTHDAY
*21 JUNE*

## KNOLLYS ROSE CEREMONY
*24 JUNE*

The descendants of Sir Robert Knollys continue to pay his fine of one red rose every year to the Lord Mayor for leave to build a footbridge across Seething Lane. Write to: The Clerk to the Company of Waterman and Lighterman of the River Thames at Waterman's Hall, 16 St. Mary at Hill, EC3R 8EE or telephone (020) 7283 2373.

## LORD'S TEST MATCH
*3-5 DAYS IN JUNE OR JULY*

At Lord's Cricket Ground, St. John's Wood, NW8. For general information telephone: (020) 7289 1611/5. Ticket Office: (020) 7432 1066.

## HENLEY ROYAL REGATTA
*LATE JUNE OR EARLY JULY*

At Henley-on-Thames, Oxfordshire. This international rowing event is also a popular social occasion, with a stringent dress code. Dress rules are stringent (women must not wear trousers, culottes, split skirts or short skirts, and men must wear a jacket and tie at all times) in the Steward's Enclosure, which is reserved for members and their guests. The more informal Regatta Enclosure is for the general public and tickets may be purchased in advance after May 1, or upon arrival. Alternatively, take a picnic and sit alongside the towpath for free. Foe information, write to: The Secretary, Henley Royal Regatta, Regatta Headquarters, Henley-on-Thames, Oxfordshire RG9 2LY or telephone (0149) 157-2153; (www.hrr.co.uk).

## ALL ENGLAND TENNIS CHAMPIONSHIPS (WIMBLEDON)
*LAST WEEK IN JUNE OR FIRST WEEK IN JULY*

See chapter 14: Sports and Leisure for details on applying for tickets. For the public ballot, you must apply no later than December the year <u>before</u> you want to attend. Note that the tube stop is Southfields, not Wimbledon.

## ROYAL ASCOT
*USUALLY HELD THIRD WEEK IN JUNE*

Very important week for racegoers and equally important socially. Tuesday through Friday is attended by the Royal Family. Formal attire, hats and gloves required for ladies and full morning suit for men. To obtain passes for the Royal Enclosure write for an application to: The American Ambassador, US Embassy, Grosvenor Square, W1 or telephone (020) 7499 9000. Applications are then passed on to a sponsor, senator or someone else who has been on the Ambassador's list. Closing date is 30 March (30 April for those who have attended in previous years).

Tickets to the racecourse are purchased separately. Contact: Ascot Racecourse, Ascot, Berkshire; (0134) 462 2211.

### QUEEN'S CUP INTERNATIONAL POLO TOURNAMENT

The Guards Polo Club, Great Park, Windsor. For information: (01784) 434 212. Ticket Office: (01784) 437 797.

### HIGHLAND GAMES BEGIN

Many held during the summer all over Scotland. Traditional Scottish games and lots of local colour. Contact: The Scottish Tourist Board, 19 Cockspur Street, SW1Y 5BL; (020) 7930 8661.

### OUTDOOR CONCERTS

There is an annual summer opera season, featuring the Royal Philharmonic Orchestra, in Holland Park. Holland House, one of the oldest houses in Kensington, acts as a backdrop and many people picnic beforehand in the gardens – you can even collect a picnic hamper from the bar. Contact: (020) 7602 7856; (www.operahollandpark.com).

Outdoor classical music concerts in the long July and August evenings are held in the grounds of several historic houses around London, including 18th century Kenwood House in Hampstead Heath. Arrive early and bring a picnic, a rug, and plenty to drink. Advance booking is advised as most concerts are sellouts. (www.picnicconcerts.com)

Many other manor houses hold outdoor concerts during the summer. Dates vary each year so contact the individual locations. Some of the most popular are:

✓ Leeds Castle, Maidstone, Kent

✓ Hever Castle, Edenbridge, Kent

✓ Audley End House, Essex

✓ Wrest Park House, Bedfordshire

✓ Pevensey Castle, East Sussex

✓ Portchester Castle, Hampshire

✓ Marble Hill Park, Twickenham

Information is also available from English Heritage on (020) 7973 3427.

## JULY

### STREET THEATRE FESTIVAL

*THROUGHOUT JULY*

At St. Martin-in-the-Fields, Trafalgar Square, WC2.

### ROYAL NATIONAL EISTEDDFORD OF WALES
*JULY OR AUGUST*

An annual competitive festival of music, drama, literature, arts and crafts. Write to: The Eisteddfod Office, Moderator Wharf, Kinsway, Newport NP9 1EX.

### HENRY WOOD PROMENADE CONCERTS BEGIN (THE PROMS)

At the Royal Albert Hall, Kensington Gore, SW7. Celebrated series of orchestral concerts promoted by the BBC. Telephone: (020) 7589 8212. Guide books to The Proms available end of May, includes booking form.

### ROYAL INTERNATIONAL HORSE SHOW

Located in Hicksted. Foe information, telephone: The British Show Jumping Association; (0120) 369 6516.

### GOODWOOD WEEK HORSE RACING
*LAST TUESDAY TO SATURDAY IN JULY*

Race meeting at one of the most beautiful courses in the world, on top of the Sussex Downs. Details and tickets from the Goodwood Race Course, Goodwood, West Sussex on (0800) 018 8191 or visit www.goodwood.co.uk.

### BRITISH OPEN CHAMPIONSHIP

St. Andrew's Golf Course, Scotland. Top British golfing event. Write to: The Secretary, Royal and Ancient Golf Club, St. Andrews, Fife, KY16 98T.

### LADIES BRITISH OPEN CHAMPIONSHIPS

For information, write to: The Tournament Secretary, Ladies' Golf Union, The Scores, St. Andrews, Fife, KY16 98T.

### BRITISH GRAND PRIX

Premier motor racing event with the world's top drivers in action. Write to: Silverstone, Towcester, Northampton, NN12 8TN or telephone (0132) 785 7271.

### STRATFORD-UPON-AVON FESTIVAL

The Stratford Festival, featuring many literary, artistic and musical events, and a street carnival, takes place during the last 2 weeks of July and the first week of August in Stratford-upon-Avon, Warwickshire. Ring (01789) 293 127 or (01789) 267 969.

# AUGUST

## COWES WEEK
*IN JULY OR EARLY AUGUST*
On the Isle of Wight. Sailing races and festival usually attended by Royalty. Contact: The Isle of Wight Tourist Board, 21 High Street, Newport, Isle of Wight by telephoning (0198) 381 3800. Isle of Wight Tourism, Westridge Centre, Brabing Road, Ryde, Isle of Wight, PO33 1QS

## BUCKINGHAM PALACE OPENS TO VISITORS
*EARLY AUGUST TO THE END OF SEPTEMBER*
Buckingham Palace is the official London residence of Her Majesty the Queen. The Palace's staterooms and garden are open to visitors while the Queen is on her summer holidays in Scotland. Advance tickets (which will allow you to avoid some of the long queues) go on sale from the last week of July. Ring (020) 7321 2233, or book online at www.the-royal-collection.com/royaltickets. You can also purchase tickets on the day from the Ticket Office at Canada Gate in Green Park between 09:00 and 16:00.

## NOTTING HILL CARNIVAL
*AUGUST BANK HOLIDAY SUNDAY AND MONDAY*
Largest street festival in Europe. Children's events, including a costume competition, are on Sunday. Telephone: (020) 8964 0544.

## LONDON RIDING HORSE PARADE
At Rotten Row, Hyde Park. Contact: Brendan Byrne, Greater London Horseman's Association; (020) 8761 5651.

## EDINBURGH INTERNATIONAL FESTIVAL
Edinburgh, Scotland. Said to be the largest festival of the arts. Write to: The Edinburgh Festival Society, The Hub, Castlehill, Edinburgh, EH1 2NE, telephone (0131) 473 2001, or visit www.eif.co.uk.

## EDINBURGH MILITARY TATTOO
Military pageant held on floodlit grounds of Edinburgh Castle. Tickets can be purchased in London at the Scottish Tourist Board. Telephone: (020) 7930 8661.

## JERSEY BATTLE OF FLOWERS
On Jersey in the Channel Islands. A three-hour parade, held on Thursday afternoon and Friday evening by moonlight, of floats displaying thousands of flowers, bands, etc. Crowds gather along the route. Tickets required for the arena. Telephone: The Executive Officer, Jersey Battle of Flowers, Meadowbank, St. Peter's Valley, St. Lawrence, Jersey, Channel Islands, JE3 1EE; (01534) 30178.

## SEPTEMBER

### *LIBERAL DEMOCRATS PARTY CONFERENCE*

### *OBSERVANCE OF AUTUMN EQUINOX*
*21 SEPTEMBER*
Druids gather at Primrose Hill, Regent's Park, W1.

### *WINDSOR FESTIVAL*
Music and art. Write to: The Windsor Tourist Office, Central Station, Windsor, Berkshire SL4 1PJ or telephone (0175) 374 3900.

### *NATIONAL CARRIAGE DRIVING CHAMPIONSHIPS*
Windsor Castle Royal Mews. Write to: The Royal Mews, Windsor Castle, Windsor, Berkshire SL4 1NJ or telephone (0175) 386 0633.

## OCTOBER

### *Reminders:*
Send for Wimbledon Ballots. See June.

Send for Epiphany Tickets. See January.

Send for Cheltenham Hunt Meeting Tickets. See March.

### *TRAFALGAR DAY*
*21 OCTOBER*
At Nelson's Column, Trafalgar Square, WC2. The Royal Navy organises a remembrance service for Lord Nelson. Telephone: The London Tourist Board; (020) 7932 2000.

### *CONSERVATIVE PARTY CONFERENCE*

### *LABOUR PARTY CONFERENCE*

### *BRITISH SUMMER TIME ENDS*
*Clocks are set back one hour on the Sunday following the fourth Saturday in October.*

### *OPENING OF THE LAW COURTS*
At Westminster Abbey. A closed service is held at Westminster Abbey attended by Her Majesty's Judges and Queen's Counsel dressed in state robes and wigs. Afterwards, the Lord Chancellor leads the procession from the East end of the Abbey to the House of Lords. There is a reception lunch followed by a drive to the Royal Courts of Justice. The first motion of the year constitutes the official opening of the Courts. Telephone: The House of Lords Information Centre on (020) 7219

3000 or The London Tourist Board on (020) 7932 2000 or the Law Courts on (020) 7936 6000.

## COSTERMONGERS' HARVEST FESTIVAL

At St. Martins in the Fields, Trafalgar Square, WC2. The Pearly Kings and Queens, wearing their traditional pearl-buttoned covered suits, arrive in the afternoon for their annual service bearing gifts of food. Public welcome. Telephone: (020) 7930 1862.

## HORSE OF THE YEAR SHOW

*EARLY OCTOBER*

At the NEC in Birmingham. For tickets call (08700) 101 052 or book online at (www.hoys.co.uk). Tickets usually sell out quickly.

## NATIONAL BRASS BAND FESTIVAL

At the Royal Albert Hall, Kensington Gore, SW7. Telephone: (020) 7589 8212.

## NOVEMBER

## GUY FAWKES DAY (BONFIRE NIGHT)

*5 NOVEMBER*

Bonfires, fireworks and burning effigies of Guy Fawkes throughout the UK on the nearest weekend to this date, celebrate his failure to blow up the King and Parliament in the Gunpowder Plot of 1605. There is a particularly spectacular event at Leeds Castle in Kent, (01622) 765 400. The Evening Standard and Metro newspapers publish lists of bonfires and fireworks displays in the London area in the week leading up to Guy Fawkes Day.

## H.R.H. PRINCE OF WALES' BIRTHDAY

*14 NOVEMBER*

## BOUTIQUE DE NOEL

*EARLY NOVEMBER*

The Junior League of London's annual Christmas Fair features items hand crafted by members as well as unique gifts from selected vendors. Funds generated by the day and evening event support the community projects of the Junior League of London. For tickets write to: The Junior League of London, 9 Fitzmaurice Place, London W1X 6JD or telephone (020) 7499 8159.

## REMEMBRANCE SUNDAY

*ON THE SUNDAY CLOSEST TO 11 NOVEMBER*

Around the Cenotaph at Whitehall. A service is held in memory of those killed in battle since 1914. It is attended by the Queen, members of the Royal Family, the

Prime Minister, members of the Cabinet and members of the Opposition. Two minutes silence are observed as Big Ben strikes 11.00. During the week which precedes this event, volunteers sell poppies in the streets to raise money for ex-servicemen. Poppy wreaths are placed at many war memorials in village high streets and grave sites. Telephone: The London Tourist Board; (020) 7932 2000.

## LONDON TO BRIGHTON VETERAN CAR RACE
*FIRST SUNDAY*

Cars built prior to 31 December 1904 participate in the 60-mile run to Brighton. Departures from 08.00 at Hyde Park Corner. Pre-departure festivities and along the route. No tickets required. Write to: The RAC Motor Sports Association Ltd., Motor Sports House, Riverside Park, Colnbrook, Slough SL3 OHG, or telephone (0175) 368 1736.

## LORD MAYOR'S PROCESSION AND SHOW
*SECOND SATURDAY*

For the past 600 years, following the inauguration of the Lord Mayor, there is a great parade with elaborate floats through the City streets from Guildhall to the Royal Courts of Justice. No tickets required for viewing along the route. Ring the Public Relations Office; (020) 7606 3030 or (0891) 505 453.

## STATE OPENING OF PARLIAMENT

English pageantry at its finest. H.M. The Queen rides in the Irish state coach from Buckingham Palace to the House of Lords, where she reads a speech prepared by the party in power, outlining their intentions for the next session. Viewing along the route. The House of Lords is not open to the public. Telephone: (020) 7219 3000 or (0891) 505 453.

## CARAVAN AND OUTDOOR LEISURE SHOW

At the Earl's Court Exhibition Centre, Warwick Road, SW5 9TA. Contact: P. and O. Exhibitions Limited at Earl's Court Exhibition Centre. Telephone: (020) 7370 8203.

## DAILY MAIL SKI AND SNOWBOARD SHOW

The biggest consumer ski show in the world, held at the Olympia Exhibition Centre. Telephone (020) 8515 2000 or book online at www.dailymailskishow.co.uk.

## AMERICAN THANKSGIVING SERVICE
*THIRD THURSDAY IN NOVEMBER AT HIGH NOON*

St. Paul's Cathedral, St. Paul's Churchyard, EC4M. Telephone: The American Church of London; (020) 7580 2791.

# DECEMBER

### Reminders:

31st December - Last day to send in Ballots for Wimbledon. See June.

## SKATING AT SOMERSET HOUSE

In the Courtyard of Somerset House, The Strand, W1. Nearest tube Charing Cross. (020) 7845 4670 or www.somerset-house.org.uk. Ice rink at the centre of a historic London landmark, open in December and January only. A "must-visit", if only to drink hot mulled wine in the rink-side café by the light of flaming torches. Skates for hire.

## CHRISTMAS TREE LIGHTING CEREMONY

*EARLY IN THE MONTH*

At Trafalgar Square, WC2. Each year an enormous Christmas tree is donated by the people of Oslo, Norway in remembrance and thanks for British assistance during World War II. Contact: The London Tourist Bureau; (020) 7932 2000.

## HANDEL'S MESSIAH

At St. Paul's Cathedral and several other locations open to the public. Arrive early for good seats. Telephone: The Music Department at St. Paul's Cathedral, 5B Amen Court, London EC4; (020) 7236 6883.

## CHILDREN'S PANTOMIMES

Held throughout Britain in local theatres and Town Halls between mid-December and mid-January. Traditional pantomimes with male/female roles reversed, audience participation, sing-alongs and candy thrown into the audience. Especially popular in London and the seaside resort towns (e.g. Bournemouth). Check theatre listings or local newspapers for information from September.

## WINTER SOLSTICE

*21 DECEMBER*

## CHRISTMAS

*25 DECEMBER - Bank Holiday.*

## BOXING DAY

*26 DECEMBER - Bank Holiday.*

## NEW YEAR'S EVE

*31 DECEMBER*

Big Ben tolls at midnight, but do not be tempted to join in the crowds at Trafalgar Square – there is an unpleasant crush and nothing to see.

# Chapter Seventeen: Organisations

## EMBASSIES

In general, your embassy represents your government. The consular office within every embassy concerns itself with individual citizens. Most of your communication with your embassy will be through the consular office. Also, there are consular offices located in other cities where there is a high concentration of citizens of a specific nationality. In general, consular offices will help you with:

*Emergencies*

1. Death of a citizen abroad
2. Arrests (the embassy provides you with names of lawyers)
3. Financial assistance

*Non-emergencies*

1. Passports - particular help with stolen passports
2. Registering of births and deaths
3. Tax obligations (see Chapter Three)
4. Voting - help with absentee balloting
5. Notary Public

The following is a partial list of embassies in London:

*The Australian High Commission*, Australia House, Strand, WC2B; (020) 7379 4334, (www.australia.org.uk).

*The Belgian Embassy*, 103-105 Eaton Square, SW1; (020) 7470 3700, (www.belgium-embassy.co.uk).

*The Canadian High Commission*, Macdonald House, 38 Grosvenor Street, W1X; (020) 7258 6600, (www.canada.org.uk).

*The French Embassy*, 58 Knightsbridge, SW1X; (020) 7201 1000, (www.ambafrance.org.uk).

*The Embassy of the Federal Republic of Germany*, 23 Belgravia Square, SW1; (020) 7824 1300; (www.german-embassy.org.uk).

*Italian Embassy*, 14 Three Kings' Yard, Davies Street, W1; (020) 7312 2200; (www.embitaly.org.uk).

*The Embassy of Japan*, 101 Piccadilly, W1; (020) 7465 6500; (www.embjapan.org.uk).

*The Embassy of the Netherlands*, 38 Hyde Park Gate, SW7; (020) 7590 3200; (www.netherlands-embassy.org.uk).

*The New Zealand High Commission*, New Zealand House, 80 Haymarket, SW1; (020) 7930 8422; (www.newzealandhc.org.uk)

*The Embassy of Spain*, 39 Chesham Place, SW1X; (020) 7235 5555.

*The Swiss Embassy*, 16 Montagu Place, W1; (020) 7616 6000. (www.swissembassy.org.uk)

*Embassy of United Arab Emirates*, 30 Prince's Gate, SW7; (020) 7581 1281.

*The Embassy of the United States of America*, 24-31 Grosvenor Square, W1A; (020) 7499 9000 (24 hour switchboard); (www.usembassy.org.uk). For visas only, telephone (0891) 200 290. For visas, there is an operator assisted visa information service on (09061) 500 590 Monday through Friday between 08.00 and 20.00, and Saturday between 10:00 and 16:00. Calls are charged £1.50/minute. The building was designed by Eero Saarinen and completed in 1960. Guided tours may be arranged in advance.

## Hours

*Embassy and Consular Section*: Monday to Friday, 08.30 to 17.30.

*Reference Library*: Monday to Friday, 10.00 to 12.00.

## Holidays

The Embassy is closed on all official American and British holidays. If a holiday falls on a Saturday, the Embassy is closed on the preceding Friday. If the holiday is on a Sunday, the Embassy is closed on the following Monday. Official US holidays are as follows:

| | |
|---|---|
| *New Year's Day* | – 1 January |
| *Martin Luther King's Birthday* | – third Monday in January |
| *Washington's Birthday* | – third Monday of February |
| *Memorial Day* | – last Monday of May |
| *Independence Day* | – 4 July |
| *Labor Day* | – first Monday of September |
| *Columbus Day* | – second Monday of October |
| *Veterans' Day* | – 11 November |
| *Thanksgiving Day* | – fourth Thursday of November |
| *Christmas Day* | – 25 December |

**Division of Agencies.** The Embassy is divided into six sections:

Administrative (Ext. 2234)

Consular (Ext. 2515)

Defence (Ext. 2745)

Economic (Ext. 2411)

Political (Ext. 2120)

Public Affairs (Ext. 2611)

Helpful Information:

*Passport and Citizenship Branch* - Ext. 2563/ 2564 (Travel information and warnings are available from this office); Hours: 08.30 to 12.00, Monday through Friday.

*Internal Revenue Service* - Ext. 2476; Public access hours: Tuesday to Thursday, 09.00 to 16.00, closed for lunch from 12.00 to 13.00; Phone enquiries Monday to Friday, 09.00 to 12.00.

*Commercial Library* - Open to business professionals for research by appointment. Monday through Friday, 09.00 to 12.00 and 14.00 to 16.00.

**The Ambassador**

The Ambassador is the highest ranking American official in the United Kingdom and is the personal representative of the President of the United States of America to Her Majesty the Queen. The full title for the American Ambassador is *'Ambassador Extraordinary and Plenipotentiary to the Court of St. James's, His (Her) Excellency The Honorable'*. If you should write to the Ambassador, the letter should be addressed with the full title of *'His (Her) Excellency The Ambassador of the United States of America'*.

The Deputy Chief of Mission (the 'DCM'), usually referred to as 'Minister' assists the Ambassador and is responsible for the day-to-day operation of the Embassy. He becomes Charge d'Affaires in the absence from the United Kingdom of the Ambassador and assumes all responsibilities.

## PROFESSIONAL ORGANISATIONS

*The American Banks Club,* First Chicago NBD, 1 Triton Square, NW1; (020) 7903 4437.

*American Chamber of Commerce* (United Kingdom), 75 Brook Street, W1; (020) 7493 0381; (www.amcham.org.uk). Independent non-profit organisation which provides assistance to member companies in the expansion of their activities on both sides of the Atlantic. Services to members include publications, luncheons, lectures, and seminars relating to Anglo-American affairs and business.

*American Women Lawyers in London,* General Counsel, Rolls-Royce Power Ventures Ltd., Arlington House, 150 Victoria Street, SW1; (020) 7227 9000.

*Association of MBAs, 15 Duncan Terrace,* N1; (020) 7837 3375; (www.mba.org.uk).

*British-American Chamber of Commerce,* 8 Staple Inn, WC1; (020) 7404 6400; (www.bacc.org.uk).

*Enterprising Women,* 10 Stratton Street, W1X; (070) 4404 7797; (www.ew-network.com).

*Institute of Directors,* 116 Pall Mall, SW1; (020) 7839 1233; (www.iod.co.uk).

*Institute of Management,* 2 Savoy Court, The Strand, WC2R; (020) 7497 0580. (www.inst-mgt.org.uk).

## CHARITABLE, SOCIAL AND SERVICE ORGANISATIONS

*The American Society in London,* The Secretary, 37 Charles Street, W1X; (020) 7732 5225. Organisation for American expatriates which sponsors numerous social events and outings, celebrating American holidays and traditions including a July 4th picnic at the Ambassador's Residence and a Thanksgiving Dinner Dance.

*American Women's Club of London,* Connaught Room, 68 Old Brompton Road, SW7; (020) 7589 8292. (http://london.fawco.org). Social, recreational and charitable club with facilities for American women living in London.

*The American Women of Surrey,* P.O. Box 170, Cobham, Surrey KT11 2YJ; (01426) 904 307; (www.awsurrey.org). A social club and support group for American women living in Surrey.

*CARE International;* 10-13 Rushworth Street, SE1 0RB; (020) 7934 9334. www.careinternational.org.uk. Charitable organisation founded in America after World War II. Today it is a confederation of humanitarian organisations which act together to provide emergency responses and assist long-term development to the world's poorest people.

*Centre for Creative Communities,* 118 Commercial Street, E1; (020) 7247 5385. (www.creativecommunities.org.uk). Charitable organisation for professional artists. The Association is geared to strengthening links and increasing opportunities in the arts and arts administration between the United States and the United Kingdom.

*Chilterns American Women's Club*, Contact: Membership Chairman, P.O. Box 445, Gerrards Cross, Buckinghamshire SL9 8YU; 07626 927 533; (http://cawc.fawco.org). Operates in the Gerrards Cross and Beaconsfield area. A friendly mix of women from all areas of the US and Canada. Monthly meetings plus a great variety of activities and charitable fundraising.

*Cyclists Touring Club*, Cotterell House, 69 Meadrow, Godalming, Surrey GU7 3HS; (01483) 417 217; (www.ctc.org.uk). Britain's national cycling organisation. All ages welcome, though under 14's should be accompanied by an adult.

*Democrats Abroad (UK)*, Suite 240, 56 Gloucester Road, SW7; (020) 7724 9796. (www.democratsabroad.org.uk). Political interest group supporting the US Democratic Party with the power to organise and elect delegates to the National Convention.

*East Anglia American Club*, contact Riki Evans (01440) 714 748 (e-mail: rikievans@aol.com). Social club that covers areas Cambridgeshire, Sussex, Essex, and Norfolk.

*English Heritage*, 23 Saville Row, W1; (020) 7973 3000; (www.english-heritage.org.uk). Offers exhibitions, museums, guided tours as well as historical re-enactments, displays, concerts and other special events. Funds from the membership help protect and preserve England's historical legacy.

*English Speaking Union*, Dartmouth House, 37 Charles Street, W1X; (020) 7493 3328. A world-wide registered charity with facilities supported by membership and donations whose aim is to promote international understanding through a variety of social and educational activities including scholarships, lectures, outings, receptions.

*Focus Information Services*, 13 Prince of Wales Terrace, W8; (020) 7937 7799; (www.focus-info.org.uk). Monday to Thursday, 10.00 to 16.00. Information line: (020) 7937 0050; Monday to Thursday 10.00 to 14.00. Non-profit organisation that functions as a clearing-house of information concerning community services, schools, child care, organisations, etc. Offers telephone information line, career and educational services, and seminars and workshops for the international community in the United Kingdom.

*The Georgian Group*, 6 Fitzroy Square, W1; (020) 7387 1720; (www.heritage.co.uk/georgian). Special interest group concerned with the preservation of and education about Georgian England through trips, seminars and lectures.

*Hampstead Women's Club*, Margaret Rodgers, 9 Hampstead Hill Mansions, Downshire Hill, NW1; (020) 7431 2025; (www.hampsteadclub.com). Social club for women living in the Hampstead area.

*The Junior League of London*, 9 Fitzmaurice Place, W1X; (020) 7499 8159; (www.jll.org.uk). An international organisation of women committed to promoting voluntary service and improving the community through the effective action and leadership of trained volunteers. A registered charity active in the areas of social welfare, the education and welfare of children and the arts and culture.

*The Kensington Chelsea Women's Club,* PO Box 567, 28 Old Brompton Road, SW7; (020) 7863 7562; (www.kcwc.org.uk). Since 1983 the KCWC has provided social contact and cultural exchange for women in London, both expatriates and British nationals. Monthly meetings with prominent guest speakers promote exchange among membership of 1,700. Newsletter contains active monthly calendar from Antiques to Working Women.

*Lansdowne Club,* 9 Fitzmaurice Place, W1X; (020) 7629 7200; (www.lansdowne-club.co.uk). A private club which offers a swimming pool, squash courts and a fencing salle as well as a ballroom, restaurant and regular activities such as Scottish country dancing, chess and bridge.

*London Ladies Club,* P.O. Box 3870, SW1W; (020) 7730 4640. Contact: Membership Chairman.

*National Trust for Places of Historic Interest or National Beauty,* (known as the National Trust), 36 Queen Anne's Gate, SW1; (0870) 609 5380; (www.nationaltrust.org.uk). A non-profit organisation and special interest group which purchases or is bequeathed historic properties or places of great natural beauty that are preserved for the nation. Membership by subscription entitles anyone to free entry to properties, various publications, etc. There are also local branches which sponsor activities and trips.

*The Pilgrims,* The Savoy Hotel, The Strand, WC2R; (020) 7836 1533. Anglo-American dining club which meets at the Savoy and was founded in 1902 to improve Anglo-American relations. Membership by election.

*Republicans Abroad* (UK), 56 Prince's Gate, SW7; (020) 7590 9244; (www.republicansabroad.org). Political interest group supporting the US Republican Party with the power to organise and elect delegates to the National Convention.

*Rotary Club of London,* 6 York Gate, NW1; (020) 7487 5429; (www.londonrotaryclub.org.uk).

*St. John's Wood Women's Club,* (020) 7266 2237, (www.sjwwc.org.uk). Social club for women living in the St. John's Wood area.

*United Oxford and Cambridge University Club,* 71 Pall Mall, SW1Y; (020) 7930 5151; (www.uocuc.co.uk). World-wide reciprocal agreements. Telephone for information on club facilities and extensive activities.

*United Kingdom Panhellenic Association.* Contact: Dena Lee Crooke on (020) 7937 1771 for information.

*University Women's Club,* 2 Audley Square, W1Y; (020) 7499 2268; (www.the-university-womens-club.co.uk). Social club with facilities for women university graduates or women who are not graduates but professionally qualified.

*Victoria and Albert - Art of Living Club,* Decorative Art Exhibitions and Lecture Programmes, 79 Hurlingham Court, Ranelagh Gardens, SW6; (020) 8741 8691.

*Victorian Society,* 1 Priory Gardens, W4; (020) 8994 1019; (www.victorian-society.org.uk). Special interest group concerned with the preservation of and education about Victorian England through trips, seminars and lectures.

*W&G Foyle Literary Lunches,* 113 Charing Cross Road, WC2; (020) 7440 3227; (www.luncheons.foyles.co.uk). Afternoon events with lectures by newsmakers and world leaders.

## PLACES OF WORSHIP

### Baptist

*Bethesda Baptist Church,* Kensington Place, W8; (020) 7221 7039. International congregation with an American pastor.

### Buddhist

*West London Buddhist Centre,* 94 Westbourne Park Villas, W2; (020) 7727 9382.

*The Buddhist Society,* 58 Eccleston Square, SW1; (020) 7834 5858.

### Catholic

*Archdiocese of Westminster,* (www.westminsterdiocese.org.uk).

*Brompton Oratory,* Brompton Road, SW7; (020) 7589 4811. Largest Catholic church in London. High Church and Latin Mass.

*Holy Cross Catholic Church,* Ashington Road, SW6; (020) 7736 1068.

*St. Mary's RC Church,* Cadogan Street, SW3; (020) 7589 5487.

### Church of England

Diocese of London, 36 Causton Street, SW1; (020) 7932 1100. (www.london.anglican.org).

*Holy Trinity Brompton,* Brompton Road, SW7; (020) 7581 8255. Evangelical church with contemporary worship style and Sunday school for children. Located behind Brommpton Oratory.

*St. Lukes and Christ Church,* Sydney Street, SW3; (020) 7351 7365. Traditional worship style but not High Anglican. Sunday school for children.

*St. Michael Church of England Church,* Chester Square, SW1; (020) 7730 8889. Family-oriented worship style with children's Sunday school.

**Hindu**

*Shree Swaminarayan Mandir,* 105-119 Brentfield Road, Neasden NW10, (020) 8965 2651.

**Interdenominational**

*American Church in London (ACL),* 79 Tottenham Court Road, W1P; (020) 7580 2791. An international and interdenominational, Christ-centred community of faith located in the heart of London. Sunday worship service held at 11.00 a.m. with coffee hour following.

**Islam**

*Islamic Universal Association,* 20 Penzance Place, Holland Park Avenue, W11; (020) 7602 5273.

**Jewish - Orthodox**

*United Synagogue,* High Road, Finchley, N12; (020) 8343 8989.

Also contact *The Reform Synagogues of Great Britain;* (020) 8349 4731.

**Jewish - Reform**

*West London Synagogue,* Upper Berkeley Street, W1; (020) 7723 4404.

Also contact *Joint Israel Appeal;* (020) 8446 1477.

**Methodist**

*Methodist Central Hall Westminster,* Storeys Gate, SW1; (020) 7222 8010.

**Mormon**

*Church of Jesus Christ of Latter Day Saints,* 64-68 Exhibition Road, SW7; (020) 7589 8561.

# Recommended Reading

The number of books and publications available regarding information on Britain must number thousands. The listings below form a good basis for research. As you settle in and find your neighbourhood bookstore be sure to explore the wealth of information available to you. The books on Britain's villages, historical homes and heritage make wonderful keepsakes, as they are often beautifully printed as well as informative.

## ACCOMMODATION AND RESTAURANTS

✓ *Egon Ronay's Cellnet Guide to Hotels and Restaurants*, published by Pan Macmillan Publishers Ltd.

✓ *The Good Bed and Breakfast Guide*, by Elsie Dillard, Susan Causin.

✓ *The Good Food Guide*, edited by Drew Smith.

✓ *Johansens Recommended Hotels in Great Britain and Ireland*, edited by Adrian Bridgewater. Revised yearly.

✓ *Johansens Recommended Inns and Restaurants in Great Britain*, edited by Adrian Bridgewater. Revised yearly.

✓ *Signpost Hotel Guide*, published by Signpost Ltd. Revised annually.

✓ *Time Out Guide: Eating and Drinking in London*, Timeout Publishing Ltd. Revised annually.

✓ *Zagat Survey: London Restaurants.* Revised annually.

## BACKGROUND
### Insights into being a Foreigner in a Foreign Land

✓ *ASA Citizens Abroad; A Handbook*, Written by American Citizens Abroad, Gannett News Media Services, Available from USA Today Books: P.O. Box 450, Washington DC, 20044, USA: 703-276-5978.

✓ *Brit-think - Ameri-think*, by Jane Walmsley.

✓ *Dictionary of Britain; An A to Z of The British Way of Life*, by Adrian Room.

✓ *The English Companion; An Idiosyncratic A-Z of England and Englishness*, by Godfrey Smith. (Available in the US only).

### Social and Political History of Great Britain: Both Past and Contemporary

✓ *Britain: An Official Handbook*, HMSO Publications Centre (revised yearly).

✓ *British Politics Today*, by Bill Jones, Dennis Kavanagh.

✓ *Contemporary British Politics, An Introduction*, by Bill Coxall, Lynton Robins.

✓ *A Dictionary of British History*, edited by J. P. Kenyon.

✓ *Introduction to British Politics*, by John Dearlove, Peter Saunders.

✓ *The Lives of the Kings and Queens of England*, edited by Antonia Fraser.

✓ *The Oxford History of Britain*, edited by Kenneth O. Morgan.

✓ *A Social History of England*, by Asa Brigg.

✓ *The Story of England*, by Christopher Hibbert.

✓ *A Vision of Britain*, by Prince Charles.

## CHILDREN AND MOTHERS

✓ *Good Nanny Guide*, by Charlotte Breese, Hilaire Gomer.

✓ *The Good Schools Guide*, by Amanda Atha, Sarah Drummond.

✓ *Look Out, London*, by Louise Nicholson, an illustrated guide to London for children to use.

✓ *Nicholson's Children's Guide*, Robert Nicholson Publications Ltd.

✓ *Working Mother: A Practical Handbook for the Nineties*, by Sarah Litvinoff and Marianne Velmans.

✓ *When I Go to Work I Feel Guilty: Working Mothers Guide to Sanity and Survival*, by Jenney Mosley and Eileen Gillibrand.

## CULTURE

✓ *Fodor's London Companion*, by Louise Nicholson, winner of the London Tourist award.

✓ *London's Best Kept Secrets*, by Mike Michaelson.

✓ *The London Encyclopedia*, edited by Ben Weinreb, Christopher Hibbert.

✓ *London Museums and Collections*, edited by G. M. S. Scimone, M. F. Levey.

✓ *The Time Out Guide*, Penguin Books.

## HOUSING

✓ *Evening Standard Where to Live in London*.

✓ *Sunday Telegraph Guide to Commuterland*, by Caroline McGhie.

✓ *The New London Property Guide*, by Carrie Segrave.

✓ *Where to Live in London*, by Sara McConnell.

✓ *Where to Live in London*, edited by Liz Veroce (revised yearly).

## 'HOW TO . . .' GET BY

✓ *AA Citypack: London*, by Louise Nicholson, part of a new series providing essential information in a clear format.

✓ *An American's Guide to Living Abroad*, published by Living Abroad Publishing Inc.

✓ *The British Puzzle*, Beaconsfield/Chiltern Women's Club.

✓ *The Companion Guide to London*, by David Piper.

✓ *Going International: How to Make Friends and Deal Effectively in the Global Marketplace*, by Lennie Copeland, Lewis Griggs. (Available in the US).

✓ *Living and Working in Britain, A Survival Handbook*, by David Hampshire.

✓ *Moving and Living Abroad*, by Sandra Albright, Alice Chu, Lori Austen. (Available in the US).

✓ *USA Citizens Abroad*, USA Today Books, Code CAI, P.O. Box 450, Washington DC, 20044.

## MEDICAL SERVICES

✓ *The Good Doctor Guide*, by Martin Page

## SERVICES

✓ *A Time Out Guide: Services in London*, Time Out Publications Ltd.

## SHOPPING

✓ *Sheila Chichester's London Woman, Her Shopping and Fashion Guide*, by Sheila Chichester.

✓ *A Time Out Guide: Shopping in London*, Time Out Publications.

## SPORTS AND FITNESS

✓ *Where to Ride*, British Horse Society.

# Notes

# Glossary

See Chapter Nine: Cooking, Food and Drink for Glossary of food-related words. See Chapter Two: Housing for Glossary of housing-related words. See Chapter Eight: Children for Glossary of words specific to children's items. See page 285 for British to American Glossary.

| AMERICAN | BRITISH |
|---|---|
| **A** | |
| antenna | aerial |
| appetizer | starter |
| attic | loft |
| advice columnist | agony aunt |
| Australian | Aussie |
| **B** | |
| baby carriage or buggy | pram |
| baked potato | jacket potato |
| ball point pen | biro |
| band-aid | plaster/elastoplast |
| bangs | fringe |
| baseboard | skirting board |
| bathrobe | dressing-gown |
| bathing suit | swimming costume |
| bill (account) | invoice |
| bill (money) | banknote, note |
| blanket (travelling) | travelling rug |
| blender | liquidizer |
| bobbie pin | hair grip/kirby grip |
| boots (waterproof) | wellies (wellington boots) |
| broil/broiler | grill |
| buddy | mate |
| **C** | |
| cake | gateau (or cake) |
| calendar (personal) | diary |
| call (telephone) | ring up |
| call collect | reverse charges |
| can | tin |
| candy/candy bar | sweets/chocolate bar |
| candy store | confectioners/sweet shop |
| cash register | till |

| | |
|---|---|
| change purse | purse |
| check (restaurant) | bill |
| checkers (game) | draughts |
| checkroom | cloakroom |
| cleaning lady | domestic help |
| closet (hanging clothes) | wardrobe |
| clothes pin | clothes peg |
| cocktail party | drinks party |
| college/university | university |
| comforter | duvet |
| contractor | builder |
| coveralls (workmen's) | boiler suit |
| cookie | biscuit |
| costume | fancy dress |
| cotton balls | cotton wool |
| crib/baby bed | cot |
| crosswalk | zebra crossing |
| cuffs (pants) | turn-ups (trousers) |
| curb (sidewalk) | kerb (pavement) |
| curling iron | curling tongs |

**D**

| | |
|---|---|
| daycare center | creche |
| delivery truck | delivery lorry/van |
| denatured alcohol | methylated spirits |
| dessert | pudding/sweet |
| detour | diversion |
| diaper | nappy |
| dime store/five and ten | Woolworths |
| directory assistance | directory enquiries |
| dishes, do the | washing up |
| dishwashing liquid (hand) | washing up liquid |
| divided highway | dual carriageway |
| Do-It-Yourself | DIY |
| doctor's/dentist's office | surgery |
| doorman | porter |
| drapes/draperies | curtains |
| drugstore/pharmacist | chemist |
| drunk | pissed |
| drygoods store | (materials) draper |
| dump (garbage) | tip (rubbish) |
| dumpster (construction) | skip |
| duplex/triplex | maisonette |
| dust ruffle | valance |

# E

| | |
|---|---|
| eggplant | aubergine |
| electric cord/wire | lead |
| electric golf cart | golf buggy |
| elevator | lift |
| elementary school | junior school |
| eraser | rubber |
| Europe | Continental Europe/The Continent |
| extension cord | extension lead |

# F

| | |
|---|---|
| faucet | tap |
| fender (car) | bumper |
| first floor | ground floor |
| flashlight | torch |
| freeway/super highway | motorway |
| F.T.D. (florist) | Interflora |
| furnace/hot water heater | boiler |
| French fries | chips |

# G

| | |
|---|---|
| garbage (trash) | rubbish/refuse |
| garbage/trash can | dustbin/bin |
| garden hose | hose pipe |
| garter belt | suspenders |
| gas | petrol |
| gear shift (car) | gear lever |
| glasses (eyes) | spectacles/specs |
| grade (school) | class/form |
| grocery cart | trolley |
| ground wire | earth wire/earth |

# H

| | |
|---|---|
| half-bath/powder room | cloakroom |
| hamburger/ground beef | mince |
| hardware store | ironmonger |
| hat check girl | cloakroom attendant |
| homework | prep (or homework) |
| hood (car) | bonnet |
| housewares | hardware |

# I

| | |
|---|---|
| incorporated/Inc. | limited/Ltd |
| information (phone) | enquiry |
| installment payment plan | hire purchase plan |
| intermission | interval |

## J

| | |
|---|---|
| janitor | cleaner |
| jello | jelly |
| jelly | jam |
| jump rope | skipping rope |
| jumper | pinafore dress |
| jumper cables (car) | jump leads |

## K

| | |
|---|---|
| kerosene | paraffin |
| knickers | knickerbockers/plus fours |

## L

| | |
|---|---|
| lawyer/attorney | solicitor |
| lawyer (trial) | barrister |
| leash (dog) | lead |
| legal holiday | bank holiday |
| lemonade | lemon squash |
| licence plate | number/registration plate |
| line (stand in) | queue |
| linen closet | airing cupboard |
| liquor | spirits |
| liquor store | off licence |
| living room | sitting/reception room/lounge |
| lost and found | lost property |
| lounge suit | business suit |

## M

| | |
|---|---|
| maid | cleaner/domestic |
| mail/mailman | post/postman |
| mailbox | pillar box (antiquated)/post box |
| main street | high street |
| make out (kiss) | snog |
| make reservations | book |
| martini | gin or vodka martini |
| mezzanine | dress circle |
| milk truck | milk float |
| money order | postal order |
| monkey wrench | adjustable spanner |
| motorcycle | motorbike |
| motor vehicle inspection test | M.O.T. |
| movie | film |
| movie house/theatre | cinema |

| | |
|---|---|
| moving van | removal van/ pantechnicon (antiquated) |
| moving company | removal company |
| muffler (car) | silencer |

**N**

| | |
|---|---|
| napkins | serviettes/napkins |
| newsdealer/newsstand | newsagent |
| nipple (baby bottle) | teat |
| notions | haberdashery |
| number used twice (55) | double number (double 5) |
| number used three times (555) | treble number (treble 5) |
| nursery | creche |

**O**

| | |
|---|---|
| on the prowl | on the pull |
| one way ticket | single ticket |
| orchestra seats (theatre) | stalls |
| outlet/socket (electrical) | point/power point/plug socket |
| oven | cooker |
| overpass (highway) | flyover |

**P**

| | |
|---|---|
| pacifier (for baby) | dummy |
| package | parcel |
| packing tape | parcel tape |
| paint (interior house) | emulsion |
| painter | decorator |
| panty hose | tights |
| pantry | larder |
| pants | trousers |
| paper towels | kitchen roll |
| parka (lined) | anorak |
| parka (unlined) | kagoule |
| parking brake | hand brake |
| parking lot | car park |
| pass (vehicle) | overtake |
| pavement | tarmac |
| pay telephone | phone box |
| period (punctuation) | full stop |
| ping pong paddle | table tennis bat |
| pit (fruit) | stone |
| pitcher | jug |
| porch (enclosed) | conservatory |
| pot holder/gloves | oven gloves/mitt |

| | |
|---|---|
| potato chips | crisps |
| precinct | district |
| principal (school) | headmaster/mistress |
| private school | public/fee paying school/private |
| public school | state school/grammar school |
| pull-off (driving) | lay-by |
| pump (shoe) | court shoe |
| purse/pocketbook | handbag |

## R

| | |
|---|---|
| raincoat | mackintosh (mac) |
| range | cooker |
| real estate agent | estate agent |
| rear view mirror (outside) | wing mirror |
| recess (school) | break, holiday |
| rent (goods) | hire |
| rent (real estate) | let |
| repairman | engineer |
| restroom/toilet | cloakroom/.W.C./loo/toilet |
| roast (meat) | joint |
| roomer/boarder | lodger |
| round trip ticket | return ticket |
| rubber bands | elastic bands |
| rubber cement | cow gum/studio gum |
| rubbing alcohol | surgical spirit |
| run (for public office) | stand |
| run (in nylons) | ladder (in tights) |

## S

| | |
|---|---|
| sack lunch | packed lunch |
| sales clerk | shop assistant |
| Santa Claus | Father Christmas/Santa Claus |
| Saran Wrap | cling film |
| schedule | time-table |
| scotch tape | cellotape |
| scratch pad | scribbling pad/book/jotter |
| second floor | first floor |
| sedan (car) | saloon |
| semester (school) | term (three yearly) |
| Seven-Up/Sprite | lemonade |
| sewer pipe/soil pipe | drain |
| shade (window) | blind/roller blind |
| sheers (under drapes) | net curtains |
| shopping bag | carrier bag |

| | |
|---|---|
| shorts (underwear) | pants |
| shot/injection | jab |
| shoulder (highway) | hard shoulder |
| sideburns | sideboards |
| sidewalk | pavement |
| sink | basin |
| slash (/) | stroke/oblique |
| snaps (sewing) | press studs/poppers |
| sneakers/tennis shoes | trainers/plimsolls |
| soccer | football |
| sod (new grass) | turf |
| soft shoulder (road) | verge/hard shoulder |
| spool (thread) | cotton reel |
| sports clothes/equipment | kit |
| stamped addressed envelope | S.A.E. |
| stand in line | queue |
| station wagon | estate car |
| sterling (silver) | hallmarked/solid |
| stove/cooktop | hob |
| straight (cocktail) | neat |
| stroller | pushchair/buggy |
| subway | tube/underground |
| supper | tea/supper |
| surgery (medical) | theatre/operating theatre |
| suspenders | braces |
| sweatpants | tracksuit bottoms |
| sweater/pullover | jumper/jersey |
| swimming pool | baths |
| swindler (home repair) | cowboy builders |

**T**

| | |
|---|---|
| thanks | ta/cheers (or thanks) |
| take out (food) | take-away |
| tag | label |
| tea | afternoon tea |
| tea cart | tea trolley |
| warm-up (tennis) | knock-about |
| thread | cotton |
| thumb tack | drawing pin |
| tic-tac-toe | noughts and crosses |
| tired | knackered |
| time payment | hire-purchase |
| toilet/bathroom/john | lavatory/toilet/loo |
| tour bus | coach |
| traffic circle | roundabout |

| | |
|---|---|
| trailer/camper/mobile home | caravan |
| training wheels | stabilizers |
| truck | lorry |
| truck (semi) | juggernaut |
| trunk (car) | boot |
| t-shirt | vest |
| T.V. | telly |
| two weeks | fortnight |

**U**

| | |
|---|---|
| umbrella | brollie |
| underground/pedestrian passage | subway |
| underpants/panties | knickers/pants |
| undershirt | vest |

**V**

| | |
|---|---|
| vacation | holiday |
| vacuum (cleaner) | Hoover |
| valance (drapes) | pelmet |
| vest | waistcoat |

**W**

| | |
|---|---|
| wade | paddle |
| Wall Street (financial industry) | The City |
| wall-to-wall carpet | fitted carpet |
| wallet | purse |
| wash cloth | face flannel/face cloth |
| wash up | wash your hands |
| water heater (electric) | immersion heater |
| water heater (gas) | geyser |
| wax paper | grease proof paper |
| wharf/pier | quay (pron. 'key') |
| whining | whinging |
| windbreaker | windcheater/kagoul |
| windshield | windscreen |
| with or without? | white or black? |
| (milk or cream in coffee) | |
| wrench | spanner |

**Y**

| | |
|---|---|
| yard | garden |

**Z**

| | |
|---|---|
| Z | 'zed' (pron.) |
| zero | nil/nought/zero |
| zip code | post code |

| | |
|---|---|
| zucchini | courgette |

**A**

| | |
|---|---|
| adjustable spanner | monkey wrench |
| aerial | antenna |
| afternoon tea | tea |
| agony aunt | advice columnist |
| airing cupboard | linen closet |
| anorak | parka (lined) |
| aubergine | eggplant |
| Aussie | Australian |

**B**

| | |
|---|---|
| bank holiday | legal holiday |
| banknote, note | bill (money) |
| barnet | haircut |
| barrister | lawyer (trial) |
| basin | sink |
| baths | swimming pool |
| bill | check (restaurant) |
| biro | ball point pen |
| biscuit | cookie |
| blind/roller blind | shade (window) |
| boiler | furnace/hot water heater |
| boiler suit | coveralls (workmen's) |
| builder | contractor |
| bonnet | hood (car) |
| book | make reservations |
| boot | trunk (car) |
| braces | suspenders |
| break, holiday | recess (school) |
| brollie | umbrella |
| Brummie | accent or person from Birmingham |
| bumper | fender (car) |
| business suit | lounge suit |

# C

| | |
|---|---|
| car park | parking lot |
| caravan | trailer/camper/mobile home |
| carrier bag | shopping bag |
| cellotape | scotch tape |
| chemist | drugstore/pharmacist |
| chips | French fries |
| cinema | movie house/theatre |
| class/form | grade (school) |
| cleaner/domestic | maid or janitor |
| cling film | Saran wrap |
| cloakroom | checkroom/half-bath/powder room |
| cloakroom attendant | hat check girl |
| clothes peg | clothes pin |
| coach | tour bus |
| Cockney | accent or person from East End of London |
| confectioners/sweet shop | candy store |
| conservatory | porch (enclosed) |
| Continental Europe/The Continent | Europe |
| cooker | oven/range |
| cot | crib/baby bed |
| cotton | thread |
| cotton reel | spool (thread) |
| cotton wool | cotton balls |
| courgette | zucchini |
| court shoe | pump (shoe) |
| cowboy builders | swindler (home repair) |
| cow gum/studio gum | rubber cement |
| creche | daycare center/nursery |
| crisps | potato chips |
| curling tongs | curling iron |
| curtains | drapes/draperies |

# D

| | |
|---|---|
| decorator | painter |
| delivery lorry/van | delivery truck |
| diary | calendar (personal) |
| directory enquiries | directory assistance |
| district | precinct |
| diversion | detour |
| DIY | Do-It-Yourself |
| domestic help | cleaning lady |
| double number (double 5) | number used twice (55) |

| | |
|---|---|
| drain | sewer pipe/soil pipe |
| draper (materials) | drygoods store |
| draughts | checkers (game) |
| drawing pin | thumb tack |
| dress circle | mezzanine |
| dressing gown | bathrobe |
| drinks party | cocktail party |
| dual carriageway | divided highway |
| dummy | pacifier (for baby) |
| dustbin/bin | garbage/trash can |
| duvet | comforter |

**E**

| | |
|---|---|
| earthwire/earth | ground wire |
| elastic bands | rubber bands |
| emulsion | paint (interior house) |
| engineer | repairman |
| enquiry | information (phone) |
| estate agent | real estate agent |
| estate car | station wagon |
| extension lead | extension cord |

**F**

| | |
|---|---|
| face flannel/face cloth | wash cloth |
| fancy dress | costume |
| Father Christmas/Santa Claus | Santa Claus |
| film | movie |
| first floor | second floor |
| fitted carpet | wall-to-wall carpet |
| fiver | five pound note |
| flyover | overpass (highway) |
| football | soccer |
| fortnight | two weeks |
| fringe | bangs |
| full stop | period (punctuation) |

**G**

| | |
|---|---|
| garden | yard |
| gateau (or cake) | cake |
| gear lever | gear shift (car) |
| Geordie | accent or person from North Eastern England |
| geyser | water heater (gas) |

| | |
|---|---|
| gin or vodka martini | martini |
| golf buggy | electric golf cart |
| grease proof paper | wax paper |
| grill | broil/broiler |
| ground floor | first floor |

### H

| | |
|---|---|
| haberdashery | notions |
| hallmarked/solid | sterling (silver) |
| handbag | purse/pocketbook |
| hand brake | parking brake |
| hard shoulder | shoulder (highway) |
| hardware | housewares/hardware |
| hair grip/kirby grip | bobbie pin |
| headmaster/mistress | principal (school) |
| high street | main street |
| hire | rent (goods) |
| hire purchase | time payment |
| hire purchase plan | installment payment plan |
| hob | stove/cooktop |
| holiday | vacation |
| hoover | vacuum (cleaner) |
| hose pipe | garden hose |

### I

| | |
|---|---|
| immersion heater | water heater (electric) |
| Interflora | F.T.D. (florist) |
| interval | intermission |
| invoice | bill (account) |
| ironmonger | hardware store |

### J

| | |
|---|---|
| jab | shot/injection |
| jam | jelly |
| jelly | jello |
| joint | roast (meat) |
| jug | pitcher |
| juggernaut | truck (semi) |
| jumper/jersey | sweater/pullover |
| jump leads | jumper cables (car) |
| junior school | elementary school |

### K

| | |
|---|---|
| kagoule | parka (unlined) |
| kerb (pavement) | curb (sidewalk) |
| kit | sports clothes/equipment |

| | |
|---|---|
| kitchen roll | paper towels |
| Kiwi | New Zealander |
| knackered | tired |
| knickers/pants | underpants/panties |
| knickerbockers/plus fours | knickers |
| knock about | warm-up (tennis) |

**L**

| | |
|---|---|
| label | tag |
| ladder (in tights) | run (in nylons) |
| larder | pantry |
| lavatory/toilet/loo | toilet/bathroom/john |
| lay-by | pull-off (driving) |
| lead (dog) | leash (dog) |
| lead | electric cord/wire |
| lemon squash | lemonade |
| lemonade | Seven-Up/Sprite |
| let | rent (real estate) |
| lift | elevator |
| limited/Ltd | incorporated/Inc. |
| liquidizer | blender |
| lodger | roomer/boarder |
| loo/toilet/W.C. | restroom/toilet |
| lorry | truck |
| lost property | lost and found |

**M**

| | |
|---|---|
| mackintosh (mac) | raincoat |
| maisonette | duplex/triplex |
| mate | buddy |
| methylated spirits | denatured alcohol |
| milk float | milk truck |
| mince | hamburger/ground beef |
| M.O.T. | motor vehicle inspection test |
| motorbike | motorcycle |
| motorway | freeway/super highway |

**N**

| | |
|---|---|
| nappy | diaper |
| neat | straight (cocktail) |
| net curtains | sheers (under drapes) |
| newsagent | newsdealer/newstand |
| nil/nought/zero | zero |
| noughts and crosses | tic-tac-toe |
| number/registration plate | licence plate |

## O

| | |
|---|---|
| off licence | liquor store |
| on the pull | on the prowl |
| oven gloves/mitt | pot holder/gloves |
| overtake | pass (vehicle) |

## P

| | |
|---|---|
| packed lunch | sack lunch |
| paddle | wade |
| pants | shorts (underwear) |
| paraffin | kerosene |
| parcel | package |
| parcel tape | packing tape |
| pavement | sidewalk |
| pelmet | valance (drapes) |
| petrol | gas |
| phone box | pay telephone |
| pillar box (antiquated)/post box | mailbox |
| pinafore dress | jumper |
| pissed | drunk |
| plaster/elastoplast | band-aid |
| point/power point/plug socket | outlet/socket (electrical) |
| porter | doorman |
| postal order | money order |
| post code | zip code |
| post/postman | mail/mailman |
| prep (or homework) | homework |
| press studs/poppers | snaps (sewing) |
| public/fee paying school/private | private school |
| pudding/sweet | dessert |
| purse | change purse/wallet |
| pushchair/buggy | stroller |

## Q

| | |
|---|---|
| quay (pron. 'key') | wharf/pier |
| queue | line (stand in) |

## R

| | |
|---|---|
| removal van/pantechnicon (antiquated) | moving van |
| removal company | moving company |
| return ticket | round trip ticket |
| reverse charges | call collect |
| ring up | call (telephone) |
| roundabout | traffic circle |
| rubber | eraser |

| | |
|---|---|
| rubbish/refuse | garbage (trash) |

**S**

| | |
|---|---|
| S.A.E. | stamped addressed envelope |
| saloon | sedan (car) |
| Scally | accent or person from Liverpool |
| scribbling pad/book/jotter | scratch pad |
| serviettes/napkins | napkins |
| shop assistant | sales clerk |
| sideboards | sideburns |
| silencer | muffler (car) |
| single ticket | one way ticket |
| sitting/reception room/lounge | living room |
| skip | dumpster (construction) |
| skipping rope | jump rope |
| skirting board | baseboard |
| snog | make out (kiss) |
| solicitor | lawyer/attorney |
| spanner | wrench |
| spectacles/specs | glasses (eyes) |
| spirits | liquor |
| squaddie | young person in the military (e.g. ROTC) |
| stabilizers | training wheels |
| stand | run (for public office) |
| stalls | orchestra seats (theatre) |
| state school/grammar school | public school |
| stone | pit (fruit) |
| stroke/oblique | slash (/) |
| subway | underground/pedestrian passage |
| surgery | doctor's/dentist's office |
| surgical spirit | rubbing alcohol |
| suspenders | garter belt |
| sweets/chocolate bar | candy/candy bar |
| swimming costume | bathing suit |

**T**

| | |
|---|---|
| ta/cheers (or thanks) | thanks |
| table tennis bat | ping pong paddle |
| take-away | take out (food) |
| tap | faucet |
| tarmac | pavement |
| tea/supper | supper |
| tea trolley | tea cart |
| teat | nipple (baby bottle) |

| | |
|---|---|
| telly | T.V. |
| tenner | ten pound note |
| term (three yearly) | semester (school) |
| theatre/operating theatre | surgery (medical) |
| tights | panty hose |
| The City | Wall Street (financial industry) |
| till | cash register |
| time-table | schedule |
| tip (rubbish) | dump (garbage) |
| tin | can |
| torch | flashlight |
| tracksuit bottoms | sweatpants |
| trainers/plimsolls | sneakers/tennis shoes |
| travelling rug | blanket (travelling) |
| treble number (treble 5) | number used three times (555) |
| trolley | grocery cart |
| trousers | pants |
| tube/underground | subway |
| turn-ups (trousers) | cuffs (pants) |
| turf | sod (new grass) |

**U**

| | |
|---|---|
| university | college/university |

**V**

| | |
|---|---|
| valance | dust ruffle |
| verge/hard shoulder | soft shoulder (road) |
| vest | t-shirt/undershirt |

**W**

| | |
|---|---|
| waistcoat | vest |
| wardrobe | closet (hanging clothes) |
| washing up | dishes, do the |
| washing up liquid | dishwashing liquid (hand) |
| wash your hands | wash up |
| wellies (wellington boots) | boots (waterproof) |
| whinging | whining |
| white or black? | with or without (milk or cream in coffee) |
| windcheater/kagoul | windbreaker |
| windscreen | windshield |
| wing mirror | review view mirror (outside) |
| Woolworths | dime store/five and ten |

## Z

| | |
|---|---|
| zebra crossing | crosswalk |
| 'zed' (pron.) | Z |

# INDEX

## V

## W

## X

## Y

## Z

# Reader's Questionnaire

## LIVING IN LONDON
## Ninth Edition

*Dear Reader,*
To help us to continue to improve and update *Living in London*, we would appreciate you taking a few moments to complete the following and mail to: The Junior League of London, 9 Fitzmaurice Place, London W1X 5JD.

1.   Are you currently living in or moving to London?

2.   If you live in London, how long have you lived here?

3.   Where did you get your copy of *Living in London*?

4.   Which sections/chapters were most helpful to you?

5.   Is there any topic you would like to see covered in greater depth?

6.   Are there any other topics or services you would like us to consider including in the next edition of *Living in London*?

Thank you!

# The Junior League of London

The Junior League of London is an international organisation of woman committed to promoting voluntary service and improving the community through the effect action and leadership of trained volunteers. The members offer their services to the London community in the areas of social welfare of children and families, and the arts and culture. As a registered charity, the League's are exclusively educational and charitable.

If you would like to receive more information about the League, or be invited to an informational session (held twice a year), please complete the following:

NAME: _____

ADDRESS: _____

_____

CITY: _____

POSTAL CODE: _____

COUNTRY: _____

TELEPHONE NUMBER: _____

E-MAIL: _____

And return to:

The Junior League of London
9 Fitzmaurice Place
London W1J 5JD
Tel: (020) 7499 8159
Fax: (020) 7629 1996

# Living in London: A Practical Guide

## Ninth Edition    ISBN 0-9525195-3-4

**The Junior League of London**  9 Fitzmaurice Place, London W1J 5JD   **T** 020 7499 8159   **F** 020 7629 1996   **W** www.jll.org.uk

## Price  *(Includes postage and packing)*

| Destination of the Order | Cost Each | How Many | Total Cost |
|---|---|---|---|
| Shipments within the UK | £16 | | |
| Airmail to Europe | £17 | | |
| Airmail Overseas | £20 | | |
| **Total Order: £** | | | |

*There is a 10% discount available for purchases of over 50 books.*
*You will be invoiced accordingly.*

## Payment

☐ by sterling cheque (please make payable to JLL Enterprises Ltd)   *OR*   ☐ by credit card

Credit card no: ☐☐☐☐ ☐☐☐☐ ☐☐☐☐ ☐☐☐☐

Expiry date: ☐☐ / ☐☐    Issue date (if debit card): ☐☐ / ☐☐

Please print name as it appears on the card

Signed    Contact tel. no (important)

## Card billing address

Name

Address

City    Postal code

Country

## Shipping address  *(If different from billing address)*

Name

Address

City    Postal code

Country

Profits from the sale of this book enable The Junior League of London to develop, fund and staff its community projects.
Registered UK Charity Number 288427.   JLL Enterprises VAT No. 461582541.   Prices subject to change.

307

# DRY MEASURES

|  | US | UK | Metric |
|---|---|---|---|
| Flour | 1 cup | 5 oz. | 140 gms. |
| Sugar | 2 Tbsp. | 1 oz. | 25 gms. |
|  | 1 cup | 8 oz. | 225 gms. |
| Brown Sugar | 1 cup | 6 oz. | 170 gms. |
| Breadcrumbs or Nuts | 1 cup | 4 oz. | 115 gms. |
| Butter | 2 rounded Tbsp. | 1 oz. | 25 gms. |
|  | 1 cup (2 sticks) | 8 oz. | 225 gms. |
| Yeast | 1 US pkg. (21/2 tsp.) | 1/4 oz. | 7 gms. |

In measuring dry ingredients such as flour or sugar, when using a British recipe remember to weigh the items as the ingredients will be listed in ounces or grams. (Remember 8 ounces of two different ingredients may have distinctly different volumes).

Butter is sold in the UK in blocks weighing 250 grams. If approximately 3/8" is cut off one end of the block, the remainder will equal 2 sticks of butter in a US recipe. (One stick of US butter contains 8 US tablespoons).

# LIQUID MEASURES

|  | oz. | ml. |
|---|---|---|
| US/UK 1 teaspoon | 1/6 oz. | 5 ml. |
| UK 1 dessert spoon | 1/3 oz. | 10 ml. |
| US/UK 1 tablespoon | 1/2 oz. | 15 ml. |
| US 1 cup | 8 oz. | 240ml. |
| UK 1 cup | 10 oz. | 300 ml. |
| US 1 pint | 16 oz. | 470 ml. |
| UK 1 imperial pint | 20 oz. | 585 ml. |
| US gill | 5 oz. | 150 ml. |

# COOKING TEMPERATURES

| C | F | Gas Mark | Description |
| --- | --- | --- | --- |
| 110 | 225 | 1/4 | Very Slow |
| 125 | 250 | 1/2 | Very Slow |
| 140 | 275 | 1 | Slow |
| 150 | 300 | 2 | Slow |
| 165 | 325 | 3 | Moderate |
| 180 | 350 | 4 | Moderate |
| 190 | 375 | 5 | Moderate/Hot |
| 200 | 400 | 6 | Moderate/Hot |
| 220 | 425 | 7 | Hot |
| 230 | 450 | 8 | Hot |
| 240 | 475 | 9 | Very Hot |

# MEASUREMENT CONVERSIONS

| | |
| --- | --- |
| Ounces to grams | Multiply ounces by 28.35 |
| Quarts to litres | Multiply quarts by 0.95 |
| Grams to ounces | Multiply grams by 0.03527 |
| Pounds to grams | Multiply pounds by 453.6 |
| Pounds to kilograms | Multiply pounds by 0.4536 |
| Kilograms to pounds | Multiply kilograms by 2.205 |
| Centigrade to Fahrenheit | Multiply C by 1.8 and add 32 |
| Fahrenheit to Centigrade | Multiply F by 5, subtract 32 and then divide by 9 |
| Stones to pounds | Multiply stones by 14 |

# The IHT
# hand
# delivered
## to your door

**Save up to 38%** off the cover price –
subscribe to the IHT today and have
every copy delivered to you for as little
as **£0.75 per issue.**

**Enjoy these benefits when you subscribe:**
- a free replacement copy if your issue is not delivered
- have your subscription redirected or suspended if you are away on business or vacation
- we will refund the cost of all unserved issues if you decide to cancel
- toll free customer service line: 0800 895 965
  (Open Mon-Fri 09:00 – 17:00 CET)

**Early Morning Hand Delivery**
Copies will be hand delivered to your home or
office within the M25 area and selected parts
of south east England.

---

## YES, I'd like the World's Daily Newspaper delivered to me every morning.

| Your Details | Payment Details |
|---|---|

**Your Details**

Title:  ☐ Mr. ☐ Mrs. ☐ Ms. ☐ Dr.   Other _____
Family Name: _____
First Name: _____
Address: ☐Home   ☐ Office
_____

City: _____ Postal Code: _____
Country: _____
Telephone: (inc. prefix) _____
E-mail: _____

**Return your completed coupon to:**
Circulation Director UK-Ireland,
International Herald Tribune,
40 Marsh Wall, London E14 9TP
Fax: (+44) 20 7987 3462  E-mail: subs@iht.com

☐ I do not wish to receive information from other carefully
  screened companies.

**Payment Details**

Yes, I'd like to subscribe and pay for the following term:
☐ 12 months (+ 2 months free): £270
  Saving off cover price: 38%
☐ 3 months (+2 weeks free): £75
  Saving off cover price: 31%

Please charge my credit card:
☐ Amex  ☐ Diners  ☐ **VISA**  ☐ Euro/MasterCard
Cardholder's Name: _____
Card Number: _____

Expiry Date: _____ Signature _____

☐ My check is enclosed (payable to the International Herald Tribune).
☐ Please start delivery and send invoice.

Residents of other countries call
(+33) 1 41 43 93 61 for your local price.

This offer is valid for new subscribers only. Expires December 31, 2002.

## Call toll free on 0800 895 965 and quote reference LIL